Networks of Corporate Power

A Comparative Analysis of Ten Countries

EDITED BY

Frans N. Stokman
Rolf Ziegler
John Scott

POLITY PRESS

HD
2844
N48
1985

First published 1985 by
Polity Press, Cambridge, in association with Basil Blackwell, Oxford

Editorial Office: Polity Press
                Dales Brewery, Gwydir Street, Cambridge, CB1 2LJ

Basil Blackwell Ltd
108, Cowley Road, Oxford, OX4 1JF, UK.

Basil Blackwell Inc.
432 Park Avenue South, Suite 1505, New York, NY 10016, USA.

British Library Cataloguing in Publication Data
Networks of corporate power: a comparative analysis of ten countries.
1. Corporations   2. Interorganizational relations
I. Stokman, Frans N. II. Ziegler, Rolf
III. Scott, John, *1949–*
338.7'4 HD2741

ISBN 0-7456-0115-4 case

Library of Congress Cataloging in Publication Data
Networks of corporate power.

  Bibliography: p.
  Includes index.
  1. Interlocking directorates – Europe – Addresses,
essays, lectures. 2. Directors of corporations – Europe –
Addresses, essays, lectures. I. Stokman, Frans N.
II. Ziegler, Rolf. III. Scott, John, 1949-
HD2844.N48 1984   338.8'7'094   84-23730
ISBN 0-7456-0115-4

96,399

Typeset by Communitype, Wigston, Leicester.
Printed in Great Britain by Bell and Bain Limited, Glasgow.

To Robert J. Mokken

Contents

List of Tables and Figures

TABLES

x *List of Tables and Figures*

FIGURES

List of Contributors

JAMES BEARDEN MA, PhD is the author of *The Functions of the Boards of Directors in Large US Corporations* (PhD thesis, State University of New York, Stony Brook, 1982) and of 'Bank Boards of Directors and Social Capital' in *The Corporate Elite as a Ruling Class* (Holmes and Meier). He has taught at the Universities of Edinburgh and Wisconsin (Madison).

DONALD BENDER is Research Assistant at the University of Munich (Sociology Institute, Konradstraße 6, D8000, Munich 40). He is co-author of *Software zur Clusteranalyse, Netzwerkanalyse und verwandten Verfahren* (with H.P.Ohly and H.H.Bock).

HERMANN BIEHLER, Dipl.-Volkswirt, Dr.rer.pol. is Research Assistant at the University of Munich (Sociology Institute, Konradstraße 6, D8000, Munich 40). He is co-author of *Arbeitsmarktsegmentation in der Bundesrepublik Deutschland* (Campus, 1981), *Arbeitsmarktstrukturen und -prozesse* (Mohr, 1981) and *Neue Mikroökonomie* (Physica, 1979).

ANTONIO M. CHIESI has a degree in political science. He is co-author of *I Grandi Imprenditori Italiani* (with A.Martinelli and N.Dalla Chiesa, Feltrinelli, 1981) and *Il Sistema Degli Orari* (Angeli, 1981), and is editor of *Le Ricerche sui Lavoratori Non Manuali e il Sindacato in Italia* (Angeli, 1983). He is Assistant Professor at the University of Trieste (Institute of Political Science, P. le Europa 1, 34127 Trieste).

LUDO CUYVERS has a doctorate in applied economics. He is the author of 'Keynes Collaboration with Erwin Rothbarth' in *Economic Journal* 1983, 'A Mathematical Interpretation of Marxian Unproductive Labour' in *Economica* 1978 and (with W.Meeusen) 'The

Structure of Personal Influence in the Belgian Holding Companies' in *European Economic Review* 1976. He is currently Assistant Professor in economics at the University of Antwerp.

DONALD ELSAS is drs. Sociology and teaches research methodology at the University of Groningen (Sociology Institute Oude Boteringestraat 23, NL9172, GC Groningen).

MEINDERT FENNEMA teaches political science at the University of Amsterdam. In the field of network research he has published 'Analyzing Interlocking Directorates: Theory and Methods' in *Social Networks* 1979 (with H. Schijf), *International Networks of Banks and Industry* (M. Nijhoff, 1982) and *Het Nederlands belang bij Indië* (with H. Baudet et al., Spectrum, 1983).

CATHERINE GRIFF MA is a graduate of the Australian National University and of the University of Leicester. Until 1982 she was Research Associate at the University of Leicester.

ILKKA HEISKANEN PhD is the author of *Theoretical Approaches and Scientific Strategies in Administrative and Organizational Research* (Commentationes Humanarum Litterarum, 1967), *Julkinen, Kollektiivinen ja Markkinaperusteinen* (Valtion Painatuskeskus, 1977) and (with R.Mitchell) 'Defining the Objectives of Cultural Development' in *Planning for Cultural Development* (UNESCO Documentary Dossier 9–10). He is Professor of Political Science at the University of Helsinki (Department of Political Science, Aleksanterinkatv 7, SF0100 Helsinki 10).

ERKKI JOHANSON MA is the author of 'Poliittia – hallinnollisesta Rakennetut Kimuksesta ja Eliittitutkimuksesta sen Välineenä (With I.Heiskanen, E.Hänninen and R.Mitchell) in *Politiikka* 1976. He is doctoral student in political science at the University of Helsinki.

WIM MEEUSEN has a doctorate in economics and is the author of 'Efficiency Estimation from Cobb-Douglas Production Functions with Composed Error' (with J. van den Broeck) in *International Economic Review* 1977, 'On the Maximal Number of 2-cliques in a Graph with n Vertices' in *Belgisch Tijdschrift voor Statistiek* 1980 and (with L.Cuyvers) 'The Structure of Personal Influence of the Belgian Holding Companies' in *European Economic Review* 1976. As well as lecturing at the Free University of Brussels, he is Senior Researcher in macro-economics at the University of Antwerp (Faculty of Applied Economics).

BETH MINTZ PhD is the author of 'The President's Cabinet 1897–1972' in *The Insurgent Sociologist* 1975, (with M.Schwartz) 'Interlocking Directorates and Interest Group Formation' in *American Sociological Review* 1981 and *The Structure of Power in American Business* (University of Chicago Press, 1984). She is Associate Professor at the University of Vermont (Department of Sociology, 31 South Prospect Street, Burlington, VT 05405).

GERHARD REISSNER has a doctorate in law and has worked as Research Assistant at the University of Vienna. He is now a court judge in Hainburg (Bezirksgericht Hainburg Donau, A-2410, Hainburg Donau).

PETER RUSTERHOLZ Lic.phil. is Assistant at the University of Zurich (Sociology Institute, Zeltweg 63, CH-8032, Zürich).

HUIBERT SCHIJF studied political science at the University of Amsterdam. He is lecturer at the Department of Sociology of the same university. He has done research on interlocking directorships in the Netherlands at the turn of the century and participated in the development of the program package GRADAP. Among his publications are 'Analyzing Interlocking Directorates: Theory and Methods' in *Social Networks* 1979 (with M. Fennema) and chapters in the manual for GRADAP.

JOHN SCOTT BSc(Soc), PhD is the author of *Corporations Classes and Capitalism* (Hutchinson, 1979), *The Anatomy of Scottish Capital* (with M.Hughes, Croom Helm, 1980) and *The Upper Classes* (Macmillan, 1983). He is Lecturer in Sociology at the University of Leicester (Department of Sociology, University Road, Leicester LE1 7RH).

FRANS STOKMAN is the author of *Graven naar Macht* (with others, Van Gennep, 1975), *Roll Calls and Sponsorship* (Sijthoff, 1977) and *GRADAP Users Manual* (with J. van Veen, Interuniversity Project Group GRADAP, 1981) and editor of *Modellen in de Sociologie* (with S. Lindenberg, Van Loghum Slaterus, 1983) and *Nederlandse Elites in Beeld* (with J. Dronkers, Van Loghum Slaterus, 1984). He is Professor of Research Methodology in the Social Sciences at the University of Groningen (Sociology Institute).

DAVID SWARTZ PhD, Maîtrise Sociologie, Licence Sociologie is the author of 'Classes, Educational Systems and Labour Markets' in *European Journal of Sociology* 1981 and 'Pierre Bourdieu: The

Cultural Transmission of Social Inequality' in *Harvard Educational Review* 1977. He is currently based at the University of Boston (Department of Sociology, Boston, MA).

FRANS WASSEUR drs. Economics is the author of 'Personeelsfunctionarissen en Beroepsverenigingen' (with A.Buitendam) in *Professionalisering van het personeelsbeleid* (Kluwer, 1982). He is Research Assistant at the University of Groningen (Sociology Institute).

ROLF ZIEGLER, Diplom-Volkswirt, Dr.rer.pol. is the author of *Kommunikationsstruktur und Leistung sozialer Systeme* (Verlag Hain, 1968) and *Theorie und Modell* (Verlag Oldenbourg, 1972), and is the co-editor of *Korrelation und Kausalität* (3 Volumes, Enke Verlag, 1976) and of 'Analyse sozialer Netzwerke' (special issue of *Kölner Zeitschrift für Soziologie und Sozialpsychologie, 1984.* He is Associate Editor of *Social Networks*, Advisory Editor of *Quality and Quantity* and sits on committees of the German Sociological Association and the European Science Foundation. He is Professor at the University of Munich (Sociology Institute, Konradstraße 6, D8000, München 40).

Preface and Acknowledgements

This book presents the results of work carried out over a number of years by the Research Group on Intercorporate Structure. This group included member teams from a number of countries and its efforts have throughout been directed towards a truly comparative study – the first such study in the area of interlocking directorships. Behind the various chapters in this book, therefore, lies a complex and continuous process of discussion and co-ordination. Given the practical problems involved in such research, it might be valuable to point to the means through which a truly comparative approach was effected. This can best be seen in terms of the four stages of selection, processing, analysis and editing.

The initial decision was to make the *selection* of companies and individuals in each country as comparable as possible. The earliest meetings of the research group were concerned with arriving at a set of selection criteria which could be applied with the minimum of changes in each of the participating countries. Each team then proceeded to carry out the time-consuming and labour-intensive task of compiling its data set. Using the relevant published and unpublished sources lists of companies and their directors were drawn up. These extremely long lists had then to be checked and cleaned before they could be used. The basic unit in our study – the interlocking directorship – is based on the presence of one person on two or more company boards and the first step in identifying interlocks is to construct a list of all names appearing more than once in the master list. Anyone who has carried out this kind of research will realize the difficulties involved. It is necessary, for example, to ascertain whether J.B.Smith is the same person as James B. Smith and whether either of these is the same person as J. Brown Smith. Completion of this task requires recourse to further data sources and may even involve writing to the persons concerned. Additional problems arise over the time period studied and these are discussed in chapter 1. No doubt some errors remain in the data sets but the researchers feel that the number of errors is far lower than the level accepted as normal in survey research.

Only when selection has been completed is it possible to go on to the stage of *processing*. This involved the use of a common package of computer programs with similar runs carried out for each country. An important contribution to the success of the project was made by the centralized computing facilities used. Each team had to produce similar data files, from which were produced standardized computer runs. On the basis of these data, each team could request further, tailor-made processing of their files. Such standardized processing, together with the local processing carried out by each team, maximized the comparability of the *analyses* produced. Analysis involved discussions of detailed working papers by all members of the research team, and these discussions could be centred on the specific features of each national study. There was no need to explain the selection and processing of the data themselves in each national paper. The discussions of the research group epitomized the operation of collegial authority which is at the heart of scientific research.

Collective responsibility extended to the *editing* of the final reports for publication. Although the various chapters show the names of individual authors, all the reports are the outcome of collective discussions ranging over a number of years. The editors have sought to emphasize this by becoming far more involved in the content of individual chapters than is normal in collective works. In matters of style and terminology a necessary degree of uniformity was aimed at and the various contributors have accepted many substantive changes suggested by the editors. While individual authors take responsibility for the particular arguments which they present in their chapters, the authors take a collective responsibility for the approach and methods employed.

The editors are glad to have this opportunity of expressing the gratitude of themselves and their fellow contributors to the many people and organizations who have helped in the preparation of this book. First of all we must thank Rob Mokken, who was in many ways responsible for initiating this project. He was actively involved in all the early planning and it was only his move from Amsterdam University to the Central Bureau of Statistics which forced him to withdraw from active involvement. He has remained a constant source of inspiration and encouragement and many of the ideas contained in the book are due to his work. Last, and by no means least, Rob kindly allowed the editors to meet at his country farmhouse to complete the preparation of this manuscript. For all these reasons we have dedicated this book to Rob Mokken.

Our thanks must also go to the European Consortium for Political

Research which sponsored our original meetings and has continued to provide an all-important framework for our loosely structured network. Valerie Stewart did much to ease the administrative aspects of our interlocking activities. The support of the Werner-Reimers-Stiftung was essential to the success of our work. By financing meetings and providing congenial surroundings for our discussions, the Stiftung ensured the maximum degree of co-operation between the research teams. A particular debt of gratitude is due to Herr Krosigk for the interest and enthusiasm which he has shown for our research.

Groningen University and its Institute of Sociology provided material support for computing and the secretariat of the group (particularly Carola Ubben-Verbraak) and showed great hospitality towards the various foreign visitors who went to Groningen to collect their latest stack of print-out. A special word of thanks must be said for the Herculean efforts of Frans Wasseur, who knows more about all the data sets than do the research teams themselves.

Use of the word-processor at the Sociology Institute, University of Munich, greatly facilitated the editing and correcting of the text.

The whole of the manuscript has been typed – and retyped – by Frauke Wilkens and all tables and figures by Carola Ubben-Verbraak. We are grateful to them for transforming the untidy copy that we produced into a readable typescript.

The editors would like to add a personal note of gratitude to their families for enduring our absence not only during the main meetings but also during our last 'holiday' at Wapse.

The work presented in this book is an outcome of the loose, but co-ordinated, links between the various research teams and the myriad connections that each team had with its home institution. For this reason the book is a monument to the strength of weak ties.

Frans Stokman, Rolf Ziegler and John Scott, Wapse, May 1983

1

Theoretical Framework and Research Design

JOHN SCOTT[1]

The phenomenon of the interlocking directorship has exercised a peculiar fascination for many social researchers, perhaps reflecting the apparent ease with which information can be collected and subjected to some kind of crude analysis. Such research seems to lead all too easily to conclusions about the concentration of economic power. At the same time – and perhaps for the same reasons – this kind of research has encountered considerable scepticism from other re-searchers and also from company directors themselves. Interlock research is criticized for equating positions with power, for resorting uncritically to some kind of conspiracy theory, and for being politically motivated – as if the latter were not true of all social research. Over the last decade or so, however, a new sophistication has become apparent in interlock research. This has involved an awareness of both its potential and its limitations and a willingness to subject research findings to minute theoretical and empirical criticism. The study of interlocking directorships is no longer the 'one-off' rapid way to academic success (or notoriety). It is now becoming a legitimate and respectable area of scientific specialization. The work presented in this book reflects this new trend in interlock research, and a number of the participants in the research group have been actively involved in research on interlocking directorships during the last ten years.[2] It is hoped that the publication of this volume will contribute further to the re-orientation of work on interlocking directorships.

But first things first: what is an interlock? An *interlock* is simply the social relation that is created between two enterprises when one person is a member of the board of directors in each enterprise. Such a person is termed a *multiple director*. These two concepts – interlocking directorship and multiple director – are the building blocks of the edifice constructed in this book. An interlocking directorship (or simply an interlock) is one link in that complex chain of connections that is termed the network of interlocking directorships. If A is interlocked with B, B with C, C with D and so on, there is a simple chain of connections. But if D is also connected to B and C also to A, the network begins to acquire a much more complex structure. As the number of interlocks carried by each enterprise increases, so the structure of the resulting network becomes more complex. It is a basic assumption of all contributors to this book that research on interlocking directorships must concern itself not only with dyadic relations between particular enterprises, but also with the global features of network structure. It is held that the features of the intercorporate network play an important and generally unrecognized role in the structuring of economic power and in wider social processes.

The study of interlocking directorships, therefore, is relevant not only to those interested in the question of industrial organization, but also to those whose main concern is with the structuration of capitalist classes and with their political organization. One of the most refreshing features of recent work on interlocking directorships has been the close connection that it has had with 'power structure' research (see Domhoff, 1980). In this book the contributors employ data on various national economies to produce descriptions of the network of interlocks in each country studied and to draw conclusions as to the implications of their work for some of these wider issues. The research has brought together sociologists, economists, and political scientists in a fruitful interchange of ideas, and each national report reflects something of the disciplinary concerns of the national team. For some, the issues of interlocks between competitor firms and the contribution of interlocks to overall concentration are central; for others the role of the public sector and the consequences of state intervention are important topics; while for others the issues of corporate ownership and control are paramount. The contributors are united, however, in their general approach to this research and in their belief that only through comparative research can theoretical and empirical advances be made. Most interlock research to date has been concerned with the USA; far less research has been carried out on other societies. This book represents the results of the first attempt to carry out comparative research on a co-ordinated basis by research teams based in each of the countries studied. The number of countries involved in this comparative exercise – a total of ten nations – makes the research a unique example of international and interdisciplinary cooperation. However, this introductory chapter is not intended as an eulogy for the research group. Its aim is to outline the research strategy adopted to make the project work, and to make clear the areas of agreement and disagreement which have emerged in the course of the research. While there is a broadly shared theoretical framework, many hotly contested points of dispute have arisen within this framework. Disagreements between members of the research group – many of which will be apparent from the various chapters – reflect a wider conflict of perspectives and models within the social-scientific community. The purpose of the first section of this chapter is to clarify some of the major points of contention in existing studies of economic power and to document the role that interlock research can play in resolving these disputes.

PERSPECTIVES AND MODELS OF ECONOMIC POWER

The study of economic power is not a unified area of research, but has involved a number of competing perspectives and theoretical models. Perhaps more than any other area of social science, contending perspectives have been associated with rival political positions, and discussion of theoretical problems has been inextricably intertwined with ideological contention. Concern over the problem of economic power had an important point of origin in the work of Marx, and the subsequent development of Marxist theory and practice has both informed and criticized much of the academic work in the area. Attempts to study economic power through investigations of inter-locking directorships had an independent source in the anti-trust concerns of the American liberal tradition, which eventuated in a series of official enquiries (Fennema and Schijf, 1979; Andrews, 1982). The recent upsurge of interest in interlocks and economic power in Europe and the USA continues to show the signs of its origins in these political traditions. One sign of the increased sophistication of such research has been a willingness to break with political dogma in an attempt to grasp the real significance of the phenomena under investigation. The perspectives which have come to dominate this area, therefore, confront one another on the theoretical and empirical terrain and permit the important questions to be posed and answered in a far more adequate way.

Figure 1.1   Perspectives on Economic Power

Level of analysis	Units of analysis	
	Enterprise	Person
Agent	1 Organizational perspective	2 Social-background perspective
System	3 Interorganizational perspective	4 Class-hegemony perspective

Studies of economic power have involved a differentiation of focus along two main dimensions: the *unit* of analysis and the *level* of analysis. The units of analysis have been seen as either enterprises or persons, and the level of analysis has been either the level of the agent or the level of the system. A cross-classification of these two dimensions generates the four major perspectives on economic power (see figure 1.1). Each box in the diagram represents the particular combination of features defining a specific perspective. Box 1 defines the organizational perspective, within which the organizational features of enterprises are placed in the centre of the analysis. This perspective has evolved out of the traditional economic view of the firm through the work of writers such as Simon (1961) and it has led to recent work on multidivisional organization (Chandler, 1962; Channon, 1973; Dyas and Thanheiser, 1976) and on the so-called market and hierarchy relationship (Williamson, 1975; Francis et al., 1982). Within this perspective, interlocking is treated as an attribute of the enterprise which can be related to economic performance as measured by such things as profit rates, debt – equity ratios, and so on (Pennings, 1980; Burt, 1980b). It is also assumed that measures of interlocking and performance can be aggregated over industrial sectors to show, for example, whether highly interlocked sectors are more profitable than sectors with a lower level of interlocking (Burt, 1982, ch.8; Ziegler, 1982). Box 2 defines the social-background perspective, within which the education, club memberships and attributes of business leaders are studied as a major aspect of their formation into a corporate 'elite'. In the work of writers such as Mills (1956) and Domhoff (1967) this perspective has proved a fruitful way of viewing the holders of economic power (but see Mintz et al., 1976). Within the social-background perspective the number of directorships held and the types of firms in which they are held are treated as attributes of the persons studied and are related to their level and type of education, their wealth, and so on.

The organizational perspective and the social-background perspective, which have dominated the area for some time, share a focus on the role of social agents and tend to isolate this concern from the wider system of relationships within which actions take place. For this reason, social relations tend to be reduced to the *attributes* of the enterprises and persons studied (Berkowitz, 1982, chapter 1) and much important information is lost. The recent growth of interest in interlock research has encouraged the development of the perspectives defined in boxes 3 and 4 of figure 1.1, both of which start out from an explicit attempt to theorize the *relational* features of economic power in order to arrive at an understanding of its systemic character. Box 3 defines the interorganizational perspective advocated by writers such as Aldrich (1979) and Benson (1975, 1977). Relations between enterprises are seen as constitutive of the environment within which they are located, and therefore as determinants of their possibilities of action. Box 4, the class-hegemony perspective, is perhaps the least well developed. It emerged from the 'structuralist' arguments of such writers as Poulantzas (1975) and Wright (1978), who were critical of what they termed the 'instrumentalism' of Miliband (1969) and Domhoff (1967), and it presents relations between people as defining the structure of a capitalist class. This class exists as a system of positions to which agents are recruited and class 'fractions' are seen as clusters of structurally defined positions rather than as groups of individuals possessing particular attributes. So far, interlock research has had little impact on these concerns, though Zeitlin and Ratcliff (1975) have suggested that it is possible to analyse the structure of relations between enterprises which result from the kinship relations between people.

These four perspectives have structured much of the research on economic power and interlock researchers have worked within each one of them. But, regardless of the perspective within which they work, all interlock researchers have had to come to grips with one fundamental question What does an interlocking directorship signify? Although rarely addressed explicitly, this question is implicit in all attempts to use interlock data to study economic power. The minimum inference which can be made about *any* interlock is that it is intrinsically meaningful as a channel of communication and that the network of interlocks constitutes a web of communication through which general business information and opinion can be transmitted (Mills, 1956, pp. 122ff.). The mere fact of sitting on two boards opens up possibilities of communication which might not otherwise be present. This is indeed a *minimum* inference: it is possible to say little a priori about the quality and quantity of information which is communicated or about what else the interlock might signify. It is clearly necessary to go beyond the minimum inference and treat interlocks as indicators on the basis of which it might be possible to infer the existence of significant social relations between enterprises and people. Not all interlock researchers have realized the importance of this point, and it has often been assumed that interlock research gives immediate and direct access to the channels of power. It is a sign of the increased sophistication of interlock research that the majority of researchers have gradually come to realize that interlocks are most usefully treated as indicators of social relations. Thus, one of the most productive teams of researchers outside the USA entitled their first publication Digging for Power (Helmers et al., 1975) and have entitled their series of working papers Traces of Power. Their argument is that interlocks may be regarded as signs of possible power relations but that demonstrating the actual existence of such relations requires the researcher to 'dig' beyond the mere fact that interlocks exist. The significance of particular interlocks, therefore, is always a question which must be answered empirically with substantiating evidence.

Assessing the significance of an interlock is a process of inference which consists of hypothesizing the existence of a relation on the basis of interlock evidence and then devising tests for the existence of this relation. Although such hypotheses can be arrived at by any method from blind intuition to systematic literature search, most researchers have drawn their hypotheses from a limited number of theoretical models. Five main models, each of which postulates distinct mechanisms and processes in the exercise of economic power, have guided inferences about the significance of interlocking directorships:

(1)　the finance-capital model;
(2)　the co-ordination and control model;
(3)　the resource-dependence model;
(4)　the managerial model; and
(5)　the class-cohesion model.

These models have often been developed within one or other of the four theoretical perspectives, yet some have their origin outside this area and have been taken up by researchers seeking to interpret the interlock data which they have collected. The finance-capital model, for example, developed within the Marxist tradition, though its assumptions are well suited to the interorganizational perspective. The managerial model, by contrast, was an internal development of the organizational perspective. Some of the models have been taken up by researchers in more than one perspective: the resource-dependence model has been used in both the organizational and the interorganizational perspective and the class-cohesion model developed within the social-background perspective but is now mainly associated with the class-hegemony perspective. In order to approach the question of how to infer the significance of interlocks it is necessary to review briefly the central tenets of each model.

The Finance-capital Model

This model developed within Marxism, with the earliest-known study of interlocks (that of Jeidels, 1905) being influential in the formulation of Hilferding's classic statement of the model. Hilferding (1910) argues that the concentration of banking and industry leads to their fusion into the monopoly form of money capital. Although banks, insurance companies and other credit-granting companies take on a particularly important role in systematic capital mobilization, these companies at the same time become parts of diversified enterprises spanning the banking, industrial and commercial sectors. Finance capital, the form taken by this fusion of banking and industry, is not limited to one sphere of activity and it is not possible to identify distinct 'financial' and 'industrial' enterprises. Finance capital forms itself into units of capital with varying mixes of banking and industrial interests, ready to shift the balance of their activities as opportunities present themselves.[3] These units need not be integrated enterprises, but may be looser alliances tied together through intercorporate shareholdings, indebtedness and various kinds of 'Personalunion' (especially interlocks). These trends enhance the possibility for a systematic co-ordination of the capitalist system through what have been described as distinct 'empires' or 'spheres of influence' (Rochester, 1936; Perlo, 1957; Aaronovitch, 1961). These empires are seen as organized groups of companies pursuing a relatively autonomous corporate strategy through the co-ordinated actions of the constituent elements. Hilferding held that the tendency of this organized capitalism was towards the general cartelization of the whole national economy. Internationally, the tendency towards finance capital has variously been seen as involving anarchic international competition between tightly integrated national centres or as involving the formation of transnational alliances by the separate empires to form a closely integrated (but unstable) international network.[4]

A number of conclusions about the expected patterns of interlocks can be drawn from this model. Banks and insurance companies should be the organizing pivots of the structure and there should be a division of the network into relatively distinct cliques or clusters around these companies.[5] These clusters may perhaps be identified by the existence of multiple interlocks between companies. The network should have a moderate density because of the relative sparsity of interlocks between clusters and cliques. It is assumed that there would be a high correspondence between interlocking, on the one hand, and financial participations and indebtedness on the other. It is also to be expected that there would be a strong tendency for interlocks which disappear with the death or retirement of a director to be reinstated by the recruitment of another director.[6] The majority of the interlocks within the network should be expected to run between financial and non-financial companies rather than being confined within each sector. Multiple directors would be regarded as the finance capitalists, who may have a home base in a particular company but who also play a role on behalf of the system of finance capital as a whole.

The Co-ordination and Control Model

This model depicts the economy as structured into competing groups of co-ordinated companies, each group being subject to a specific locus of control. There are essentially two variants of the model: the bank-control model, which derives from a specific interpretation of the finance-capital model; and the family-control model. The two variants are not, however exclusive, and writers such as Sweezy (1939), Allen (1974, 1978), and Knowles (1973) have described bank-controlled 'interest groups' in which the bank is family-owned.

The bank-control model is often mistakenly equated with the finance-capital model but in fact differs in that it holds that banks are the decision-making centres within the 'empires' of high finance. Banks are seen as having an independent base of power because of the level of their shareholdings (especially in their trust departments) and because of their ability to grant or to withhold long- and short-term loans. Banks seek board representation on those companies whose affairs they wish to control, the interlock both expressing and effecting this control. In this way, banks build up interest groups subject to co-ordination or control by themselves. The bank subordinates the interests of the various corporations to a common strategy aimed at maximizing its own interests. The strongest statement of this viewpoint is to be found in Fitch and Oppenheimer's (1970) discussion of 'banking terrorism', though a weaker form of the argument can be found in Kotz (1978). As in the case of the finance-capital model, the interlock network should be structured into clusters or cliques, but it is further assumed that the interlocks will be created by bankers sitting on industrial boards rather than vice versa, i.e. interlocks are seen as directional indicators of the flow of power. Banks should, therefore, be centrally placed in a network of directional interlocks.

In the family-control variant it is held that the interest groups need not be centred around a bank but will always be based on the shareholdings and influence of a particular family, which may form a more or less extended 'kinecon group' (Zeitlin et al., 1975). Family holdings bound together through trusts, foundations and the family office are the basis upon which unified control can be exercised over the companies in which the family is interested. The model is sometimes specified as simply involving the dominance of the '60 families' or the '200 families' (Lundberg, 1937; Baumier, 1967), but in Zeitlin's work it is made clear that the model implies a view of these families as members of a propertied class (Zeitlin, 1974). In the USA the capitalist class has been seen as a network of intermarrying kinecon groups based on local business centres and integrated loosely into a national upper class (Baltzell, 1958); in societies with less of a regional structure it might be expected that the families would have relatively stronger national ties. If it is held that the families operate through banks, the interlock network should look little different from that expected on the basis of the bank-control variant. Where this does not hold, it might be expected that the central positions in the network would be taken by family investment or holding companies, each of which would lie at the centre of a clique or cluster.[7] The multiple directors, according to this model, are entrepreneurial capitalists (Scott, 1982a, p. 125) with executive positions in their base company and generating interlocks which radiate out from the base company to the other members of their interest group. It should be possible to divide the set of multiple directors into relatively distinct family groups (e.g. Rockefeller, Mellon, DuPont; Solvay, Empain; Boël; Siemens, Flick) and so the network of connections between persons would be extremely disconnected.

The Resource-dependence Model

The model of resource dependence starts out from the assumption that large enterprises depend upon one another for access to valued resources and therefore seek to establish links in an attempt to regulate their interdependence. At its extreme, the unregulated market relations are controlled by the complete fusion of the companies into a hierarchically organized enterprise. In this sense, interlocking director-ships are midway between 'market' and 'hierarchy' (Williamson 1975; Aldrich, 1979; Pennings, 1980; Burt, 1980a). Interlocks may signify a 'no competition' liaison or a coalition aimed at facilitating joint action, and it is assumed that the number of interlocks between two enterprises is an indicator of the strength of the relation. The links established can involve dyadic reciprocities or broader alliances of reciprocal interests. In the latter case there is a 'community of interest' between the constituent companies but they do not form a co-ordinated 'interest group'.[8] The most important resources sought by enterprises are capital and trading advantages but corporate information may also be considered as a resource. Sitting on the board of another company gives access to the details of its finances and operations and the specific corporate information garnered by a director may be utilized for enhancing the position of the other enterprise of which the person is a director. The implication of the model at the international level is that the control over the crucial resources of capital and technology which multinationals possess makes them independent of local banking and industrial firms. Multinationals will create alliances within their home economy but have no need to ally their foreign subsidiaries with local firms.

According to this model the network of interlocks should have no systematic structure. It should consist of dyads, triads and other communities of interest which are perhaps linked to one another through a sparse nexus of random interlocks. The model would therefore predict a low network density, a low level of centralization, and a correspondingly high degree of fragmentation. Although many of the interlocks would be directed according to the degree of power imbalance, it would not be predicted that there would be many multiple interlocks between enterprises. When dyadic interlocks are broken because of death or retirement they will tend to be replaced, but when they are broken deliberately because of the surfacing of a deep conflict of interest they will not be replaced. There should therefore be a significant but not complete replacement of broken interlocks. The model would predict that most interlocks would be carried by executives rather than by outsiders but that there should be little sign of clustering in the network.

The Managerial Model

This model is based on the general managerial view of the firm, which holds that the top executives of large enterprises have achieved almost total autonomy from control by shareholders and lenders (for a criticism see Scott, 1979). The board of directors, it is held, has little or no say in the management of a large company, the outside directors being passive and subject to manipulation by the insiders who actually run the firm (Mace, 1971; Pahl and Winkler, 1974; but see Scott, 1982b). For this reason, whatever links may exist between boards are irrelevant to the question of control over corporate strategy. Outside directors are recruited to serve two main functions: to enhance the 'environmental scan' of the enterprise and to enhance its prestige. All enterprises must monitor or scan their environment and the recruitment of prominent and well-placed outsiders to their boards enables them to accumulate relevant business and political information in a way that optimizes the scanning of the environment. Recruiting such people also enhances the social standing of the enterprise in the corporate world and so serves a useful public-relations function (Andrews, 1982). Where 'figureheads', 'token' women and so forth are recruited to the board, the public-relations function outweighs the environmental-scan function.

It is to be expected that the larger and more prestigious enterprises would have chief executives who are in high demand by other enterprises and that they will, therefore, have a large number of interlocks. Conversely, a large enterprise is unlikely to find the chief executive of a small firm attractive as an outsider on its own board. For these reasons the model predicts that most interlocks will be directed from large to smaller enterprises and that the big enterprises will have a large number of mutual interlocks. Apart from this, the network will have little structure and will simply be the outcome of stochastic processes. Since dyadic interlocks are regarded as contingent consequences of director recruitment, those which are broken would be unlikely to be replaced. To the extent that an economy is regionally organized with a major financial centre, this structure might be reproduced in the network of interlocks: a number of outside directors will be recruited through the regional contacts of the head office (especially local banks and other national firms based in the same region), but many will be recruited from the financial centre owing to its prestige in the national economy. Although the network may include a number of 'big linkers' with many directorships, this does not indicate that they are powerful. Rather, it indicates that they are persons in high demand because of their particularly prized qualifications (business knowledge, legal expertise, political contacts, etc.).

The Class-cohesion Model

This model holds that directors are recruited from an upper class and that the patterns of interlocks express and contribute to the cohesion of this class. Directors have a common educational background and they are associated with particular clubs and with the governance of charitable and educational bodies. The directorships which they hold are part of this pattern of privilege in that frequent meetings on company boards encourage informality and easy interaction amongst those who regard themselves as social equals and so enhance the opportunities of furthering business deals. This accumulation of meetings in myriad settings reinforces common experiences and definitions of the situation and so strengthens the business ethos of class members. The network of interlocks is expected to be extensive and diffuse, paralleling the diversification of investment portfolios characteristic of wealthy families in modern capitalism. The major structural feature of the network should be a separation between an 'inner circle' (or 'corporate elite') of multiple directors and the bulk of the directors. This inner circle epitomizes the relationship between social background and board membership and they are likely to be the brokers between business and the political system (Useem, 1982). The big linkers are the opinion leaders of business and their interlocks are the means through which information and opinion is communicated and accumulated. The network of connections between companies should be relatively dense. Particular dyadic interlocks are unimportant and there would be a low probability of their being replaced when broken. Interlocks simply map the cohesion of the capitalist class and their significance has to be assessed alongside the other inter-corporate and interpersonal relations which express this class cohesion.

These five models are the main sources upon which researchers have drawn in the search for the significance of the interlocking director-ships. The general strategy, however, has been either to assume the a priori validity of one particular model or to carry out tests in the attempt to select one model as being superior to all the others. The strategy suggested here is different. The point is not to choose one from among the various models but to discover the relative contribution which each can play in a full interpretation. The models are not simple alternatives but may be complementary to one another. Interlocks must be studied in such a way that it is possible to say, for example, that one type of interlock indicates relations of the kind posited by the finance-capital model and a second type indicates relations of resource dependence. Different models may be useful for explaining different aspects of the intercorporate system. Social reality is the outcome of a complex mixture of structuring mechanisms (Bhaskar, 1979) and various of the models – or elements of them – may be used to explain different features of the observable world. The mechanisms and proc-esses described in the models of economic power must be combined in varying ways to explain the different structures found in the countries studied. It is more than likely that detailed empirical research into the merits and demerits of the various models will lead to the discovery of new structuring mechanisms which have not so far figured in any of the available models. Such research may give a new meaning to elements of one model by placing them alongside mechanisms derived from radically different models.

In view of the importance of this argument to the comparative research reported in this book it is necessary to illustrate the way in which elements of the various models might be combined. Such an illustration serves the heuristic purpose of exemplifying the research strategy but it should not be regarded as pre-empting any of the findings presented in the national or comparative chapters. The finance-capital model, for example, is compatible with certain elements of the model of class-cohesion which can be taken as an extension of it. The finance-capital model posits the existence of a group of finance capitalists, those who are simultaneously involved in both the credit sector and the industrial sector and who personify the fusion of banking and industry. These finance capitalists might be expected to form a distinct grouping within the capitalist class, the inner circle around which its other members gravitate. The members of the inner circle may have their bases in privately owned family companies which stand at the head of interest groups and which form parts of larger 'empires' in which the credit institutions play a key role. These credit institutions control a resource – capital – upon which other enterprises are dependent and for this reason dyadic relations between banks and industrials might be comprehensible in terms of the resource-dependence model. To the extent that the inner circle of finance capitalists defines itself as an elevated status group and seeks to protect and enhance its own social standing, the recruitment of directors to top corporate positions may be expected to approximate to those features described in the managerial model.

This is, of course, simply one scenario. It has been outlined in order to show the way in which elements of the various models must be combined. The models must not be regarded as radically opposed either/or alternatives but as contributions to the resolution of a common problem: understanding the mechanisms structuring the exercise of economic power. National variations in economic circumstances might be expected to lead researchers to combine elements of the models in varying ways to approximate to the reality that they have observed. But it is also possible that certain generic features of advanced capitalist economies might be discovered from a comparative exercise of the kind presented in this book. The concluding chapter takes up some of these possibilities.

Interlocking directorships, it has been argued, are indicators of social relations between enterprises and individuals and it is unlikely that any one of the existing models of economic power can give a satisfactory view of the significance of the interlock patterns discovered in modern capitalist societies. A major theme of the chapters which follow is that different types of interlock may signify different types of social relation: dyadic interlocks carried by an executive in one of the companies (termed primary interlocks) might be expected to play a different role in the exercise of economic power to that played by interlocks carried by those without executive positions. A basic problem with much of the earlier research into interlocks has been a failure to realize this crucial point. Although the notion of a primary interlock, for example, was introduced almost 50 years ago (Sweezy, 1939), the importance of this conceptual innovation has rarely been recognized. Only in the recent upsurge of interest in interlocks has the attempt begun to classify them according to such criteria as whether they involve an executive, whether they imply a particular 'direction', whether they are multiple, and so on. Quite apart from the question of national variations in interlocking, each of the partial networks defined by these types of interlock will have their own distinct structures. Only through a study of such partial networks is it possible to move beyond the superficial aggregation of interlocks to a systematic account of the mechanics of economic power.

The research reported in this book has its origins in the inter-organizational perspective (see figure 1.1), based as it is around the concept of social networks with certain distinct systemic properties that can be analysed independently of the orientations and actions of the enterprises and persons involved in them. It is this distinctive concern of social-network analysis which has made it such a fruitful and powerful approach to sociological investigation (Berkowitz, 1982). However all the contributors are aware that a separation between agents and systems is artificial, that networks exist only through the active agency of people and collectivities. For this reason, each chapter moves out in a slightly different direction from a base in the interorganizational perspective. For some contributors there is an interest in showing that although the logic of the market situation facing individual enterprises is determined by the network structure, the actual courses of action followed by these enterprises are responsible for the reproduction or transformation of that structure.[9] Other contributors push the analysis in the direction of showing what the structure of relations between enterprises can tell us about the class relations between people. Indeed, the implication of the work reported here is that an adequate understanding of economic power requires a transcendence of both of the dichotomies presented in figure 1.1. A sign of the maturity of interlock research has been an increasing tendency for research to do just this.

RESEARCH DESIGN OF THE PROJECT

The comparative research project began in 1978 when a number of people who had been working on the topic of interlocking director-ships came together at a meeting of the Joint Sessions of Workshops of the European Consortium for Political Research at Grenoble.[10] Contact between these researchers at various international meetings, in the professional journals and through correspondence had led to the idea of carrying out a comparative inquiry into international variations in interlock patterns. From the beginning it was decided that the immediate end-product of the research should be a single volume which did not simply juxtapose independently written papers but would represent the outcome of a common research design and a uniform programme of data analysis. This required a tightly co-ordinated organization of the research group, and the ECPR sponsored a second meeting at Mannheim (in 1978) which enabled the details of the research to be hammered out. A meeting in Amsterdam (1979) between various members of the research group followed and initial research reports were presented at Joint Sessions of the ECPR in

Brussels (1979) and Florence (1980). As it had not proved possible to finance the project from one single source, each participating research team raised funds in its own country to support its contribution to the overall research effort. A particularly important feature of the research design had been the intention to utilize the GRADAP computer package (see below) for the analysis of the data of each national team, and it was fortunate that it was possible for this to be carried out at the University of Groningen. Each team forwarded its data to Groningen and then visited the University to discuss the results with GRADAP analysts. A major contribution to the ability of the research group to pursue the intended common analysis was financial support from the Werner Reimers Stiftung for three meetings of the group at Bad Homburg during 1981 and 1982. These meetings provided an essential focus for the work of the research group and offered opportunities for resolving many of the theoretical and empirical problems which emerged in the course of the research. Together with a final meeting in Nijmegen (1982) supported by the ECPR, these meetings enabled this book to take a much more structured form than would otherwise have been possible.

The initial concern of the research group was to arrive at a set of selection criteria which could be applied in all the participating countries and which was justified in terms of the underlying theoretical principles of the group. First of all it was necessary to decide upon which enterprises to select for analysis. Previous research had tended to take, say, the 50, 100 or 200 largest enterprises in a particular country, where 'largest' was defined in terms of a specific economic variable. It was decided to follow this practise and to select a similar number of large enterprises in each country. Although various possible measures of size were discussed, it was decided that 'turnover' (the monetary value of sales) was the only reliable measure of the size of non-financial companies that was readily available in all countries. In view of the tendency of this measure to overestimate the importance of the distributive sector – as compared, for example, with a measure based on employment – it was initially thought possible to apply a weighting to the turnover of trading companies prior to selection. This strategy was abandoned, however, on the grounds that any such weighting procedures would be arbitrary and that because many manufacturing enterprises had important trading activities the weighting could not be consistently applied. Selection was, therefore, based on unadjusted turnover.[11] A target of 200 non-financial companies was adopted, this number being chosen partly for purpose of comparability with previous research and partly because of practical limitations on the number of companies which could realistically be handled in the time allowed. Here a serious problem of cross-national comparability was encountered. In most countries consolidated results are reported at the level of the parent company, whereas in other countries, such as Belgium, non-consolidated results are reported at the level of the working companies. A selection of the 200 largest non-financials ranked by turnover would have given serious distortions if these national differences were not taken into account. It was decided to exclude, in all countries, those non-financials that would have been consolidated in another national non-financial under the usual consolidation rules because more than 50 per cent of their shares were owned by that company.

In the case of financial companies, information on turnover was neither appropriate nor available, and it was decided to take assets as the basis of selection. A total of about 50 financial enterprises were to be aimed for, taking into account clear-cut breaks in the rank distribution of assets. In rare cases, important companies from financial sectors whose assets underestimated their role in the economy were included. In general the rules of consolidation were also applied to financials, deleting the financials that would have been consolidated in another national financial company, because of a majority particip-ation. Deviations from these general rules are reported in the national chapters. Lack of adequate information on assets for all financial companies and the need to make subjective but informed judgements on the relative importance of different types of financial enterprise meant that the final selection of the 50 financials could not be made as precise and unambiguous as was possible for non-financials. As the Belgian holding companies cannot strictly be considered to belong either to the financial or to the non-financial sector, it was necessary to select them as a separate category. The Belgian data set was therefore supplemented with the 20 largest holding companies.

It was decided to collect data with 1976 as the target year. At the time of the initial planning meetings this was the most recent year for which the relevant data were available in directories, handbooks and official sources in each of the countries. Data were to be collected on the directors of the selected companies together with various items of economic information on the companies. An immediate problem became apparent. Although companies report their financial results annually, the date on which they report is not uniform. Companies can publish their results in any of the 12 months in the year and these results may be a number of months out of date by the time of their publication. Results purporting to relate to the year ending 1976 could in fact relate to the year ending in the last half of 1975. Equally, annual handbooks which reprinted this information under the date 1976 were frequently even more out of date. Each team agreed to try to compensate for these factors by using sources which were most appropriate to the target date of 1976. The problems of not being able to collect all data for a particular day in 1976 are that a number of changes in board membership will have occured during the course of a year and that in a time of rapid inflation the results of companies reporting at the end of the period may not be strictly comparable with the results of those reporting at the beginning. Where relevant, the distortions introduced by this selection criterion are discussed in the following chapters.

Having resolved to collect the names of all the directors of the selected companies holding office in 1976, it was necessary to decide on which corporate positions were to be taken as 'directors'. The word director has a relatively unambiguous meaning in British and American law but is not used in the same way in other countries, and therefore selection criteria for positions had to be adopted. These criteria had to be based on variations in the board systems operating in the various countries. In Britain and the USA there is a single board system of corporate administration, whereby all legal responsibility for corporate affairs is vested in a board of directors headed by a chairman. The chief executive or managing director (president in the USA) is normally a member of this board along with other top executives. The board meets frequently and regularly to take responsibility for determining and monitoring corporate strategy. The British and American teams selected all members of the single board. In Austria, West Germany, the Netherlands and Switzerland a form of two-board management operates. The executives of a joint stock company form an executive board (Vorstand, Raad van Bestuur) and a supervisory board (Aufsichtsrat, Raad van Commissarissen) has responsibility for appointing the executive board and for overseeing the general management of the company. The supervisory board, in turn, is selected by the shareholders.[12] The distinction between the two boards comes very close to the distinction between executive and non-executive directors in the Anglo-American system and therefore members of both boards were included in the analysis. Belgium, Finland, France and Italy have two-board systems of a rather different type, involving a distinction between an auditing board (Commissaires aux comptes, Collegio Sindacale) and an administrative board (Conseil d'administration, Consiglio d'amministrazione). The auditing board is appointed by the shareholders and is responsible for monitoring the financial probity of the enterprises but has no management responsibility and the administrative board functions very much as the single board of the Anglo-American system.[13] For the general analysis only members of the administrative board were selected.[14] Thus, the directors chosen for analysis in the case of the joint stock companies were members of the single board in Britain and the USA, members of both boards in Austria, Germany, the Netherlands and Switzerland, and members of the administrative board in Belgium, Finland, France and Italy. Not all the companies selected, however, were joint stock companies (Aktiengesellschaft, Societé Anonyme, and their equivalents) and the various partnerships, mutual companies, co-operatives, and so on were treated in such a way that the principle of selection would approximate to that used for joint stock companies.

The enterprises and directors selected for study were to be treated from the standpoint of social-network analysis and therefore the specific form of processing had to reflect the assumptions of this approach. It was decided to employ graph theory as a formal analogue of network theory and to use the specific implementation of graph theory available in the GRADAP computer package.[15] In GRADAP, enterprises were treated as points in a graph, with the interlocks between enterprises being treated as 'lines' between the points. The various points and lines in the national networks were coded with information on the type of enterprise, the type of positions directors held (executive or non-executive), industrial base, and financial variables such as turnover, assets, profits, etc. On this basis it was straightforward to analyse both the overall features of the networks and the attributes of individual enterprises. It was also possible to separate out specific types of enterprise or types of interlock for more detailed analysis. Various standard analyses were computed for all national networks and the results of many of these analyses are presented in chapter 2. Each team could request additional analyses and was encouraged to extend the standard analysis in those directions which seemed most interesting and appropriate to them. For some teams this involved an examination of the relationship between interlocks and economic performance, while for others the analysis was pursued in a more historical direction. A particularly important feature of the research was the formation of a separate team to study the links between the national networks. Drawing on earlier research by a member of the group (Fennema, 1982) and utilizing the national data sets, an attempt was made to explore some of the transnational links which are often missing from national studies.

The members of the research group would not see the research reported in this book as offering any definitive solutions to the many problems raised in the first section of this chapter. Rather, it is hoped that it can be seen as part of the reorientation of interlock research which has taken place in recent years and that it will stimulate others to continue the movement towards an adequate understanding of the mechanisms through which economic power is exercised in a capitalist society.

NOTES

1 This chapter was written by John Scott on the basis of earlier drafts prepared by Meindert Fennema and Huibert Schijf.

2 References to the relevant works produced by research-group members will be found in the list of references. More extensive bibliographies are to be found in Fennema and Schijf (1979), Scott (1979) and Mizruchi (1982a).

3 It is important to distinguish between 'finance' capital as defined here and the usage of 'financial' to refer to companies operating in banking, insurance and investment. Both usages are too well entrenched to make any alternative terminology acceptable.

4 See Fennema (1982) for a discussion of these two variants.

5 The terms 'cliques' and 'clusters' will be given technical meanings in the course of this book. In the present context the common-sense meanings are sufficient for the development of the argument.

6 On the analysis of such 'broken ties' see Palmer (1983) and Ornstein (1982).

7 Where the family base is a private foundation which has not been selected for study the cliques or clusters should exhibit an absent centre. This is a general problem involved in determining selection criteria.

8 The fact that the unequal distribution of resources leads to power imbalances between enterprises might be expected to suggest that a community of interest could be transformed into an interest group through the rise to dominance of one of its members.

9 The general form of this argument is contained in Giddens (1979, 1981).

10 References to the previous work of the participants will be found in Fennema and Schijf (1979) and in the following chapters.

11 In general this was world-wide turnover but for foreign subsidiaries operating in a participating country only the turnover within that country was taken into account.

12 In Germany the laws of 'co-determination' permit a proportion of the supervisory-board members to be appointed by the employees. In the Netherlands the shareholders have only the right of veto.

13 In Britain and the USA the auditing function is performed by firms of accountants in professional practice. They hold no board or other position in the companies which they audit.

14 In France a variant of the German two-board system has been optional since 1966.

15 GRADAP is the Graph Definition and Analysis Package developed by the interuniversity project group of the universities of Amsterdam, Groningen and Nijmegen. It uses SPSS format and can be used as an appendix to SPSS. Further details are available from Technical Centre FSW, University of Amsterdam, Roetersstraat 15, 1018 WB Amsterdam.

2

National Networks in 1976: A Structural Comparison

FRANS N. STOKMAN and FRANS W. WASSEUR

This chapter is concerned with the overall patterns of relations between the corporations that result from interlocking directorships in the various countries cited in chapter 1. Because interlocking directorships result from the accumulation of positions by directors, the chapter starts with a comparison of this cumulation for the ten countries. Subsequently, the resulting structure of relations, or lines, between the corporations is given. The overall structures of the networks in the ten countries will be compared in terms of two major aspects: their density and their centralization. A third major aspect, that of clustering, will be dealt with in the national chapters, as the basis of the clustering is different from country to country. Not all relations between corporations based on interlocking directorships can be considered of the same importance, however. The strength of a relation will depend both on the number of interlocks between two corporations and on the combination of positions held by a multiple director in the two corporations. This will be the subject of the second section. The final section will be concerned with the contribution of the primary interlocks to the overall network structures. During this chapter it will become apparent that the overall structures of the national inter-corporate networks are shaped quite differently. The following chapters will show the peculiarities of each national network in more detail, particularly with respect to positions of individual corporations and sectors in the national network and the national economy as a whole. Similarities and differences of network positions of certain categories of corporations will be the main subject of chapter 15.

ACCUMULATION OF POSITIONS: MULTIPLE
DIRECTORS AND THE NETWORK OF INTERLOCKING
DIRECTORSHIPS

In chapter 1, different perspectives have been introduced from which interlocking directorships have been studied (see figure 1.1). Whether interlocking directorships are studied from the point of view of the person or the organization, it is of the utmost theoretical and analytical importance to realize that interlocking directorships are generated by the distribution of positions over people. In this process both organizations and individuals play an active role. From the (inter) organizational point of view the active role of the organization (its role in the selection of individuals at the top levels of decision-making) is emphasized and is placed in the context of the two functions that large corporations have to perform: the supervisory function, related to the representation of shareholders and other financial interests, and the executive function, related to the management of the corporation and to the representation of the firm towards third parties (Fennema, 1982, p. 87). The organizations in the environment of the focal organization play an important role in the distribution of a certain proportion of the positions, either as constraints (if the enterprise is dependent on other organizations), or as loci of control. From the point of view of the person, ambitions and career planning determine the acceptance or refusal of positions offered to him or her. It should be realized, however, that organizational demands and constraints often play an important role in the personal choices, as personal motivations do so in the decision-making process of the organization. This is for the simple reason that decision-making within organizations is carried out by groups of individuals. Theoretically, the personal and organizational perspectives should be seen as two sides of the same coin. As it is useless to discuss which side of a coin is most important and determines its value, so it is useless to argue the predominance of one of the perspectives over the other.

Analytically it is important to start with the distribution of positions over individuals, as this defines the structure of the resulting network between organizations and people. Within a network of interlocking directorships between corporations, only persons with two or more positions – the multiple directors – generate interlocks. Figure 2.1 shows that multiple directors were a small minority of all directors, their proportion varying from 11 to 20 per cent. The largest proportions of multiple directors were observed in France, Italy, Finland, the USA and Belgium. With the exception of the USA, all these countries had a Latin variant of the European two-board system. These four countries also had the highest mean number of positions per director and this *cumulation ratio* was surprisingly constant over these countries. In the countries with the German variant of the European two-board system, the cumulation ratio was systematically lower than in the Latin variant but showed more variation. There was, however, a striking similarity between Austria and Germany. The two countries with the one-board system were very different: Great Britain had a low percentage of multiple directors and a very low cumulation ratio, whereas the USA scored high on both measures.

Figure 2.1   Multiple directors as a proportion of all directors

	A	B	CH	D	F	GB	I	NL	SF	US
(Number of multiple directors)	(271)	(373)	(405)	(420)	(378)	(282)	(322)	(357)	(564)	(564)
Country code	A	B	CH	D	F	GB	I	NL	SF	US
(Number of directors)	(2,430)	(2,203)	(2,999)	(3,943)	(1,931)	(2,682)	(1,737)	(2,321)	(3,110)	(3,108)
(Number of positions)	(2,939)	(3,000)	(3,681)	(4,727)	(2,625)	(3,091)	(2,358)	(2,950)	(4,178)	(3,976)
Cumulation ratio	1.21	1.36	1.23	1.20	1.36	1.15	1.36	1.27	1.34	1.28

Note: Countries are placed in alphabetical order of the official international abbreviations used in all the figures and tables in this chapter.

A high cumulation ratio can be due to a large proportion of multiple directors but also to a high number of directorships per multiple director. If table 2.1 is compared with figure 2.1 it can be seen that a high cumulation of positions by multiple directors was unrelated to the proportion of multiple directors. Great Britain, Germany and Austria had the same low proportion of multiple directors, but the number of directorships held by them was higher in Germany and Austria than the very low figure for Great Britain. A similar observation can be made for the USA and Finland. Both countries had a large proportion of multiple directors but the accumulation of positions in the USA was very low in comparison with Finland. In fact, table 2.1 reveals a great similarity between the USA and Great Britain, the two countries with the one-board system. The differences between these two countries in figure 2.1 are almost entirely due to the substantially larger proportion of multiple directors in the USA.

Taking figure 2.1 and table 2.1 together, it can be concluded that the distribution of positions over persons was substantially different in each of the three board systems: the Latin system (Belgium, France, Italy and Finland) combined a high proportion of multiple directors with a high cumulation of positions by them; the Anglo-American system (Great Britain and the USA) showed the lowest cumulation of positions by multiple directors; and the German system (Austria, Germany, the Netherlands and Switzerland) was located somewhere between the other two systems but the four countries showed considerable variation in terms of both the proportion of multiple directors and their cumulation of positions.

Table 2.1   Accumulation of positions by multiple directors

| | Number of positions (%) | | | | | | Total | Total number of multiple directors |
	2	3	4	5	6-10	11 or more		
Austria	65	17	9	4	4	2	100	271
Belgium	57	19	9	6	6	2	100	373
Switzerland	67	19	6	2	5	1	100	405
Germany	60	20	9	5	5	0.5	100	420
France	60	19	9	6	6	0	100	378
Britain	69	21	6	3	1	0	100	282
Italy	63	17	7	5	7	1	100	322
Netherlands	64	17	8	6	5	0	100	357
Finland	61	20	6	6	7	0.4	100	564
USA	64	24	8	3	1	0	100	564

The differences discovered in the cumulation of positions by multiple directors is of considerable importance for the structure of the networks of interlocking directorships, as the number of interlocks is a quadratic function of the number of positions held by a person. A multiple director with 16 positions, as found in both Austria and Italy, creates 120 interlocks between corporations.[1] In Great Britain no multiple director held more than six positions, generating only 15 interlocks between corporations. A substantial part of each network was, therefore, due to the interlocks of a few individuals with a large number of positions. Except for Great Britain and the USA with their low accumulation of positions, more than 60 per cent of all interlocks were carried by the multiple directors with four or more positions – between a quarter and one-fifth of the multiple directors. These multiple directors are designated 'big linkers'. Table 2.2 clearly reveals that the network of interlocking directorships cannot be analysed without a consideration of the main affiliation of the persons who carry the network: again one side of the coin cannot be studied in isolation from the other.

Table 2.2 *Interlocks carried by multiple directors*

	Interlocks % carried by multiple directors with			Total number of big linkers
	2 or 3 positions	4 or more positions	All multiple directors	
Austria	25	75	100	(1,238)	50
Belgium	19	81	100	(2,049)	92
Switzerland	38	62	100	(1,314)	56
Germany	31	69	100	(1,629)	82
France	33	67	100	(1,326)	80
Britain	63	37	100	(591)	27
Italy	27	73	100	(1,380)	65
Netherlands	35	65	100	(1,173)	68
Finland	30	70	100	(2,248)	110
USA	59	41	100	(1,308)	69

Note: Absolute numbers are in parentheses.

Before going on to this in the next section and in the national chapters, it is first necessary to compare the overall stuctures of the ten national networks. In this comparison, relations, or lines, between corporations are considered. Such a line can be due to the existence of more than one personal interlock. If two corporations share two directors (if there are two interlocks) the *multiplicity* of the line between the two corporations is said to be 2. Table 2.3 gives the multiplicities of the lines in ten countries. With the exception of France, the countries with the Latin board system showed the highest multiplicities and again Great Britain scored lowest. Multiple interlocks between corporations indicate a strong relation between two corporations and may indicate a shared system of co-optation, which gives strong possibilities of policy co-ordination and shared information. For this reason a number of analyses in the national chapters are confined to the network of multiple interlocks between corporations. In the chapter on Finland (chapter 9), for example, such an analysis made it possible to discover different groups of corporations, connected through strong, long-standing institutional links. For the first comparison of the networks, however, lines between corporations of the networks will not be differentiated according to their strength, as the main affiliations of the persons who carry the interlocks are also still to be considered. At first, equal weight will be given to all lines.

Table 2.3   Multiplicities of lines

	Multiplicity (%)					Mean number of
	1	*2*	*3*	*4 or more*	*Total lines*	*interlocks per line*
Austria	78	15	4	3	100	(909)	1.36
Belgium	67	18	7	8	100	(1,219)	1.68
Switzerland	81	12	5	2	100	(1,002)	1.31
Germany	81	14	4	2	100	(1,278)	1.27
France	85	10	3	2	100	(1,065)	1.25
Britain	94	5	2	0	100	(542)	1.09
Italy	70	17	7	7	100	(891)	1.55
Netherlands	87	11	2	1	100	(980)	1.20
Finland	75	15	5	5	100	(1,498)	1.50
USA	84	13	2	1	100	(1,086)	1.20

Note: Absolute numbers are in parentheses.

At this level of analysis the network of interlocking directorships can be interpreted as at least constituting a communication or information network between corporations. A major aspect of the structure of such a communication network is its *density*, i.e. the fraction of pairs of points (corporations) between which a line exists.[2] Two corporations, connected through a line, have a direct link between their highest decision-making organs. Such corporations with direct access are located at *distance* 1 from one another in the network. If two corporations have no direct access to one another, they may be linked indirectly through other corporations. Of special empirical importance is the proportion of pairs of corporations that are linked with one or more common third corporations. When one or more directors of two corporations meet each other in a third corporation to participate in its .policy-making, the first two corporations are said to be located at distance 2 from one another. They have one or more meeting-points in the network. Pairs of corporations at a greater distance from one another can hardly be assumed to communicate through such personal interlocks.

Figure 2.2 shows only a small variation in the densities of the ten national networks. Not surprisingly the British network showed the lowest density (0.02, or 2 per cent). Finland and Germany had a

Figure 2.2 Percentages of pairs of corporations at distances 1 and 2

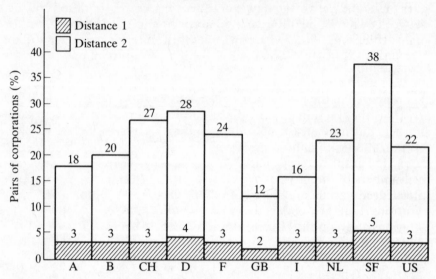

somewhat higher density than the other countries. The small differences are partly due to the very large number of pairs within each country; if 250 corporations are selected, the total number of pairs is 31,125. A further reason is that the two countries with the highest numbers of interlocks, Belgium and Finland, had the highest average multiplicity of lines, whereas Great Britain had the lowest (see table 2.3). Due to its high multiplicity of lines the Italian network had the lowest number of lines after Great Britain, although Italy had the largest number of interlocks after Finland, Belgium and Germany. In consequence, the different board systems do not result in significantly different densities in the network.

The ten networks reveal more differences with respect to the percentages of pairs of corporations at distance 2, but no systematic differences can be observed between the different board systems. The low percentage for Great Britain can be attributed to its low density. The low percentage in the Italian network, however, is surprising and hints at a low 'efficiency' of the lines in terms of indirect connections. This might well be due to the bipolar structure of the Italian network described in chapter 11.

A second major aspect of the structure of a communication network is its *centralization* – the concentration of relations around a small number of corporations. A first comparison can be made on the basis of table 2.4. The second column contains the numbers of isolated corporations in the networks – the corporations that have no interlocks with any other corporation in their own national network.

Sometimes a few corporations are connected with one or two corporations but have no indirect links with others; the numbers of these corporations are given in the third column. In all countries the bulk of the corporations were contained in one large component, in which they were directly or indirectly linked through interlocking directorships.[3] The numbers involved are given in the fourth column. Within these large components two structural aspects of the networks are compared in the last two columns: density and centralization. The density is the fraction of pairs of corporations at distance 1 from one another, but now measured only within the largest component. The centralization within the largest components is measured with Snijders' index H of graph heterogeneity. This index is based on the variation in the numbers of directly connected corporations for each corporation (the degree variance). If a component contains a number of corporations that are connected with a large number of other corporations and a number of corporations that are connected with only a few of them, then a large variation in these numbers exists and the lines in the graph will be concentrated around a small number of corporations. The measure reaches its maximum value of 1 in a component in which a completely connected centre exists and in which all other corporations are connected with all corporations in the centre without direct mutual connections. The measure is 0 if the variation in the numbers of connected corporations is as expected under random distribution of the lines between the corporations. This index makes it possible to compare the heterogeneity of networks with different numbers of corporations and lines (Snijders, 1981).

Table 2.4   Components in the networks

	Number of corporations				Density	H index
	Selected	*Isolated*	*In small components[a]*	*In largest component*	*(largest component)*	*(largest component)*
Austria	241	90	4	147	0.08	0.30
Belgium	270	80	8	182	0.07	0.35
Switzerland	250	44	0	206	0.05	0.26
Germany	259	62	2	195	0.07	0.27
France	250	30	0	220	0.04	0.13
Britain	250	61	4	185	0.03	0.12
Italy	247	53	14	180	0.06	0.22
Netherlands	250	56	4	190	0.05	0.24
Finland	237	27	0	210	0.07	0.30
USA	252	24	2	226	0.04	0.13

Note:
a There were only small components of size 2 or 3.

Four countries had only a small number of isolated corporations and a large component of 200 or more corporations: the USA, France, Finland and Switzerland. The small numbers of isolated corporations was mainly due to the relatively small numbers of subsidiaries of foreign enterprises among the selected corporations in these countries. In all countries these subsidiaries tended to be isolated or only very loosely connected with other corporations. In the USA only a few subsidiaries of foreign parents were sizeable enough to be selected, whereas the small number of subsidiaries of parents in the other three countries can be attributed to a strong nationally oriented economic policy by their governments. Of these four countries, two had dense and centralized components: Finland and Switzerland. The levels of centralization and density in Finland were particularly due to the existence of a small number of national, integrative forums that knitted together different ideological and economic groups and which were, in turn, densely connected (see chapter 9). In Switzerland, the banks were the main integrators of the network (see chapter 7). The lower density and centralization in the USA was due to the existence of various regional centres, around which the American network was built (see chapter 13), whereas the predominance of different financial groups was the main reason for the low centralization and density found in the French network (see chapter 10).

The remaining six countries had a large component of less than 200 corporations. In Austria and Belgium in particular, the number of isolates was very large. At the same time, however, these two countries had the most dense and centralized components. The Belgian network was very centralized because of the very strong position of the holding companies, which integrated the traditional financial and industrial sectors (see chapter 8). In Austria, the centralized structure was due to the predominance of the nationalized sector in the economy (see chapter 4). In both countries a large number of subsidiaries of foreign enterprises were sizeable enough to be selected and this is the main reason for the small size of the large components. In Germany and the Netherlands, the banks were the main integrators of the network, though the German network was both denser and more centralized than the Dutch. Historically, the German banks have played an important role as industrial banks with large, direct financial participations in German industry (see chapter 5) and this contrasts with the Netherlands, where the banks were strongly oriented towards trade and, by consequence, towards the provision of short-term credits (see chapter 6). Although the large component of the Italian network was denser than that of the Netherlands, the Italian network was less centralized. This was due to the fact that it had two centres: a state and a private centre (as is shown in chapter 11). The British network had the loosest network of all countries: a moderately sized large component with a low density and a low level of centralization. In chapter 12 several arguments are given for this sparse and less integrated network, two of which are the presence of other forums of business discussion and the high frequency of British board meetings in comparison with the practice in most other countries.

Although the value of H is independent of the density of a graph, it can be seen in table 2.4 that there was an almost perfect association between centralization and density over the ten countries: less dense networks tended to be less centralized. This association did not occur in Italy however, due to the very clear bipolar structure of the Italian network. The association can partly be explained by the fact that lines in a network of interlocking directorships are not created independently of one another. A new board position for a multiple director who already occupies ten positions creates ten new lines, unless a number of these corporations were already connected by one or more interlocks. Centralization and density are both strongly dependent on the accumulation of positions shown in table 2.1. This dependency will be eliminated in the third section, where only primary interlocks are considered.

Because of the special empirical meaning of distance 1 (direct access) and distance 2 (one or more meeting points), the relative centrality of corporations in the network can best be determined on the basis of their immediate neighbourhood.[4] Centrality measures based on all

Table 2.5 Distribution of lines over corporations in the large components

	Percentage of lines							Number of lines carried by the most central corporation[a]
	1	2	3–5	6–10	11–25	26–50	51 or more	Total	
Austria	10	7	20	17	33	12	0	100	47
Belgium	10	9	22	14	27	15	3	100	64
Switzerland	8	13	25	21	26	5	1	100	59
Germany	6	4	22	24	30	14	1	100	66
France	4	7	25	23	38	3	0	100	34
Britain	16	11	31	29	12	1	0	100	28
Italy	13	10	19	23	30	6	0	100	41
Netherlands	9	10	21	24	30	6	1	100	56
Finland	7	10	16	21	29	15	2	100	74
USA	5	7	16	37	30	4	0	100	37

Note:
a In graph theory the number of lines carried by a point is called adjacency or degree.

distances or on information flows over all shortest paths in a network (Freeman, 1979) do not seem applicable in this empirical situation, because distances larger than 2 have little meaning for communication or control between corporations. Table 2.5 gives the distribution of lines over the corporations in the ten large components. The number of lines with which a corporation is incident corresponds to the number of corporations to which it has direct access (distance 1). Table 2.5 shows how the differences in centralization and density in the large components of the ten countries resulted in quite large differences in the distribution of lines over corporations. In Finland the most central corporation was directly connected with no less than 74 other corporations through one or more interlocks, whereas in Britain the most central corporation was directly linked with only 28 other corporations. Another significant aspect of the distribution of lines over corporations is the fact that in some countries this distribution seems to have been double peaked. In Austria, Belgium and Finland, the three most centralized networks, corporations had either a very few or a rather large number of lines, a fact that of course results in a high degree variance for the component.

The existence of central corporations in a network, i.e. corporations that are directly connected with a large number of other corporations, is not identical to the existence of a *centre* in the network. Central corporations may well have their own spheres of influence, in which case one can hardly speak of one overall centre. The concept of a centre is, rather, associated with the existence of a number of central corporations having a high number of mutual connections: the network between central corporations is densely connected, and all central corporations are able to communicate with each other. As communication in the network of interlocking directorships is confined to distances 1 and 2, central corporations were seen as constituting one centre if they had either direct access or meeting points with *all* other central corporations. In other words, to determine whether central corporations constitute one centre, the maximal subset of central corporations, in which all pairs of central corporations had distances 2 or less in the graph as a whole, was investigated. Graph-analytically this is equivalent to ascertaining which points with the highest number of lines are contained in one or more 2-cliques in the overall graph (Alba, 1973; Mokken, 1977; Mokken and Stokman, 1979).[5] The sizes of these centres varied considerably: 58 corporations in Finland, 48 in Belgium, 38 in the Netherlands, 35 in Germany, 34 in Austria, 28 in Switzerland, 21 in Italy, 15 in France, 12 in the USA, and 9 in Britain.

For a further analysis of the degree of centralization in the network, the larger national centres were split into two groups – the *core* and *inner margin.* A core consists of those corporations that are most important in terms of the diffusion of information between them within its centre; this is measured by the rush. The *rush* of a point is a measure of the probability that a unit of information between two randomly chosen points over the shortest paths passes through the

Table 2.6   Size and density of centrality groups

(a) Size of centrality groups[a]

	Centre		Outer margin	Periphery	Total
	Core	Inner margin			
Austria	11	—	23	85	28	147
Belgium	21	—	27	100	34	182
Switzerland	12	—	16	137	41	206
Germany	15	—	19	121	39	195
France	—	15	—	161	44	220
Britain	—	9	—	137	39	185
Italy	7	—	14	125	34	180
Netherlands	16	—	22	118	34	190
Finland	23	—	35	109	43	210
USA	—	12	—	167	47	226

(b) Density of centrality groups

	Centre		Outer margin	Periphery	Total
	Core	Inner margin			
Austria	0.84	—	0.33	0.05	0.02	0.08
Belgium	0.72	—	0.25	0.03	0.02	0.07
Switzerland	0.79	—	0.23	0.03	0.01	0.05
Germany	0.74	—	0.30	0.03	0.03	0.07
France	—	0.45	—	0.05	0.02	0.04
Britain	—	0.39	—	0.03	0.01	0.03
Italy	0.67	—	0.42	0.05	0.02	0.06
Netherlands	0.56	—	0.23	0.03	0.03	0.05
Finland	0.59	—	0.19	0.03	0.01	0.07
USA	—	0.35	—	0.03	0.01	0.04

Notes:
a   In France, Britain and the USA the centres were too small for further division into core and inner margin.
—   Throughout the book a dash has been used in the tables to indicate that an entry is not available or not applicable.

point in question (Anthonisse, 1971). In this case an overall centrality measure can be used because the centre contains no large distances.[6] The sets of non-central corporations were also split into two groups. The corporations with the highest sum distances are considered to belong to the *periphery* of the network, their rows in the distance matrix containing a quarter of the sum of all distances in the network. The other non-central corporations are termed the *outer margin*.

Table 2.6a gives the sizes of the different centrality groups in the ten countries, and the densities within these centrality groups are given in Table 2.6b. The relatively low densities of the British, French and American centres are very significant. Although these centres were about the same size as the cores in the other countries, their densities were much lower. In these three countries one can hardly speak of a true network centre, and for other reasons this was also the case in Italy (see chapter 11). In the other six countries, the network of interlocking directorships can be said to have been built around a densely connected centre of corporations. This is corroborated by the fact that the bipartite densities between core and inner margin were higher than the densities within the inner margin. If the bipartite densities between core and outer margin, between inner margin and outer margin and within the outer margin are compared, a decreasing order from the first to the third can be observed for all countries with a true centre.

The composition of the cores and centres will be considered in detail in the national chapters and will be compared in chapter 15. For the moment it can be concluded that six countries had a true centre, three countries had no centre and one country (Italy) had two centres. The six countries with a true centre had a more dense and more centralized network structure than the three countries without centres. The density of the Italian network, however, was similar to that of the six countries with a single centre.

TYPES OF INTERLOCKS AND STRENGTH OF LINES

In the preceeding section the total network of interlocking directorships has been studied. This discussion of the overall structure of the network did not distinguish between different types of interlocks. In general, interlocks were considered as indicators of the existence of communication channels between corporations, possibly to be used for the direct exchange of information between their highest levels of decision-making. This is only partly true, however. For certain interlocks this interpretation is too weak, while for others it might be too strong. It is well known that in certain situations interlocking directorships have a one-sided character, particularly if they coincide with financial participations. Such interlocks indicate that the potential for financial *control* is being effected. In other situations, however, interlocks just result from the fact that two corporations have a common third orientation. An executive of a bank, for example, might be appointed as a director of two corporations, B and C, because of a common bank-orientation of the two corporations. These relations may be due to financial links between the bank and the corporations or just to a need to bring financial expertise into their boards, and it is doubtful whether the resulting interlock between B and C will be used for the direct exchange of information between them. Such interlocks are termed *induced interlocks*[7] because they are due to a common third orientation. Three variants can be distinguished.

First is the situation where corporation A has long-standing economic links, such as financial participations or relatively permanent supplier/buyer relations, with several other enterprises. Such relations can be termed *institutional* links, and the interlocks between corporation A and the other corporations can be considered as *primary interlocks*. If the personal interlocks which effect the institutional links between A and the other corporations are equally divided among A's directors, then only a few induced interlocks will result among the other corporations. If, on the other hand, only one or two individuals in A are specially qualified to carry the primary interlocks, a large number of induced interlocks will result. The number of induced interlocks grows rapidly with the number of positions held by a person. Induced interlocks may also arise because several corporations have a common institutional orientation outside the selected corporate system, e.g. in the government.[8] In this second situation *all* interlocks between corporations should be considered as induced, as they are not created specifically in order to establish communication channels between the corporations. The number of these induced interlocks increases, as above, if only a few people are considered to be specially qualified to carry the primary links with the outside organizations. In the two situations discussed, the importance of induced interlocks for the network increases if institutional links, inside or outside the network, coincide with the special qualifications of the few people carrying the primary links. This leads to a consideration of a third situation that has to be distinguished, namely that the third orientation of the corporations is simply to the highly qualified person. In this situation the primary orientation is completely *personal*. Again, all interlocks between corporations should be seen as induced.

Due to a lack of information about institutional links among the selected corporations (only financial participations are known and only for some countries) an indirect method had to be used to determine the relevance of different types of interlocks as indicators of institutional links. For this purpose interlocks were classified according to the combination of positions of the multiple director in the two corporations. For a comparative analysis of the intercorporate structure on the basis of interlocking directorships, such a classification should be based on criteria that are independent of the different board systems. As stated in chapter 1 and earlier in this chapter, two functions have to be carried out at the top decision-making levels in large corporations: the supervising and the executive. The way in which these two functions are organized differs from country to country and depends on the legal structure of the corporation. The theoretical importance of the distinction between them makes it desirable to classify positions according to whether they are primarily executive or supervisory. Involvement in all major decisions within a corporation on a day-to-day basis was taken as the determining characteristic of *inside positions*. These positions are usually held by persons who are employed full time by the corporation. In the German system all positions on the executive board were considered to be inside positions and in the Anglo-American system the executive directors were considered as insiders. In the Anglo-American system the distinction between executive and non-executive directors is a clear-cut distinction and all non-executive directors were defined as holding *outside positions* in the corporation. In the continental European systems, however, further distinctions can be made. In the Latin system, positions on the first board that were usually occupied by full-time directors were classified as inside positions. A number of members of the first board, along with members of governing boards of co-operatives, and the chairmen and delegated directors of the supervisory board in the German system were designated as holders of *intermediate positions*. This designation was made on the basis of their involvement in major decisions on a more regular basis than the true outside directors. These definitions are further specified in the various national chapters. In certain analyses the intermediate positions were considered as a separate category, but in all other cases they were counted with the outside positions as they did not correspond to the strict criterion of day-to-day involvement in major decisions.

In the first part of table 2.7 the percentages of inside, intermediate and outside positions in the ten countries are given. It shows that in the Latin variant of the continental European board system the number of inside positions was considerably smaller than in the other board systems. This difference disappears, however, if only those positions that are held by multiple directors are considered. No systematic differences between the various board systems can be observed any longer, although important differences between countries (such as the

Table 2.7　Inside, intermediate and outside positions

| | All directors (%) | | | | Multiple directors (%) | | | |
	Inside	Inter-mediate	Outside	Total	Inside	Inter-mediate	Outside	Total
Austria	37	5	58	100 (2,939)	27	9	63	100 (780)
Belgium	18	10	71	100 (3,000)	21	13	66	100 (1,170)
Switzerland	39	11	50	100 (3,681)	38	34	28	100 (1,087)
Germany	39	5	56	100 (4,727)	20	10	70	100 (1,204)
France	13	8	79	100 (2,625)	14	8	77	100 (1,072)
Britain	—	0	—	100 (3,091)	26	0	74	100 (691)
Italy	25	0	75	100 (2,358)	26	0	74	100 (972)
Netherlands	31	15	54	100 (2,950)	16	12	72	100 (984)
Finland	11	26	62	100 (4,178)	15	21	64	100 (1,632)
USA	29	0	71	100 (3,976)	17	0	83	100 (1,432)

Note: Absolute numbers are in parentheses.

very high percentage of inside positions for multiple directors in Switzerland) can be observed. The larger number of executive positions found in the German board system and in the USA was related principally to the internal management of the corporation and was not associated with representation of the firm on third-party boards.

Figure 2.3　Types of interlocks

| | | Position in corporation B | | |
		Inside	Intermediate	Outside
	Inside	ININ interlocks	INMED interlocks	INOUT interlocks
Position in corporation A	Intermediate		MEDMED interlocks	MEDOUT interlocks
	Outside			OUTOUT interlocks

On the basis of all possible combinations of types of positions held by a multiple director in two corporations, interlocks can be classified into the six types shown in figure 2.3. This typology is based on the assumption that different types of interlocks correspond with the exchange of differing amounts of information. If one multiple director has an inside position in two corporations, then the two corporations are very strongly tied together. In such rare cases the interlock is clearly used to exercise control. At the other extreme, an interlock created by a multiple director who has outside positions in two corporations can be assumed to involve only communicative functions, unless such an interlock coincides with other interlocks to create a line of high multiplicity. *The more 'outside' the combination of positions, the looser the interlock can be assumed to be.* This is confirmed if the types of interlocks that are used in combination with financial participations are considered. For eight countries data on financial participations were available and table 2.8 gives an overview of the types of interlocks that co-occur with them. This analysis suggests that INOUT interlocks, either alone or in combination with others were used to effect the possibilities of control created by financial participations. Finland and Belgium deviate from the other countries in terms of both the low percentage of financial participations without interlocks and the lower frequency of use of INOUT interlocks to effect them. Particularly in Belgium, multiple interlocks were an alternative mechanism for effecting intensive and mutual control relationships by the holding companies and their associated corporations. In other countries one of the executives of a parent tended to be an outside director in its subsidiary, whereas in Belgium and Finland the reverse was quite often the case. In these latter networks, therefore, it is dangerous to assign a direction to the INOUT interlock, although this might well be done for other countries. In all networks, however, INOUT interlocks were clearly tighter than MEDMED interlocks. It was, therefore, decided to consider ININ, INMED, and INOUT interlocks as *primary* interlocks and the other types of interlocks as *secondary*.

These results confirm that the combination of positions in two corporations is related to the strength of the relation between them, as was assumed in earlier studies on the basis of the following theoretical arguments.

(1)   A corporation is likely to use an insider to effect its institutional links.

(2)   A corporation is not likely to allow its executives to spend a great amount of time on other boards unless such positions serve certain institutional links.

(3)   An executive of a corporation in a supervisory position in another corporation has the right to receive all relevant financial information about that corporation, whereas the corporation has no such right of access to information about the base company.

If primary interlocks can be associated in general with institutional

Table 2.8 Co-occurence of types of interlocks with financial participations

| | Interlocks/participation co-occurences (%) | | | | | | | | | | Financial participations without interlocks as percentage of all financial participations |
| | Single types of interlocks | | | | | | Combination of types of interlocks[a] | | | Total | |
	ININ	INMED	INOUT	MEDMED	MEDOUT	OUTOUT	INOUT and one another	Other combinations of 2	Combinations of at least 3		
Austria	4	10	27	0	3	4	37	4	11	100 (73)	27
Belgium	2	4	16	0	7	5	20	14	33	100 (220)	17
Switzerland	0	0	27	0	4	4	27	15	23	100 (26)	41
Germany	1	9	39	0	4	8	29	5	5	100 (98)	24
Britain	0	—	65	—	—	12	23	0	0	100 (26)	54
Italy	1	—	38	—	—	20	29	6	6	100 (93)	46
Netherlands	0	6	57	2	0	4	23	2	4	100 (47)	45
Finland	5	7	22	2	6	11	23	10	15	100 (155)	25

Notes: Absolute numbers are in parentheses.
a The combinations in this table refer to the number of types and not to the multiplicity of interlocks.

links, as the above results strongly support, it makes sense to consider two types of secondary interlocks in further analyses. If a person is an executive in corporation A and an outside director in corporations B, C, etc., it will be clear that all his or her interlocks between A and the other corporations are primary interlocks. All the interlocks of that person between the corporations B, C, etc., will be classified as *induced* by his primary interlocks. All the remaining interlocks, i.e. all interlocks created by persons who are not executives in any corporation, are considered to be induced by common institutional orientations outside the selected corporations or to be due to personal qualifications only. These interlocks are, for the moment, designated as 'unclassified'. In table 2.9 the distribution of these types of interlocks are given for all ten countries, and the primary and induced interlocks are further subdivided according to whether the main affiliation of the multiple director was located in a financial corporation (including the Belgian holdings), in a production corporation, or in both. Only in Austria and in countries with the Latin board system was this last combination of executive positions frequent enough to give measurable values. Table 2.9 shows that the distribution of these types of interlocks was quite different for the ten countries. Moreover, it shows that the unclassified interlocks contribute significantly to the density of the networks. In Switzerland, the USA, the Netherlands, and France more than 50 per cent of all interlocks were carried by persons who had no executive positions in any of the selected corporations. In several of the following chapters a number of these unclassified interlocks are classified on the basis of biographies of individuals.

Table 2.2 showed that, in general, a small number of big linkers – directors with four or more directorships – were responsible for a very large number of interlocks. In particular, a small number of multiple directors with four or more directorships, but without any inside positions, carried most of the unclassified interlocks:

156 interlocks by 11 network specialists in Austria;
270 interlocks by 28 network specialists in Belgium;
514 interlocks by 31 network specialists in Switzerland;
378 interlocks by 32 network specialists in Germany;
378 interlocks by 42 network specialists in France;
 37 interlocks by 4 network specialists in Great Britain;
272 interlocks by 16 network specialists in Italy;
380 interlocks by 34 network specialists in the Netherlands;
423 interlocks by 41 network specialists in Finland; and
307 interlocks by 39 network specialists in the USA.

These multiple directors will be denoted *network specialists*, by virtue of their important role in communication through the intercorporate network as a whole. They are the opinion leaders in business and their positions in many different corporations can provide them with information from many different sources. Often playing the role of the *eminence grise*, their prestige in business circles is such that they may well represent large sections of the business world. Their function is, then, to 'supply some order and co-ordination in place of anarchy' (Barratt Brown, 1973, p. 103). This, of course, does not hold for all big linkers. A big linker may hold these positions because of membership in a minority ethnic group or because of his or her gender. Increased concern over equal opportunities might be expected to result in greater numbers of such people. This distinction between those big linkers who are and those who are not network specialists must be drawn in each case on the basis of detailed biographical information.

Those big linkers who hold an inside position in one corporation tend to be more than simply representatives of their base company and take on the communication role attributed to network specialists. This idea were expressed long ago by C. Wright Mills, when he argued that:

> On the higher levels, those in command of great corporations must be able to broaden their views in order to become industrial spokesmen rather than merely head of one of the greater firms of industry.
>
> In short, they must be able to move from one company's policy and interests to those of industry. There is one more step which some of them take: they move from the industrial point of interest and outlook to the interests and outlook of the class of all big corporate property as a whole. (Mills, 1956, p. 121)

The concept of big linkers is an empirical elaboration of the idea that 'on the higher levels' industrial spokesmen are more than just the heads of the large firms. Since the big linkers carry a disproportionate part of the network it may be assumed that the network as a whole is more important for communication than for domination and control. From an individual corporation's point of view this function has been called 'environmental scanning' (Useem, 1982) but from the point of view of the corporate *system* this concept stresses the passive side of the big linker's function. The industrial spokesmen constitute the inner circle of the corporate directorate and historical research has demonstrated that the big linkers are decisive in promoting new ideas on political and economic issues, new answers to urgent problems and ways out of economic problems which confront several, if not all, corporations (Baudet and Fennema, 1983).

Table 2.9 Distribution of types of interlocks (%)

	Financial		Production		Financial and production		Unclassified	Total number of inter-locks
	Primary	Induced	Primary	Induced	Primary	Induced		
Austria	15	27	10	8	8	8	23	100 (1,238)
Belgium	10	13	13	15	13	11	25	100 (2,049)
Switzerland	8	8	13	8	0	0	63	100 (1,314)
Germany	13	20	15	14	0	0	38	100 (1,629)
France	7	11	15	12	3	3	50	100 (1,326)
Britain	23	13	25	12	0	0	28	100 (591)
Italy	7	8	18	13	14	8	32	100 (1,380)
Netherlands	10	13	14	9	0	0	53	100 (1,173)
Finland	5	7	22	18	5	4	38	100 (2,248)
USA	6	4	23	12	0	0	55	100 (1,308)

Note: Absolute numbers are in parentheses.

The next section analyses that part of the network than can most directly be connected with institutional links: the networks of primary interlocks. Although *multiple* unclassified interlocks between corporations are sometimes used as an alternative instrument to maintain institutional links, as table 2.8 showed and further analyses in the national chapters will demonstrate, they will not be considered in the analysis of the overall structures in the following section.

STRUCTURAL FEATURES OF THE NETWORK OF PRIMARY INTERLOCKS

What are the consequences of the elimination of secondary interlocks for the network structures in the ten countries? This question can be approached by considering again the two major structural concepts of density and centralization, referring to the chapters on individual countries for further details and for discussions of clustering. In table 2.10 density and centralization in the network of primary interlocks are given for the ten countries, as they were given in table 2.4 for all lines. It should be stressed that the results are based on analyses in which no direction from inside to outside positions has been attached to primary interlocks. While this may be done in some of the separate national analyses, it is not done in this comparative analysis because of the particular features of the Belgian and Finnish networks reported in the previous section.

The structures of the networks of primary interlocks did not deviate significantly from the structures of the overall networks. The three countries without an overall centre, Great Britain, the USA and France, were again found to be the least centralized networks, as their low values for the H-index of graph heterogeneity indicate. These three countries were followed by Italy with its two centres in the overall network. Of the six countries with an overall centre, Belgium had by far the most dense and centralized structure in its network of primary interlocks. The correlation between centralization and density in the networks of primary interlocks is no longer an artefact of dependency on the number of lines, as was the case in the networks of all interlocks. Each line is, in principle, created independently from any other by each new position taken by an inside director. This implies that the correlation should be seen as an important empirical finding. Inspection of table 2.10 shows that the correlation is disturbed in three countries: Italy had a dense network with a low centralization, whereas Germany and the Netherlands had a centralized network of primary interlocks with a low density. While the first can be attributed to the two centres in Italy, the latter finding is due to the very central position

Table 2.10 Components in the networks of primary interlocks

	Number of coporations					Density (largest component)	H index (largest component)
	Selected	Isolated	In small components[a]	In medium-sized components[a]	In largest component		
Austria	241	108	7	0	126	0.038	0.20
Belgium	270	109	12	12	137	0.054	0.30
Switzerland	250	87	7	5	151	0.022	0.16
Germany	259	79	6	0	174	0.027	0.21
France	250	69	13	0	168	0.020	0.06
Britain	250	84	10	0	156	0.021	0.07
Italy	247	88	0	4	155	0.036	0.11
Netherlands	250	100	9	0	141	0.026	0.21
Finland	237	46	4	0	187	0.035	0.19
USA	252	49	13	0	190	0.019	0.05

Note:
a Small components refer to components of size 2 or 3 as in table 2.4. Medium-sized components refer to all other components except the largest one; their sizes vary between 4 and 8.

in each network of a few banks that rely heavily on the interlocks of their own executives, as will be demonstrated in chapters 5 and 6.

It can, therefore, be concluded that the contours of an overall national network were determined by the pattern of its primary interlocks, even though these interlocks generally constituted far less than half of all interlocks. Even if the remaining interlocks can be interpreted in terms of general business communication, they can be seen to correspond to the institutional preferences and constraints on the basis of which the primary interlocks were established. The primary interlocks can, therefore, be interpreted as the skeleton around which the body of a network is formed and which thus determines its shape. In the following chapters, the shapes of the 'skeletons' and 'bodies' will be analysed in far more detail than was possible in this comparative chapter.

In this chapter it was demonstrated that the network structures and board systems in the ten countries were strongly associated. For this reason, the national chapters have been ordered according to board system. First the four countries with a German board system will be analysed: Austria, Germany, the Netherlands and Switzerland. Next the four countries with the Latin board system will be considered in more detail: Belgium, Finland, France and Italy. Finally, the two countries with the Anglo-American board system will be examined: Britain and the USA. First, however, interlocks will be related to the economic performance of corporations in the next chapter. Because of the association between board system and network structure, three countries that represent three different board systems have been selected for this analysis: Belgium, the Netherlands and the USA. Readers who are not acquainted with the techniques of chapter 3, may go straight to chapter 4 and the other national chapters as the analyses in those chapters are not dependent on those of chapter 3.

NOTES

1 The general formula is $m(m-1)/2$, where m is the number of positions held.
2 In an undirected graph with N points, the potential number of lines is the total number of pairs of points, which equals $N(N-1)/2$. At several places in the book the density between disjoint (i.e. exclusive) subsets of corporations, such as financials and non-financials, are considered. In these situations, analysis is confined to pairs of points in which one point belongs to the first subset and the other to the second subset. In such a 'bi-partite graph', with N_1 points in the first subset and N_2 points in the second, the total number of pairs is N_1*N_2 (Harary et al., 1965; Harary, 1972).
3 An undirected graph is 'connected' if all its points are directly or indirectly linked with one another through sequences of lines. A 'component' in a graph is defined

as a maximally connected subgraph. In a directed graph, a point is 'reachable' from another point if it is possible to move from the latter to the former through a continuous sequence of lines running in the same direction. A 'weak component' is a maximally connected subgraph in which no direction is given to the lines. A 'strong component' is a maximal subgraph of mutually reachable points.

4   In an undirected graph, two points are 'adjacent' to one another if they are directly connected by a line. The adjacency of a point is defined as the total number of its adjacent points. The 'degree' of a point is defined as the total number of lines that are incident with the point. In a simple graph without loops and parallel lines, the adjacency and the degree are equal. In a directed graph, the 'indegree' of a point is the total number of its incoming lines and the 'outdegree' is the total number of its outgoing lines.

5   In graph theory the general definition of an N-clique is a maximal subgraph in which each pair of points has a maximum distance of N to one another in the graph as a whole. In a 1-clique, all pairs of points are directly connected by lines.

6   The split between core and inner margin is chosen where a break is observed in the values of the rush.

7   Sweezy (1939) combines these with certain other types of interlocks and terms them secondary interlocks.

8   It should be noted that any study which selects a subset of corporations for investigation, e.g. the top 250, is likely to involve cases where interlocks between selected corporations arise from common institutional links to a company outside the top 250. The technical problems raised by this possibility are discussed at the relevant points in the following chapters.

3

The Interaction Between Interlocking Directorships and the Economic Behaviour of Companies

WIM MEEUSEN and LUDO CUYVERS

The study of interlocking directorships is not without interest for economists. An early indicator of this in the USA is the famous Clayton Act of 1914, which prohibited interlocks between companies considered to be competitors. The motives behind this law were partly ideological (Pennings, 1980, pp. 1 – 2) but also there was a real concern for the possibility that firms might be able to secure through interlocks profits which would otherwise be lost.

A second pointer to the economic importance of interlocking directorships is the continuing discussion within the economics profession theories relating to the 'hierarchy' concept introduced by Williamson (1975). This discussion raises fundamental problems for the relevance of the traditional assumptions used in both micro-economic and macro-economic theory, as it has recently been stressed that the latter should be based on so-called micro-foundations. Received micro-economic theory studies market exchanges between autonomous economic entities. In the view of Williamson, hierarchical transactions may supersede the market since 'they are ones for which a single administrative entity spans both sides of the transaction' (1975, p. xi). Prices in these circumstances no longer serve as reliable (and sufficient) signals on which rational entrepreneurial action can be based and micro-economic theory looses its footing. Interlocking directorships can be seen as being mid way between markets and hierarchies and, as such, they undermine, for the same reasons, the beliefs of the micro-theorist. Small wonder that the phenomenon of interlocking directorships is often dismissed out of hand and regarded, at best, as a clumsy method for gathering information. Stigler (1966) is a leading critic in this matter.

Yet another pointer to the economic relevance of interlocks is the continuous thread that runs through this book, i.e. the confrontation of different models of business organization with the evidence from networks of interlocking directorships. It is obvious that the relevance of these models (the finance-capital model, the co-ordination and control model and the models focusing on resource dependency, managerialism or class cohesion, all described in chapter 1) is an important datum for economic theorists and economic policy-makers alike.

Important as the subject may be for economists, one is forced to conclude from the results published so far in the quickly growing literature that the existing evidence is extremely fragmentary and often contradictory. This unfortunate situation is the result of four major factors. First, while most studies pertain to the same country (the USA) and the same sector (the manufacturing sector), the period or year of observation varies widely and the sample size and the sampling method differs. Second, a large number of issues have been addressed in the literature, blurring thereby the overall picture. The analytical premises may even be different. Social scientists tend to direct the causal arrow from economic variables to interlocks, since the latter are their main interest. This leads them to focus mainly on the possible influence of indebtedness, debt structure, and solvency on the number of financial directors on the board of production companies. Economists will naturally go the other way round. They will rather be interested in the relation between interlock variables and performance indicators. Although both approaches may be sound in themselves, there are two other disturbing aspects to this inherent duality in the analysis of interlocking directorships. There is, of course, the obvious identific-ation problem familiar to econometricians. Moreover, when, as is often the case, regression techniques are used and there is a 'simultaneous-equation effect', the sign of regression coefficients as well as their statistical significance in OLS-equations may be highly misleading. There is a striking parallel with the issues involved in demand and supply modelling in economics. The third factor is that researchers often reach radically opposing conclusions with statistical material that scarcely differs. This is a consequence of the multitude of possible interlock and economic variables and of the altogether marginal explanatory power, in statistical terms, of interlock and economic variables with respect to each other. An extremely large number of variables can indeed be constructed by making use of the differences between inside and outside positions, to- and from-interlocks, inter-locks with financial or non-financial corporations, interlocks with competitors and with corporations downstream or upstream in the production hierarchy and interlocks in absolute numbers or related to board size, etc. Fourth, since no set of hypotheses has so far gained a decisive advantage over others, there is a theoretical vacuum which invites researchers to choose that particular combination of independent and dependent variables which best suits their needs in terms of the theories they want to support.

All this seems to imply a harmful positive feedback. At the present stage of theoretical development each new research effort threatens to add to the confusion and to render fruitful work more problematic. One is forced to conclude that it is probably too soon to go to the data with a clear-cut set of hypotheses for testing. There is more need for a systematic but explanatory approach. In other words, the theoretical frameworks presented in chapter 1 will not be used in any a prioristic way. Instead, a number of traditional economic ratios at the company level and a number of more or less straightforward interlock variables will be used in an attempt to generate an interpretable pattern. This will make it possible to outline a few hypotheses to be tested in future research. The choice of the interlock variables will, of course, be inspired by what has been said in chapter 2 on the theoretical bases of different types of interlocks.

The originality of the present contribution resides in three special features. First, there is, of course, its inductive strategy. Second, there is an international comparison between three countries (the USA, the Netherlands and Belgium). Third, the statistical part of the research methodology will be as systematic and uniform as possible. The latter two points will be enlarged upon in the remainder of this section and in the next.

The international comparison of the relations between economic characteristics of firms and their network characteristics in terms of interlocking directorships is, of course, interesting in its own right, but it is also an immediate by-product of the work of the research group. The choice of the USA, the Netherlands and Belgium as countries to be compared has been inspired, on the one hand, by the view that comparison with previous research requires the inclusion of the USA, and, on the other hand, by the availability of the economic data in the joint data set of the research group.[1] The choice, we believe, is a happy one, as the three countries offer a broad spectrum of different modes of business organization. The economy of the Netherlands is dominated by a relatively small number of very large and relatively independent multinational corporations of Dutch, foreign or mixed origin. Belgium, on the other hand, is a country whose economy is still for many a classroom example of the finance-capital model. A comparison of the three countries, once an inductive methodological approach has been chosen, may therefore yield a number of new insights by virtue of the stimulating diversity.

THE RESEARCH METHOD

The unit of observation in the present analysis is, of course, the firm, although it would have been possible to take a broader view and choose instead the industry level (see Daems, 1978; Poensgen, 1980). This chapter considers the number of different types of interlocks as an attribute of a corporation and not of a particular person or of a dyad of corporations. The data set consists of the 200 production and commercial corporations of each of the three national data sets. In practise, the number of observations for each country is less than 200, due to missing observations.[2] The limits of the analysis are determined by the content of the data set. In particular, the following limitations apply:

(1)   a cross-section study with only statically defined economic and interlock variables, i.e. no growth rates of performance, no replacement indicators with respect to interlocks, etc;

(2)   a core set of economic variables comprising sales, employment, total labour costs, net assets and data on the liability-side of the balance-sheet (popular and important indicators such as the so-called 'acid-test ratio' measuring solvency ['quick' assets divided by current liabilities] could therefore not be included in the analysis); and

(3)   interlock variables defined mainly in terms of the differences between inside and outside positions (and intermediate positions for Belgium and the Netherlands) and between production and financial interlocks (also holding-company interlocks in the case of Belgium).

In addition, the two-digit NACE industry codes and, in the case of Belgium and the Netherlands, ownership codes of the corporations were also available. The industry codes were, however, not used to distinguish between horizontal, vertical and other linkages, as the aggregation level of these codes was considered to be too high and the recent related tests in the literature seem to be unconvincing for the same reason (see Warner and Unwalla, 1967; Dooley, 1969; Poensgen, 1980; Schönwitz and Weber, 1980; Pennings, 1980, pp. 148 ff.). The industry and ownership codes were transformed into binary variables which were subsequently used as controlling variables in the computation of partial correlation coefficients between the economic and interlock variables and as dummies in the OLS-regression equations.

The obvious method in an inductive analysis with interval-level variables is step-wise regression. The two main problems in the setting up of a research method of this type are on the one hand the data-reduction problem and, on the other hand, the criterion-of-significance problem. The data-reduction problem arises only in the context of the 'economist's' approach, when an attempt is made to use interlock variables as explanations of performance. The mere existence of more than 100 possible candidate interlock variables in the absence of any established *ex ante* theory or hypothesis precludes the straightforward application of a step-wise regression procedure. From the alternative point of view, when interlocks are to be explained rather than used as predictors, such an approach may well be warranted. The number of candidate right-hand variables in the regression is then considerably reduced, and a step-wise regression procedure could then be repeated for as many interlock variables as one would care to explain. With regard to the first approach, it was decided not to use a principal-components or factor-analysis method because of the extreme difficulty in neatly interpreting the resulting composite variables. Instead, partial correlation coefficients were computed for each country between the set of selected economic variables (mainly performance ratios and debt – structure ratios) and the set of interlock variables, controlling for the industry to which the corporations belong, for the ownership type and for firm size as measured by net assets and sales. On the basis of a previously determined significance threshold, it was possible to define, for each economic variable, a set of interlock variables displaying minimal higher-order correlation (i.e. after taking into account the part of the variance explained by the variables being controlled but disregarding the variance explained by the other interlock variables). The industry and ownership dummies and sales and net assets were regressed on the economic ratios of interest as a first step, and in subsequent steps interlock variables were introduced which added to the overall explanatory power of the regression.[3] In the following analysis this will be referred to as A-type regressions. With regard to the second approach (when directing the causal arrow from economic to interlock variables), data reduction was, as already said, not necessary. Step-wise regression was immediately applied to each interlock variable which was considered important on account of *a priori* information or results gathered in previous stages of the analysis. In the following analysis this will be referred to as B-type regressions. The set of industry and ownership dummies was introduced in a first step, and then, one at a time, the variables in a set consisting of the economic ratios as well as firm-size variables, such as net assets and sales.

The criterion-of-significance problem arises typically in situations where no *ex ante* hypothesis or theory is at hand. The issue is one of determining an adequate value for the test statistic in deciding whether a given correlation coefficient is statistically significant. The test statistic for correlation coefficients with $H_0: p = 0$ is Student's t. There are however two points of dissent. First, some argue in cases similar to ours that the firms studied are not a random sample but a population themselves. Tests of statistical significance would therefore be meaningless (Gogel and Koenig, 1981, p. 121). This argument can be disposed of by referring to the standard practice in comparable situations: one assumes that what is observed in reality is the outcome of deterministic as well as random factors. It then naturally follows that the so-called 'population' which is observed is in fact the realization of a process which is essentially probabilistic. Second, one might contend, not without reason, that a serious epistemological issue is involved. Many statisticians regard step-wise regression methods with some suspicion. When, instead of going to the data with a specified model, repeated tests are performed so that the data determine which 'model' is reasonable, it is no longer obvious that the usual statistical tests of significance are still valid. One could indeed argue that it would then be sufficient to define 'enough' explanatory variables and perform 'enough' test runs in order to find, on purely probabilistic grounds, some which are characterized by a 'sufficiently' high t-value. Others, following Anscombe (1967), argue that significance tests on inductive models do provide some form of evidence.

In the light of this discussion 'significant' parameters will not be presented as reflecting established facts, albeit in the statistical sense of the word. But it is, perhaps, justified to use significance thresholds in a heuristic way to sift the grain from the chaff in the data, and so try to formulate consistent hypotheses on the basis of this. In the following sections we shall always implicitly be assigning this minimal interpretation to the significance concept.

The results of the two-stage procedure in the case of A-type regressions and the results of the more straightforward B-type regressions are reported in the third section. In the following section, in order to get an initial insight into the structure of the data and to gather, at the same time, a few useful hints for interpreting the regressions in the third section, the results of an introductory partial correlation analysis will be presented.

THE RESULTS: AN INTRODUCTORY PARTIAL CORRELATION APPROACH

For the sake of maximal convenience the notation has been kept as uniform as possible over the three countries studied. The relative abundance of interlock variables for Belgium (and to a lesser degree for the Netherlands) is a consequence of the necessary differentiation for that country between three types of directors (inside, outside and intermediate) and three broad types of corporations (production and commercial companies, financial companies and holding companies). The taxonomy of interlock variables is the same as used elsewhere in this book (see chapter 2). The economic and interlock variables [4] used are as follows.

Interlock Variables

X1 : the number of all interlocks

X2 : number of inside to outside and intermediate interlocks (i.e. 'outgoing')

X3 : number of outside and intermediate to inside interlocks (i.e. 'incoming')

X4 : X2 – X3

X5 : (number of) primary financial interlocks
X6 : (number of) primary financial interlocks (incoming)
X7 : (number of) primary holding interlocks
X8 : (number of) primary production interlocks
X9 : (number of) primary production interlocks (outgoing)
X10 : (number of) induced primary holding interlocks
X11 : (number of) induced primary production interlocks
X12 : (number of) intermediate production interlocks
X13 : (number of) intermediate production interlocks (incoming)
X14 : (number of) intermediate production – holding interlocks in proportion to board size
X15 : (number of) induced intermediate production interlocks in proportion to board size
X16 : (number of) induced intermediate financial – production – holding interlocks
X17 : (number of) unclassified interlocks

X18 : (number of) production-production interlocks
X19 : X18 in proportion to board size
X20 : (number of) production to financial interlocks
X21 : X20 – X18
X22 : (number of) production to holding interlocks
X23 : X20 + X22

X24 : rush

BS: : board size.

Economic Variables

S	:	volume of sales
NA	:	net assets
Y1	:	cash flow on net assets (CF divided by NA)
Y2	:	cash flow on sales (CF divided by S)
Y3	:	cash flow on net worth (CF divided by NW)
Y4	:	net profit before taxes on net assets (NP divided by NA)
Y5	:	net profit before taxes on sales (NP divided by S)
Y6	:	net profit before taxes on net worth (NP divided by NW)
Y7	:	net worth on total debts (NW divided by D)
Y8	:	debts lesser than a year on total debts (D1 divided by D)
Y9	:	total debts on net assets (D divided by NA)
Y10	:	sales on net assets (S divided by NA)
Y11	:	employment on net assets (E divided by NA)

Table 3.1 shows the partial correlations between five categories of variables: four interlock variables which are generally considered to be of importance, board size, firm size as measured by turnover and net assets, three performance variables and certain other important economic ratios. The obvious choice of X1 and X20 in the first category of variables in table 3.1 invites no additional comment. The rush (X24) was added because it is the only variable relating to positions in the network as a whole.[5] Variable X4 was added in order to assess the widely felt importance of 'directed' interlocks and its synthetic nature combines information on both ways of directing a line. The partial correlation coefficients were computed, controlling for the industry to which the corporations belonged and, in the case of the Netherlands and Belgium, for ownership type.[6] The statistical relations between these five categories of variables can now be considered.

Relations among Interlock Variables

The intercorrelation of X1, X20 and X24 was positive and highly significant as might be expected, because these three variables express different aspects of the same absolute degree of interlocking. The situation is different with respect to X4. Significantly positive correlations of the 'relative' variable X4 with the other three interlock variables in table 3.1 do not, of course, have this same obvious quality. As will be seen in the regression analyses, this variable turns out to be of some importance in the case of the Netherlands. The high correlations of the total number of interlocks with the rush for the three countries are also particularly noteworthy, since they nicely correspond with results obtained elsewhere, such as those of Mariolis (1975). He found for the USA a correlation of 0.91 with point centrality in the sense of Bonacich. The correlation of the rush with the number of financial interlocks (X20) is also relatively high. One would however be ill advised to conclude to a high interchangeability between rush and other interlock variables. As will be shown in the following section, and as can already be inferred from table 3.1, the apparent similarity breaks down from the moment that we move to the study of more subtle relations such as those with financial performance and debt structure.

In the next section it will be possible to establish the usefulness of the rush variable in explaining economic characteristics of firms only in the case of the USA. This corroborates, but at the same time limits the scope of, the optimistic conclusion of Mizruchi and Bunting (1981) with respect to the utility of centrality measures 45 compared to 'standard' interlock variables in regression analyses.

Relations between Interlock Variables and Board Size

There was a strong positive correlation between board size and the total number of interlocks for each of the three countries. The correlation with X4 should in this context again be interpreted with care. On purely logical grounds one might expect board size to be a result of the degree of interlocking rather than the other way round: a corporation will tend to enlarge its board of directors because of its practise of co-optation or because several different ownership or other interests must be represented on the board in a balanced way. There would, therefore, be no point in placing a board-size variable in the righthand side of a regression equation explaining interlocks (B-type regression), nor in placing this variable along with other interlock variables in a regression equation explaining economic performance (A-type regression). Since, however, the correlation between degree of interlocking and board size is weaker or non-existent in the case of the Netherlands an alternative strategy must be followed. It would seem appropriate to consider in this case the introduction as additional candidate explanatory variables in A-type regressions of 'relative' interlock variables, measuring interlock intensity of different types in proportion to board size. For the sake of uniformity this was done for all three countries.

Relations between Interlock Variables and Firm Size

There was positive correlation all along the line for Belgium and the USA but not for the Netherlands, although as an exception the rush

Table 3.1 *Partial correlation coefficients between interlock and economic variables*

	X4	X20[a]	X24	BS	NA	S	Y1	Y2	Y3	Y7	Y8	Y10	Y11
X1	0.02	0.92*	0.85*	0.82*	0.43*	0.26*	-0.009	0.18*	-0.11	0.11	0.30*	-0.06	-0.05
	0.28*	0.89*	0.88*	0.31*	0.18	0.15	-0.14	-0.008	-0.15	0.07	-0.08	-0.22*	-0.09
	0.17*	0.89*	0.83*	0.36*	0.52*	0.52*	0.02	0.21*	-0.05	0.13		-0.24*	
X4		0.02	0.08	0.03	0.07	0.07	-0.09	-0.16	-0.07	0.02	-0.005	0.01	0.003
		0.29*	0.37*	0.28*	0.20	0.22*	-0.07	-0.06	-0.03	-0.14	-0.26*	-0.02	-0.19*
		0.12	0.22*	-0.006	0.27*	-0.03	-0.008	0.22*	-0.03	0.04		-0.19*	
X20			0.83*	0.76*	0.30*	0.17	-0.009	0.16	-0.12	-0.07	0.26*	-0.05	-0.04
			0.78*	0.15	0.18	0.17	-0.03	0.11	-0.13	0.18	-0.02	-0.26*	-0.09
			0.68*	0.33*	0.39*	0.44*	-0.005	0.13	-0.06	0.09		-0.22*	
X24				0.72*	0.48*	0.37*	0.01	0.09	-0.09	0.02	0.29*	-0.02	-0.02
				0.32*	0.23*	0.21*	-0.08	0.01	-0.14	0.07	-0.13	-0.15	-0.03
				0.33*	0.81*	0.62*	0.03	0.20*	-0.004	0.08		-0.12	
BS					0.49*	0.34*	0.09	0.28*	-0.06	0.05	0.33*	-0.03	0.03
					0.30*	0.32*	0.006	-0.05	0.02	-0.10	-0.14	0.16	-0.05
					0.25*	0.39*	0.01	0.06	0.05	0.11		-0.22*	
NA						0.82*	0.01	0.23*	-0.08	0.04	0.18*	-0.05	-0.02
						0.94*	0.02	0.07	-0.05	0.08	-0.12	-0.13	-0.12
						0.75*	0.05	0.33*	-0.02	0.08		-0.13	
S							0.04	0.02	-0.07	-0.02	0.12	0.06	0.06
							0.06	0.05	-0.02	0.06	-0.10	-0.10	-0.08
							0.13	0.14	-0.01	0.14		-0.01	

Table 3.1 (continued)

Y1	0.69* 0.74* 0.59*	0.67* 0.45* 0.60*	0.08 0.55* 0.40*	0.07 0.25*	0.05 0.03 0.17*	0.02
Y2		0.48* 0.28* 0.32*	0.28* 0.50* 0.37*	0.16 0.16	−0.10 −0.34* −0.36*	0.06 −0.06
Y3			−0.05 −0.12 0.11	0.02 0.07	−0.03 0.11 0.15	−0.26* −0.01
Y7				−0.08 0.29*	0.14 −0.08 −0.10	0.04 0.03
Y8					−0.15 0.02	−0.03 −0.04
Y10						0.60* 0.24*

Notes:
In each cell, the first value refers to Belgium (df = 122), the second to the Netherlands (df = 94) and the third to the USA (df = 157). Asterisked values refer to significance at 0.05 level.
[a] X23 for Belgium.

correlates significantly in a positive way for the latter country. The results for the USA confirm those of Dooley (1969, pp. 315–16). In terms of a co-optation mechanism, the positive correlation between degree of interlocking and firm size may occur because directors of large corporations have the widest appeal (e.g. as a result of knowledgeability and personal influence) and are therefore the most obvious candidates for co-optation. In terms of financial participation, large firms might be regarded as the more natural controllers of relatively smaller firms and interlocks would then be used as a means of emphasizing the underlying ownership tie.

The relatively unimportant relation of firm size and network centrality in the Dutch case was, as will be verified in the next section, partly the result of the outlier position of the first and third largest corporations in terms of net assets and sales (Royal Dutch Shell and Unilever), which are only weakly connected with the main component of the graph. These corporations are typical bi-nationals, chiefly interlocking across the national border (see chapter 14).

Firm size as measured by net assets correlated positively and significantly with the gross profit margin (defined as cash flow on sales) in Belgium and the USA. In examining the possible influence of interlocking on, for example, economic performance, there is thus good reason to include firm-size variables as well in the right-hand side of the regression equation. In this way we will take due account of the part of the correlation between interlocking and profitability which should in fact be attributed to their common correlation with firm size.

Relations between Interlocking and Performance

It was again in terms of turnover and only for Belgium and the USA that significant correlations were found. There seemed to be, in these countries, a positive relation between the gross profit margin and the total number of interlocks. In the USA there was, in addition, a positive correlation of the gross profit margin with X4 and the rush. There was no correlation whatsoever between economic performance and the number of financial interlocks. In the literature there is however a heavy accent on these kind of ties. On the basis of the use of interlock variables which are generally considered as important this does not seem to be warranted. In so far as it is reasonable to assume that network features *do* influence economic characteristics of corporations, this illustrates the usefulness of an exploratory approach as opposed to a prioristic model testing.

Relations between Interlocking and Other Economic Ratios

The equity – debt ratio did not yield any significant correlations with the four interlock variables in table 3.1. The debt – structure ratio Y8 (short-term debt on total debt) on the other hand correlated positively with the three 'absolute' interlock variables (X1, X23 and X24) in the case of Belgium. Capital productivity or relative capital needs as measured by sales on net assets negatively correlated with total and financial interlocks. The relation was significant for the Netherlands and the USA. The relation with rush, on the contrary, was negative but not significant and is anyhow difficult to interpret consistently. As will be shown in the next section, the sign reverses in a significant way for the USA once rush is introduced in a regression context along with other interlock variables.

Labour intensity of production Y11 yielded a significantly negative relation to the net number of outgoing interlocks for the Netherlands, but it is hard to give a meaning to this. As the number of Dutch corporations with employment data in the file was anyhow rather small, this variable was not used in the further analysis of that country.

THE RESULTS: REGRESSION ANALYSIS

In accordance with the research methodology set out in the first section it is now possible to set out some significant relationships. On the basis of bipartite partial correlation matrices between interlock variables and economic variables, a set of interlock variables was defined for each economic variable and each country. These sets contained all interlock variables correlated at a specified threshold value. The threshold value chosen was 0.1 instead of the normal 0.05, in order to reduce, in this first stage, the chance of rejecting a variable which was actually of interest. The partial correlation tables cannot be reproduced here. Tables 3.2 – 3.5 present the final results. For the sake of clarity the tables show only those variables in the right-hand side of the equations which were significant within 95 per cent confidence limits and selected by the step-wise regression. For the same reasons, and because it would anyhow be difficult to give them a concrete meaning, the actual values of the coefficients have not been given, but only their sign and their significance level. The signs and significance of dummy variables with respect to industry and ownership status are not presented either. The same goes for firm-size variables, such as the volume of sales and net assets, as far as they were not subject to the selection procedure, but were introduced in the first regression-step for reasons of control (this holds for so-called A-Type regressions).

Table 3.2   Regression of interlock variables on economic variables for Belgium

Equation number			X4	X5	X8	X14	X16	X18	R^2
1	CF/NA	Y1					-,0.006		0.125
2	CF/S	Y2	-,0.026				-,0.000		0.295
3	NP/S	Y5		+,0.023			-,0.003		0.327
4	D1/D	Y8			-,0.028			+,0.008	0.264
5	D/NA	Y9				-,0.001			0.116

Note: The content of the table refers to the sign of the regression coefficient and the significance level of that coefficient.

With respect to the explanatory power in the regressions of the industry and ownership-status dummies a brief comment is in order. The variables concerned were introduced because there is every reason to believe that one cannot simply assume the relation between interlocking and economic characteristics of firms to be invariant to them. The evidence to the contrary is particularly well documented as far as industry differences are concerned: see, for instance, Pennings (1980, pp. 121 – 4). The same is no doubt true for differences in ownership type. For reasons of space the results concerning these variables have not been discussed in the body of the text, although a number of them were statistically significant. Little of substance is lost by this decision.[7] There is, however, a second reason. The importance of findings of interlock analyses making explicit and active use of industrial differentiation have been overstressed in general. Scepticism with respect to the analysis of horizontal and vertical interlocks has already been mentioned at the beginning of this chapter. Another example of this is the idea that interlocking is most intense in industries with intermediate levels of concentration, because there the need for interfirm communication and co-ordination will be highest

Table 3.4   Regression of interlock variables on economic variables for the USA

Equation number			X5	X9	X11	X17	X24	R^2
1	CF/S	Y2					-,0.000	0.389
2	NP/S	Y5			+,0.036		-,0.000	0.304
3	S/NA	Y10	-,0.039	-,0.001		-,0.007	+,0.006	0.457

Note: The content of the tables refers to the sign of the regression coefficient and the significance level of that coefficient.

Table 3.3 Regression of interlock variables on economic variables for the Netherlands

Equation number			X4	X6	X8	X12	X13	X15	X17	X19	X20	X21	R^2
1	CF/NW	Y3				+,026	+,003			-,032			0.209
2	NP/S	Y5										+,010	0.196
3	NP/NW	Y6		-,029									0.148
4	NW/D	Y7				-,001							0.129
5	D1/D	Y8	-,019										0.127
6	D/NA	Y9			+,043	+,000		-,033	-,013				0.293
7	S/NA	Y10									-,014		0.299

Notes: The content of the table refers to the sign of the regression coefficient and the significance level of that coefficient.

Table 3.5 *Regression of economic variables on interlock variables*

Equation number			S	NA	Y1	Y2	Y3	Y7	Y8	Y9	Y10	Y11	R^2
1	B	X1	-,001	+,000					+,023				0.432
	U		+,001	+,018									0.366
2	B	X2		+,000									0.148
	U		-,038	+,000							-,002		0.249
3	B	X3	-,031	+,000									0.274
	U		+,000	+,002							-,025		0.179
4	B	X4		+,005		-,047				+,007			0.016[a]
	N							+,043	-,005				0.180
	U		-,000	+,000								-,035	0.177
5	B	X5		+,000		+,012							0.076
6	B	X7		+,000									0.338
7	U	X8		+,000		-,002							0.222
8	B	X10		+,001									0.195
9	B	X11	-,000	+,000									0.441
	U		+,000										0.184
10	N	X12								+,006			0.259
11	N	X13					+,001			-,001			0.112[a]
12	B	X14	-,010	+,028									0.038[a]
13	B	X16	+,000	+,000									0.208
14	B	X17	-,001	+,000									0.301
	N				-,028					-,001			0.225
15	B	X18	-,000	+,000					+,019				0.384
	U		+,006	+,000						-,009			0.353
16	N	X20								-,037			0.195
	U		+,000	+,000						-,002			0.269

17	B	X22	−,0.001	+,0.000	+,0.038	0.317
18	B	X23	−,0.019	+,0.000	+,0.035	0.263
19	B	X24	+,0.000	+,0.000	+,0.020	0.313
		U		+,0.000		0.648

Note:
The content of the table refers to the sign of the regression coefficient and the significance level of that coefficient. B = Belgium, N = Netherlands, U = the USA.

a The subset of economic variables was significant at the level of 0.05 but the regression equation as a whole was not.

(Pennings, 1980, p. 12; Pfeffer and Salancik, 1978, p. 166). The problem is that this hypothesis, probable as it may be, cannot be tested in the context of an analysis where, typically, only large firms (i.e. firms in industries with a relatively high level of concentration) are selected.

Tables 3.2, 3.3 and 3.4 show the results of the step-wise regressions of the interlock variables on several economic indicators for Belgium, the Netherlands and the USA (A-type regressions). Table 3.5 presents the results of the step-wise regressions of the economic ratios, volume of sales and net assets on a number of interlock variables (B-type regressions). Only those regressions which fell into one of the following two categories are reported:

(1)   all regressions which were significant as a whole and of which at least one explanatory variable selected in the step-wise procedure was statistically significant at a level of 0.05;

(2)   all B-type regressions which were not significant as a whole (due to a relatively large number of non-significant dummies) but which predicted an interlock variable which was significant in at least one A-type regression for the corresponding country and of which at least one economic variable selected in the step-wise procedure was statistically significant.

A- and B-type regressions for the Netherlands were repeated without the two outliers (Shell and Unilever) and where relevant the main results of these additional regressions are commented upon briefly below. In the rest of this section the results in the tables will be interpreted. Since the direction of causality is often dubious, A- and B-type results will not be discussed separately. The procedure will be to deal successively with the relation between interlock variables on the one hand and economic performance, capital structure, turnover ratios and firm size on the other, and make at the same time a comparison of the three countries involved.

Interlock Variables and Economic Performance

There seems to have been a positive relation in the Netherlands and Belgium between profitability and interlocking with banks, a relation which was not found in the USA. Beneficial effects of information from and communication with bankers is a prima facie explanation. In the USA, profitability was negatively affected by rush, which can be interpreted as stemming from inertia in large complex and oligopolistic organizations with respect to new industrial and technological developments and to pricing policy. In Belgium, the negative impact of holding-company induced interlocks on profitability can best be explained by the 'industrial conservatism' of the main financial-industrial groups. Could this reflect the overall defeat of traditional Belgian capitalism, 'locking' and 'interlocking' itself up in its own shallow circles?

As table 3.2 reveals, profitability in Belgium was influenced negatively, though not always in a significant way, by interlocks initiated or induced by holding companies. The presence of directors who hold simultaneously intermediate functions (president or vice-president) in financial, holding and production companies, gives significant negative parameters for regressions on cash flow divided by net assets, net profits before taxes on sales and cash flow on sales. An explanation for these results should evidently be sought in the role that holding companies and financial-industrial groups play in the Belgian economic system (see chapter 8). Companies with relatively bad economic performance may take great pains to co-opt important finance capitalists from the group to which they belong (or intend to belong?), thereby trying to find shelter under the umbrella of powerful protectors. Alternatively, and seemingly more in accordance with the literature on the Belgian groups (CRISP, 1962; De Vroey, 1973), one can explain the negative influence of finance capital on economic performance, by reference to mechanisms of promotion and co-optation of directors *within* the main Belgian group (Société Générale de Belgique) and the industrial conservatism entailed. This explanation is in agreement with the statistical fact that the cumulation of positions by directors, together with their promotion to inside or intermediate functions in the boards of important companies within the group, led to a great number of induced interlocks which completely overshadow, by sheer number, the primary interlocks. Conversely, B-type regressions for Belgium also provide evidence for an identically signed causal mechanism in the other direction (see regression 5.13B). Companies within a group which show low profitability in terms of net assets were 'watched' by the 'network specialists' of the group.

The dominance of large financial-industrial groups by holding companies is an institutional datum which is not found in the USA or in the Netherlands. In the USA induced primary production interlocks seem to have influenced net profit margins (NP/S) positively, which would indicate that communication between production companies enhanced their respective profitability. Unfortunately the communication hypothesis was not confirmed by regressions on other performance ratios, such as gross profit margin or profit rate on invested capital. A similar situation held in the Netherlands, where intermediate production interlocks had a significant positive effect only on gross profitability in terms of net worth of the company.

The results of Pennings (1980, pp. 104 – 5) for the USA stressing the importance for good financial performance of communication with banking companies, as opposed to control, are not confirmed by the regressions. Pennings holds that, apart from positive communication effects, a strong relationship with bankers through interlocks might easily lead to loans which are then more readily available or granted on better terms (see Pennings, 1980, p. 181). In such cases, positive effects on profitability might be expected. For Belgium and the Netherlands this hypothesis seems to have had some validity, though the positive parameters were not always statistically significant. This latter was true for primary financial interlocks (X5) in Belgium and the preponderance of total financial interlocks over total production interlocks (X21) in the Netherlands. There was, however, also some 'evidence' for an inverse relation. Indeed, the A-type regressions for the Netherlands point to a negative effect of incoming *primary* financial interlocks (X6) on net profitability in terms of net worth of the company (see regression 3.4). Does this result indicate that bankers are often inadvertently squeezing the production companies, by granting loans which ultimately will depress net profits? Or is it the other way round, i.e. that bankers will sit on the board of companies to which they granted loans and which show low financial leverage, in order to keep an eye on the future potentials of the company to pay interest and redeem its debts? The second hypothesis was however not confirmed by the B-type regressions.

Neglecting the two outliers in the Dutch data set and repeating the A- and B-type regressions for that country produces only one new result: in the matter of the profitability – interlocking relation a significant negative parameter for CF/NA in the regression of the number of production interlocks (X18) was found. It seems difficult to give a consistent and unique explanation for this.

An interesting result for the USA which was not found in Belgium or in the Netherlands, is that gross as well as net profit margins were negatively influenced by point centrality as measured by the rush. With respect to the relevance of profit margins as opposed to profit rates, it can be argued that in a 'managerial' system (i.e. in a situation where the shareholders are weak) companies maximize the former but not the latter. It is therefore not surprising to find that partial correlation coefficients for the USA between interlock variables and profit rates did not give results. To explain this negativity, by using the 'industrial conservatism' hypothesis advanced previously for Belgium, would be rather dubious. Two other explanations based on a managerialist rather than a finance-capitalist model, seem to be more promising. One explanation is related to the inertia of old or mature companies in a managerial capitalist system. Pennings (1980, p. 15) has phrased it as follows:

> The markets or industries of young, innovative firms, are usually fragmented and consist of many small firms. It is likely, however, that when industries mature and move toward greater degrees of concentration, their organizations become routinized, develop oligarchical decision arrangements, acquire a divisional structure, and the senior management will become increasingly involved in developing and establishing social connections with other firms.

Along this line of reasoning it is only too natural to expect that the more central managerial companies in the USA would be the less profitable. Another explanation which might be used in addition is that big oligopolistic and mature corporations confronted with the recession of the 1970s resisted the pressures to revise their profit margins upwards for longer than the average American company. According to the theory of oligopolistic mark-up pricing, profit margins are sticky and only revised upwards when depreciation allowances and other fixed costs endanger long-run profitability and hence, growth capacity (see Schultze, 1975).

Interlock Variables and Capital Structure

As will be argued in more detail below, it seems that 'network specialists' in the Netherlands and in Belgium – though the concrete content of this category of interlockers differs between these countries – were reluctant to sit on boards of companies with a large degree of indebtedness. In both countries, some resource dependence with respect to credit from customers and suppliers can explain interlocking with other production companies. Other additional explanations might be the need for uncertainty reduction whenever the share of short-term debt is high. Very little has been found on this matter for the USA.

In Belgium, the share of debt in net assets of a company was negatively influenced by the relative importance of those finance capitalists who hold intermediate functions (but no inside functions) in both holding and production companies. Two plausible and complementary hypotheses can be formulated in this respect:

(1) for securing their long-term capital needs, companies which are part of a financial-industrial group will rely more on the issue of new shares, which are subscribed by the holding companies or other companies in the centre of the group, than on loan capital supplied by the bank of the group or an outside bank; and

(2)   companies with a low degree of indebtedness are more attractive to finance capitalists than companies which are already heavily indebted and thus show a much restricted capacity to absorb additional loans.

Both hypotheses would require, however, that the regressions on equity – debt ratios would give significant results, which they fail to do. This failure is perhaps attributable to the higher variance of equity – debt ratios and to the greater influence of omitted variables in this context. As far as Belgium is concerned, it can be argued that holding companies, by their very nature, will prefer equity financing to debt financing. This lends credibility to the first hypothesis. Moreover, the second hypothesis points to a reversed causality (indebtedness influencing the presence of captains of finance) for which an indication was found in the B-type regressions (see regression 5.12B). It would seem that both hypotheses can claim some validity at the same time.

Pennings (1980, p. 170) has formulated a hypothesis, similar to our second one, but with bankers playing the role of the Belgian finance capitalists. Unfortunately the American data which were available did not support Pennings' view. Similarly in the Netherlands, B-type regressions of capital structure on interlock variables did not support Pennings' hypothesis either. On the contrary, as inspection of tables 3.4 and 3.5 reveals, the capital structure of Dutch companies is best explained by and, conversely, explains best the intermediate production and primary production interlocks as well as the so-called 'unclassified' interlocks, which included those carried by the Dutch network specialists. In B-type regressions the parameters of the share of debt in net assets were significantly negative with respect to unclassified interlocks and financial interlocks but positive with respect to production interlocks. Repeating the A- and B-type regressions without the outliers Shell and Unilever showed a significant negative influence of capital structure on the number of network specialists. These results indicate that in the Netherlands bankers and network specialists were unwilling to sit on boards of companies with a high degree of indebtedness. The reasons for this reluctance are obvious for both categories of persons. Dutch bankers, prudent as they notoriously are, may feel the potential threat of being manoeuvred into financial adventures without perspective. Network specialists will agree on being co-opted into a board of directors for the prestige they would lend to the corporation involved, but of course would only do so if their own prestige is not negatively affected.

In A-type regressions unclassified, intermediate, and primary production interlocks gave identical signs, but the influence of financial interlocks disappeared altogether. It would appear that financial interlocks were not used to secure the capital needs of the company but that interlocks with other production companies may serve this purpose (see e.g. the importance of advance payments in building contracting and turnkey projects).

It is of course also interesting to look at the term structure of debt. Unfortunately, no results can be reported for the USA due to unreliable or missing data. In the Netherlands, A- and B-type regressions with the share of short-term debt in total debt give negative parameters with, and only with, outgoing minus incoming interlocks. If incoming interlocks are interpreted as the direct consequence of co-optation by the company and outgoing interlocks as co-optation of directors by other companies, three non-competing explanations can be advanced as far as B-type regressions are concerned.

(1) Resource dependence: companies which must satisfy important short-term capital needs by means of credits from banks, customers or suppliers will often have to allow the representatives of the latter onto their board of directors:

(2) Uncertainty reduction: companies which rely heavily on short-term capital will try to reduce uncertainty as to future performance, solvency, sales, etc., by co-opting directors from companies to which they are, in some way or another, related.

(3) As far as a high value for the debt – structure ratio expresses high vulnerability, we may assume that the attractiveness of the inside directors of the corporation involved for potential co-optation elsewhere diminishes with increasing debt – structure ratio.

A partial confirmation of these three hypotheses can be found in the corresponding partial correlation coefficients: -0.24 for the correlation with outgoing lines and 0.08 for the incoming lines (only the former is significant). Since the first two co-optation policies may be used in an anticipatory way, the above explanations can also serve as a clue for the interpretation of the results of the A-type regressions.

Resource dependence and uncertainty reduction might also explain the apparent positive relationship in Belgium between the share of short-term debt in total debts and interlocks with other production companies (irrespective of direction) in the A-type regressions, and, in addition, the results relating to the total number of interlocks, interlocks with financial companies and/or holding companies and rush in the B-type regressions. For Belgium, this result for the rush was due to the centrality of holding companies and the large number of interlocks they create.

Interlock Variables, Turnover Ratios and Company Size

It might be expected that there would be a positive relationship between firm size and such interlock variables as total number of interlocks, the number of outgoing lines, lines with financial and/or production companies, etc. This relationship was most clearly observed in the USA but certain other findings are worthy of note.

Absolute as well as relative capital needs of companies interacted with interlocking. In Belgium, absolute capital needs influenced interlocking with holding companies positively, as might be expected. In the USA, the interlocking of the large companies in the centre of the intercorporate network was positively related to their sales on net assets ratios. This might indicate a relative independence of these companies from external finance. American companies with great potential capital needs, however, seemed to try to decrease their vulnerability using primary financial interlocks.

Relative capital needs were measured by the sales on net assets ratio. This ratio indicates how fast a firm generates sales to sustain a given level of assets. Hence, a low sales on net assets ratio shows, *ceteris paribus*, a low potential for internal financing and a large potential for external capital. According to this interpretation, the constituent parts of the sales on net assets ratio need to be interpreted differently: sales can be seen as a proxy for firm size and net assets for absolute capital needs.

It was already stressed that in the Netherlands, unlike Belgium and the USA, no or only very slight correlation existed between sales or net assets and interlocking (see the second section). However, leaving the outliers Shell and Unilever completely out, greatly altered the results of the B-type regressions for the Netherlands. Sales on net assets ratios then negatively influenced the number of network specialists on the board, probably indicating that these directors were co-opted for their expertise in tapping new potential sources of finance. Moreover, whenever both outliers were neglected, sales (as a firm-size proxy) scored in a significantly positive way on the total number of interlocks, the number of outgoing lines, the number of lines with financial companies, lines to other production companies, the number of network specialists and point-centrality. All this is in line with common-sense expectations.

As is evidenced by table 3.5, regressions for Belgium of sales *and* net assets on interlock variables, frequently gave significant negative parameters for sales and significant positive parameters for net assets. Perhaps the thesis advanced by Galbraith (1967) provides a clue: the bigger sales are, the larger the size of the firm, the more complex its organizational structure and, with given capital needs, the less the need for interlocking. When large companies also show large capital needs, as they normally do, interlocking will be positively affected due to resource dependence and the need for uncertainty reduction. In the partial correlation coefficients of table 3.1, this differential effect of sales and net assets on degree of interlocking cannot be traced, because the calculation of the coefficient for one size variable did not control for the effect of the other. It is to be expected, then, that this explanation would only hold for companies that did not belong to a Belgian financial-industrial group, i.e. when holding companies were not involved. We find, indeed, in Belgium a positive parameter for net assets together with a negative one for sales, whenever they are both regressed on total number of interlocks, the number of incoming interlocks, induced production interlocks and total number of inter-locks with other production companies. Sales give no significant results when regressed together with net assets on most interlock variables related to holding companies.

In the B-type regressions for the USA, sales and net assets often gave significant positive parameters, even with negative signs for sales on net assets. This evidently points to non-linear relationships between size and capital needs on the one hand and interlock variables on the other. This is hard to ascertain in the present analysis due to the use of dummy variables. According to the A-type regressions, sales on net assets ratios of American companies seem to have been positively influenced by rush, although an opposite but not significant relation was found in the partial correlations presented in the second section. Combining the evidence of A- and B-type regressions for the USA, it was found that size, as measured by net assets, influenced rush positively and rush, in turn, influenced the sales on net assets ratio positively.

It can therefore be hypothesized that large companies in the USA were not only more central in the network but also, because of this, relatively independent from the supply of external capital. This tentative interpretation would qualify the importance of bank cen-trality in the USA. Conversely, companies with high potential external capital needs (low sales on net assets ratios) appear to generate quite a number of primary financial lines, indicating their 'resource depen-dence' with respect to loan capital from banks and other financial institutions. Pennings' findings (1980, pp. 167 – 71) do not, however, corroborate this: he found in most cases insignificant negative correlation coefficients between sales on net assets ratios and financial interlocks. Similar dependencies with respect to credit from non-financial corporations seem to have existed, as evidenced by the negative influence of primary production interlocks on the sales on net assets ratios. Since reliable American data on short-term debt were not available, the influence of production interlocks on debt structure was impossible to ascertain.

CONCLUSIONS

The analytical starting point of the present study was an original one: the situation in three different countries was compared by applying a systematic and uniform statistical methodology in an explicitly inductionist context. The latter was justified by referring to the theoretical twilight zone in which research on the relationship between interlocking directorships and economic characteristics of corporations still finds itself.

The main results were summarized at the beginning of each subsection of the third section. As a general conclusion one might on the one hand say that the great majority of statistical results have been provided with a consistent and plausible interpretation. Among the most striking are the negative relation between performance and various types of holding interlocks for Belgium, the positive relation between performance and financial interlocks for Belgium and the Netherlands and the reluctance of the network specialists in both countries to sit on boards of heavily indebted firms. A remarkable result for the USA was the positive relation between centrality in the network and turnover velocity as measured by sales on net assets. On the other hand, some results in the existing literature were not confirmed, such as the alleged positive relation between profitability and interlocking directorships with banks in the USA.

A number of consistent interpretations of inductively generated research results have thus been produced. The construction of a unified theory of the interaction between interlocking and economic characteristics of firms has however scarcely begun. On the one hand, it would seem reasonable to introduce in further research not only interlock variables defined in terms of the frequency of the different types but also variables expressing the position of the firms in the network taken as a whole. In this matter the insights which will be gained in the national chapters of this book will prove to be very valuable. On the other hand, it might be that, in order to be successful, the definition of the underlying network in terms only of interlocking directorships is insufficient to capture the essence of what economists will want to explain, namely the ways and means of the activity of firms to circumvent the market. We feel in this respect that Burt's concept of what he called 'the co-optive corporate actor network' of a corporation (Burt, 1980b) might prove to be very successful for economists in future studies. A fascinating research programme in industrial economics thus announces itself. It will indeed in our view become necessary to change from a one-sided to a multiplex approach to intercorporate networks and to add ownership ties, customer – supplier relations, credit links, interlocks with the social and political system and so on. In the meantime, apart from being interesting in its own right for the economist, the study of the intercorporate network of interlocking directorships is most surely a necessary step in a better understanding of the nature and importance of non-market factors in the activity of firms.

NOTES

1 We would like to thank Professor James Gatti, Professor Gene Laber and the School of Business Administration of the University of Vermont for access to the American economic data.

2 The problem of missing observations is more acute for the Netherlands than for the other two countries. This is due to the relatively high number of limited partnership firms in the Dutch data set. These firms are bound only by limited legal reporting rules.

3 In practice, this means that the R^2 statistic was maximized by introducing, one at a time, the variables for which the F-ratio, with respect to the variables already in the equation, exceeds unity. In order to limit the estimation problems caused by multi-collinearity a lower bound equal to 0.1 was imposed for the proportion of the variance of the variable considered for entry in the regression equation not explained by the independent variables already in the equation.

4 The interlock variables proper fall, as indicated by the spaces, into five categories: the number of all interlocks (X1); interlock variables defined in terms of the difference between inside and outside positions (X2 to X4) ; interlock variables defined in terms of the quality of the main position of the supporting director and the primary or induced character of the related interlock (X5 to X17); interlock variables defined in terms of the type of corporation on both ends of the interlock (X18 to X23); and a network variable (rush, X24). The board-size variable, BS, is of course a case apart.

5 The rush is defined in chapter 2. The particular definition used here is based on the assumption that shortest paths in the network should be of maximal length 2 in order to be meaningful. The multiplicity of the lines is taken account of.

6 Eight different ownership types were distinguished for Belgium: private domestic firms, domestic firms with a state participation less than or equal to 50 per cent, domestic firms controlled by the state (state participation greater than 50 per cent), foreign firms, mixed domestic – foreign firms, firms belonging to the Christian-Democratic sphere of influence; firms belonging to the socialist sphere of influence; and firms with unknown ownership status.

For the Netherlands there were also eight categories: majority-controlled domestic firms, firms with state ownership less than or equal to 50 per cent, state ownership greater than 50 per cent, minority-controlled domestic firms, mixed domestic – foreign firms (Dutch part less than or equal to 50 per cent), mixed domestic – foreign firms (Dutch part greater than 50 per cent), foreign firms and firms with unknown ownership status.

The industry-dummies were constructed by regrouping the relevant 2-digit

NACE sectors of the production sphere of the economy into 14 newly defined industries. Deletion of cases due to missing observations reduced this number to a maximum of ten in every regression.

7   For Belgium, no particular industry yielded consistently significant shift parameters, neither in A-type nor B-type regressions. On the contrary, several ownership-dummies scored significantly: state-controlled domestic firms (participation greater than 50 per cent) in both A- and B-type regressions and foreign firms in B-type regressions.

For the Netherlands, one sector-dummy scored significantly: the iron and steel industry in some B-type regressions (particularly on X2 and X4). In addition, the two ownership-dummies with respect to mixed domestic – foreign firms produced significant shifts.

For the USA, of course only industry-dummies showed results, because ownership-dummies were not defined for this country. Some sector-dummies scored highly, especially in B-type regressions: the chemical industry, metal manufacturing, food, drink and tobacco industries, and wholesaling.

4

Austria Incorporated

ROLF ZIEGLER, GERHARD REISSNER
and DONALD BENDER[1]

While the collapse of the Austro-Hungarian monarchy meant that the First Republic was torn apart by fierce struggles between socialist and clerical-conservative parties, the social and economic development of the Second Republic was relatively smooth and continuous after the Second World War. The common national goal of regaining sovereignty and the high degree of personal cohesion among the political elites, who had often found themselves imprisoned together by the Nazis having fought each other before, were certainly important historical causes of this development. However, there were other more enduring institutional factors involved. A high level of nationalization in both industry and banking strengthened the reciprocal influence between the political and the economic sector. The corporatist system greatly enhanced the institutionalized participation in government of all major well-organized interest groups. This interest organization was closely intertwined with the party system and kept in balance through the principle of parity. It is to be expected that these institutional peculiarities would also be reflected in the structure of the corporate network.

Following a short account of the causes and extent of nationalization, the overall structure of the corporate network will be described. Groups of enterprises will be delineated and the composition of the centre will be analysed. Special emphasis will then be given to primary interlocks and the domains they form around the four most important corporations. Relationships within and between the public, co-operative and private sector are considered next. Finally political affiliations of big linkers and their distribution over the network will be explored.

A BRIEF OUTLINE OF THE HISTORY OF NATIONALIZATION

Historically, nationalization was due far less to an outright socialist policy than to a reaction to economic crises and political constraints from abroad. Already between the two Wars a large proportion of the shares of Austrian corporations were held by foreign owners, pre-dominantly German, Italian, Swiss and French. During the Great Depression this high degree of foreign control over Austrian industry and banking led to such disastrous consequences that the first concrete plans for nationalization were discussed.

Apart from the early-nationalized railways and postal services, state control started in banking. During the last years of the Austro-Hungarian monarchy many small banks had already gone bankrupt and major financials had merged. This process of concentration continued during the 1920s, fostered by shortage of domestic capital and a heavy dependence on foreign capital which only large banks could attract. The withdrawal of foreign capital during the depression in 1929 sharpened the economic crisis and when, in 1931, France reclaimed its credits to prevent Austria from establishing a customs-union with Germany, the largest bank (Credit-Anstalt, founded in 1855) collapsed. By taking over, the government gained control of large parts of the already concentrated banking sector. In 1934 Credit-Anstalt merged with another old-established bank, Wiener Bankver-ein, forming the Creditanstalt-Bankverein (CA). Today it is still the largest commercial bank outnumbering by two thirds in total assets the second one, Österreichische Länderbank (LB), which was founded in 1880 as an Austrian-French joint venture and nationalized after the Second World War.

After the annexation in 1938 the holdings of the Austrian Republic became the property of the Deutsches Reich and at Potsdam the Allies decided to take over this 'German Property'. In order to regain control of these holdings again, there was complete agreement in both the socialist and the conservative party to nationalize the enterprises. Nationalization was facilitated as shortly after the War the provisional Austrian government had decided to manage these mostly leaderless corporations by public commissioners. Besides, there were only a few private non-German owners to be repaid. Therefore, by federal act a large part of Austrian banking, the basic goods industry and almost all utilities were nationalized in 1946 and 1947. At first these laws were only enacted in the three Western sectors, while the nationalized companies in the Russian sector were not handed over until 1955 when Austria regained its sovereignty, heavy reparations being made.

Nationalization was completed at a time of broad political consensus and a relatively stable balance of votes between the two leading parties. To keep this balance, the principle of parity was taken over from the political sphere and applied to the state-owned enterprises. A candidate for a vacant directorship therefore did not only have to show competence but to belong to the appropriate party. Even after the end of the grand coalition in 1966, which conservatives and socialists had formed since the Second World War, this practice only gradually receded.

It should not go unnoted that there were some attempts at denationalization. In 1956/57 40 per cent of the shares of both Creditanstalt and Länderbank were sold, resulting in a greater dispersal of ownerships, while the federal government kept the majority of 60 per cent. Another important outcome of these efforts was the legal requirement that all nationalized enterprises should be set up as joint stock companies under private corporate law (Langer, 1966, pp. 134ff.). To guarantee political influence several bills were passed, among other things requiring common directorships *as of right* between certain nationalized companies and between them and parts of government.

A reorganization took place in 1970 when all the industrials nationalized by the first bill in 1946 were put under the control of the 100 per cent state-owned Holding Österreichische Industrieverwaltungs-AG (ÖIAG). This had been founded in 1966 but was changed into a joint stock company in 1970. The ÖIAG and its 100 per cent subsidiaries are under the supervision of the Chancellor and constitute the so-called directly nationalized sector, together with the 100 per cent state-owned holding of public electric utilities, Österreichische Elektrizitätswirtschafts-AG, which was founded in 1947 and is under the control of the Secretary of Commerce. The three[2] nationalized banks and their subsidiaries are supervized by the Secretary of Finance and form the so-called indirectly nationalized sector.

A few figures will show the importance of the public sector for the Austrian economy. Almost 100 per cent of utilities, about two-thirds of mining, iron and mineral-oil production (measured either by number of people employed or by output) is within the public sector. It contributes about a quarter to total output of manufacturing industry and about 31 per cent to gross domestic product (excluding agriculture).[3] In 1981 19 per cent of the total working force in manufacturing industry was employed by the ÖIAG-Konzern, nine per cent by the combine of Creditanstalt and three per cent by that of the Länderbank. Within banking, public ownership is even more pronounced. In 1975 Creditanstalt and its financial subsidiaries held 34 per cent of total assets in banking while Länderbank contributed another 21 per cent (Morawetz, 1983, p. 47). Though these figures are taken from various sources and refer to different years, the overall picture seems not to be affected and demonstrates the strong position of the nationalized sector in the Austrian economy.

GROUPS OF ENTERPRISES

Besides the 209 largest, legally independent, production corporations of 1976 and the 32 largest, legally independent financials, another three banks and 15 production companies were found which – though majority-controlled by one of the 241 selected corporations – were at least as large as the smallest of them. Nine of these 18 corporations were indirectly state-controlled and five showed indirect foreign ownership. In the first analysis, which tried to delineate groups of enterprises, these subsidiaries were included.

Figure 4.1   Network Components of all 259 companies in Austria

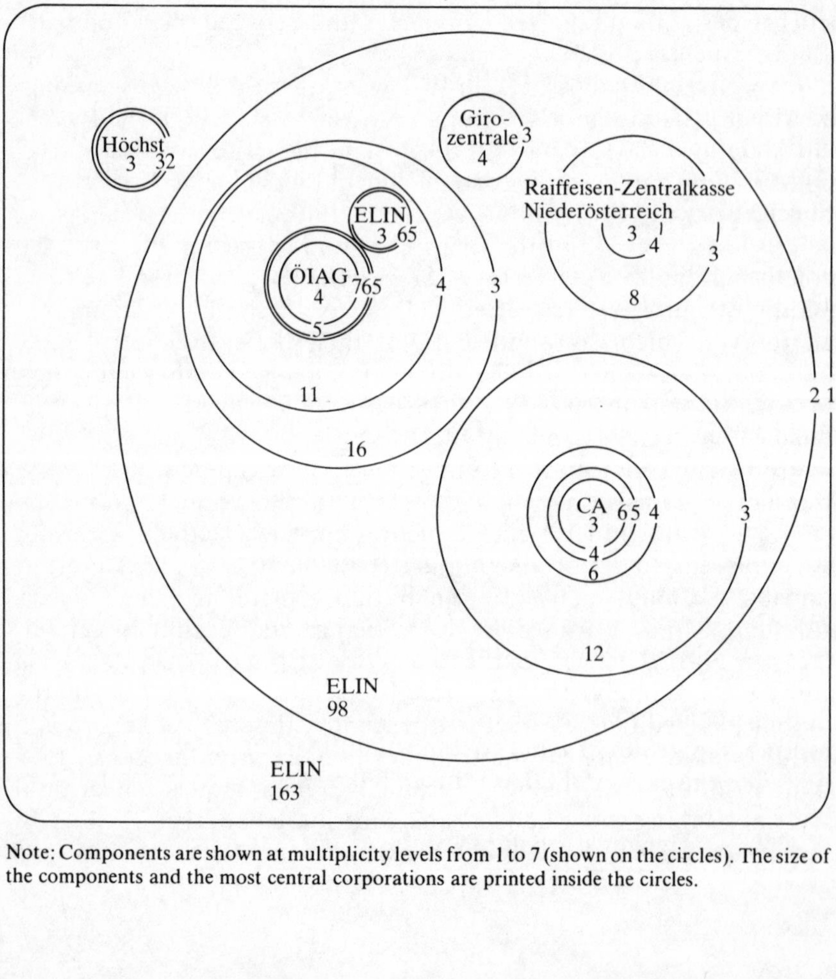

Note: Components are shown at multiplicity levels from 1 to 7 (shown on the circles). The size of the components and the most central corporations are printed inside the circles.

Multiple interlocking directorships indicate strong links between two corporations and are certainly not accidental. Figure 4.1 shows the structure of components, i.e. sets of companies connected by a series of lines at a certain level of multiplicity. Every component is named by its most central company and its size is given below it. Numbers on the circles show the level of multiplicity. Concentric circles symbolize the gradual shrinking of clusters with increasing multiplicity while excentric circles indicate that a less strongly connected subcluster was cut off at a given level of multiplicity. The clusters are placed on the figure so as to approximate their relative closeness at lower multiplicities.

The total network contained – besides four pairs and 88 isolates – one big component with 163 companies. ELIN, a subsidiary of ÖIAG, was most central, being directly linked to 53 companies through which it was connected to another 77 corporations. It still remained most central in the component of 98 companies at multiplicity level 2, where three pairs, 152 isolates and a small component of three companies were split off. The latter consisted of the German-owned corporation Höchst and its two subsidiaries. At multiplicity level 3 a very clear and simple structure appeared which should be compared with the more complex German network of figure 5.1. There was a loose grouping of financials around the Girozentrale but more important were the three other components. Raiffeisen-Zentralkasse Niederösterreich was most central among eight co-operative banks and production companies. The next largest component could be clearly identified as a group of 12 enterprises directly or indirectly controlled by Creditanstalt. This component was both strongly connected and showed a high density of 0.92 taking lines with lower multiplicity into account. At multiplicity level 4, the fourth component consisted entirely of ten companies directly or indirectly controlled by the state-holding ÖIAG. Those additional five corporations in the ÖIAG-component at multiplicity level 3 were linked to it only through one company, ELIN, forming thus a loose and somewhat separate subcluster.

It has certainly been noted that the second nationalized bank did not show up in a separate cluster. It did not even appear among the components just described. Unlike Creditanstalt the Länderbank did not keep strong ties with other corporations and was linked by three common directorships to only one of its subsidiaries. Nevertheless its traces could be found in the structure. It was connected by two common directorships with ELIN and with three of the five companies in the subcluster mentioned above. This seemed, therefore, part of a loosely tied group of enterprises around the Länderbank which was linked to the cluster of ÖIAG through the electrical engineering company ELIN.

These clusters of strongly tied enterprises were based on ownership

D

relations. The focal position of Creditanstalt was less due to its function as a bank than to its role as a holding company for indirectly nationalized corporations. The importance of financial participations for determining these groups of enterprises is also shown by the fact that six out of nine companies, which were majority-owned by one of the corporations in the five clusters, were strongly tied by multiple directorships to their respective groupings.[4] Together with the other nine majority-owned companies they were excluded from further analyses.

GENERAL STRUCTURE OF THE INTERCORPORATE NETWORK

Austrian corporation law is very similar to the German, providing similar legal types of corporations and requiring two kinds of boards for joint stock companies. In the selection, thirteen different legal types of corporations were observed which, however, might be grouped together in the following broader categories: 111 joint stock companies, 59 limited liability companies, 29 partnerships and single firms, 26 co-operatives and 16 public corporations representing various legal types under public law. The boards of these companies were classified as either managing or supervisory (e.g. Verwaltungsräte). If only one board existed it was always classified as executive.

One-hundred-and-forty-seven corporations were directly or indirectly linked together in one large component, outside of which were two pairs and 90 isolated firms. The latter predominantly belonged to one (or more) of the following categories: privately owned companies or partnerships, foreign-owned companies (e.g. ARAL, Chrysler, Citroen, Ford, ITT, Quelle, Bauknecht, Borregard, Jacobs, Knorr, Liebherr, Nestle, Unilever, Olivetti, Triumpf, Rank Xerox, Wienerwald), trading companies, especially those in the retail industry, and missing data (12 cases). Within the large component, eight per cent of all pairs of firms were directly interlocked and another 39 per cent met each other on the board of a third company, i.e. at distance 2. The largest distance was 7, the average 2.64.

In chapter 2, the partitioning of the largest component into four centrality groups was explained and their size was compared for all countries. Economic importance as measured by value added obviously determined the position of a company to a high degree: the proportion of corporations with a value added of at least 1,000 million shillings continuously declined from the core (91 per cent) to inner margin (30 per cent), outer margin (18 per cent), periphery (seven per cent), and isolates (two per cent). The core of 11 corporations consisted of the state-owned holding ÖIAG and its three largest 100 per cent subsidiaries (VÖEST-Alpine [steel and iron], ÖMV [mineral oil], and ELIN [electrical engineering]), the biggest nationalized bank Creditanstalt and its two largest subsidiaries (Steyr Daimler Puch [automobiles] and Semperit[5] [rubber]; the second largest, Italian-owned insurance company (Erste Allgemeine Versicherungs-AG) and two financial institutions which functioned as important meeting-places. By law the Österreichische Nationalbank has to recruit the members of its supervisory board from among leading figures of banking, industry, trade, agriculture and representatives of employees and workers. Actually, the Nationalbank had the largest number of executives from other corporations on its supervisory board, there being 15 incoming primary interlocks. The second meeting-place was the Österreichische Kontrollbank, a joint venture of the major Austrian banks, which acted as a clearing-house for banking, financing export and underwriting, especially public issues. There was only one comparatively small corporation, Wertheim Werke, which was operating in mechanical engineering, being majority-owned by a Swiss corporation and having a 25 per cent holding by Creditanstalt. It was part of the core because the two executives with most directorships sat on its supervisory board.

Nine production corporations had a higher value added than the second smallest one in the core, Semperit.[6] Two slightly larger corporations belonged to the inner margin: the German-owned electrical engineering company Siemens with a 44 per cent minority-holding by ÖIAG and the chemical subsidiary of ÖIAG, Chemie Linz AG. Three other large corporations being foreign owned (Philips, Shell, Mobil) were part of the outer margin which also included the state monopoly of tobacco-manufacturing, Austria Tabakwerke, and the public utility of Vienna, Wiener Stadtwerke. The nationalized railways were located in the periphery and the Austrian PTT was isolated.

The Länderbank did not appear in the core. It was linked to 27 corporations compared with Creditanstalt which interlocked with 41 companies. Nevertheless, it played an important role in the network which became more visible when the analysis was concentrated on primary interlocks only, indicating more clearly relations of co-optation and control. Those four companies which ranked top in terms of number of outgoing primary interlocks were Creditanstalt, Bankhaus Schoeller (the most important privately owned bank founded in 1833)[7], Länderbank and ÖIAG. Their executives held 80 positions on the supervisory boards of 60 corporations, i.e. were represented in more than 40 per cent of all non-isolated companies.

Figure 4.2 shows the domains of these four corporations, putting together structurally equivalent companies. The structure looks very

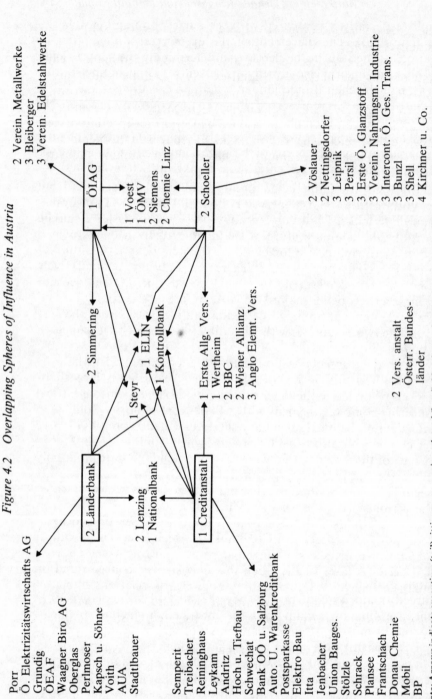

Figure 4.2 Overlapping Spheres of Influence in Austria

Note: Arrows indicate executives (tail) sitting on supervisory board (head). Numbers refer to centrality groups (1=core; 2=inner margin; 3=outer margin; 4 = periphery). Versicherungsanstalt der Österreichischen Bundesländer is in the centre but not connected by primary interlocks with the big four corporations simple, especially if compared with the corresponding German one (see figure 5.3). The placement of the executives of these four institutions turned out to be decisive in determining the centre. There was only one insurance company in the centre, Versicherungsanstalt der österreichischen Bundesländer, where no executive of any of the four institutions was represented. But even this company was linked by two common directorships with the supervisory board of Creditanstalt. Though the centre was very densely connected (density =0.48 as compared with overall density of the large component =0.08) there was only one primary interlock going from Bankhaus Schoeller to ÖIAG. It should be stressed that there were no common directorships, not even induced ones, between the three state-controlled corporations, as if government would follow the rule *divide et impera*. Integration of the centre was mainly due to the existence of two common meeting-places: the joint venture of the three banks, Österreichische Kontrollbank, and the 100 per cent subsidiary of ÖIAG, ELIN, which at that time was already heavily dependent on loans and a few years later got into serious financial trouble.

Besides these two meeting-places, the domains of the four major institutions overlapped only pair-wise and to a lesser degree than in the corresponding German network. Corporations which had executives from two or more major institutions on their supervisory board were also economically more important. Their average value added amounted to 3,400 million shillings, while those companies within exclusive domains averaged only 640 million shillings. Finally, the tendency to keep domains separate was also operating at lower levels. Primary interlocks among corporations within the same domain (these interlocks are not shown in figure 4.2) were almost three times more likely than those between companies from different domains.

CATEGORIES OF OWNERSHIPS: PUBLIC, CO-OPERATIVE AND PRIVATE SECTOR

An effort was made to determine final ownership of all 259 corporations studied. Of these, 186 could be classified as directly and 59 as indirectly majority-controlled by one of seven *categories* of owners. In eight cases final ownership had to be presumed on the basis of partial evidence. It must be stressed that, except for the federal government, majority-control here refers not to individual but to categories of owners. There were only three corporations not majority-controlled by *one type* of owner and these were assigned to the category which held the relative majority of shares. This classification resulted in the following distribution: Federal Government of Austria (49),

Table 4.1 Centrality groups and ownership categories in Austria (%)

	Public sector		Co-operative sector		Private sector			Missing data	Total number of corporations
	Federal government	Bundesländer, local communities	Co-operatives	Trade unions	Private owners	Foreign owners	Dispersed ownership		
Core	82	—	—	—	—	18	—	—	100 (11)
Inner margin	57	—	4	—	26	13	—	—	100 (23)
Outer margin	18	18	13	3	22	25	1	—	100 (85)
Periphery	7	14	32	—	25	14	7	—	100 (28)
Isolates	3	1	10	—	50	32	1	3	100 (94)
Total	17	8	13	1	33	25	2	1	100 (241)

Note: Absolute numbers are in parentheses.

Table 4.2 *(Bipartite) densities of 'subcentres' among different ownership categories and overlap with overall centre in Austria*

	Public sector	Foreign owner-ship	Private owner-ship	Co-oper-ative sector	Number of corporations		Size of subcentre	Total number of corpor-ations
					Inside overall centre	Outside overall centre		
Public sector	0.48	0.40	0.35	0.11	22	3	25	62
Foreign ownership	0.40	0.43	0.44	0.02	5	3	8	60
Private ownership	0.35	0.44	0.36	0.02	5	3	8	82
Co-operative sector	0.11	0.02	0.02	0.46	1	7	8	33

Bundesländer or local communities (22), co-operatives (30), trades unions (4), private owners (81), foreign owners (65) and dispersed ownership (5). Three companies could not be classified.

The dominant position of the state-owned corporations was quite remarkable as table 4.1 shows. The proportion of companies directly or indirectly controlled by federal government gradually fell from 82 per cent in the core to 3 per cent among the isolates. Firms owned by the nine provinces (Bundesländer) or by local communities and those belonging to the co-operative sector were concentrated in the outer margin or on the periphery. While privately owned companies dominated among isolates, foreign-owned corporations were more evenly represented among the centrality groups. An analysis of densities corroborated the focal position of nationalized industry. All categories of ownership were most densely connected with government-controlled corporations, except the co-operative sector which showed the highest density among itself.

As discussed in chapter 11, the Italian corporate network had a bifocal structure with the state and the private centre only partially overlapping. In order to test for a similar structure, 'subcentres' within four categories of ownership were determined. Table 4.2 shows their size, densities and amount of overlap with the overall centre.[8] While in the co-operative sector there existed a small but densely connected subcentre, in the other categories of ownership no tendency to form separate subcentres could be observed. Only a few corporations were added to those already belonging to the overall centre, and densities indicated no pronounced internal cohesion of the most central foreign- or privately owned companies.

To summarize, the overall centre of the Austrian corporate network was constituted by the largest nationalized enterprises to which a few big foreign- and privately owned corporations were linked, which themselves did not form separate subcentres. There existed, however, a subcentre of co-operatives located in the outer margin and connected through a single firm to the overall centre.

POLITICAL PARTISANSHIP OF MULTIPLE DIRECTORS

'Social partnership' (Sozialpartnerschaft) in Austria is often cited as an ideal-typical example of neo-corporatism. The characteristic features of this institutional form of interest aggregation are the following (Schmitter and Lehmbruch, 1979, pp. 55 ff.; Lehmbruch and Schmitter, 1982, pp. 16 ff.): the three large economic interest groups are at the same time organized into 'chambers', i.e. statutory public corporations with compulsory membership, and into voluntary associations. Labour is represented by the Chambers of Workers and Employees (Kammern für Arbeiter und Angestellte) and about 60 per cent of all employed are members of the trades unions (Österreichischer Gewerkschaftsbund [ÖGB]). Employers are organized into the Chambers of Business (Kammern der gewerblichen Wirtschaft) and the Austrian Economic Federation (Österreichischer Wirtschaftsbund). The two kinds of farmers' organizations are the Chambers of Agriculture (Landwirtschaftskammern) and the Austrian Farmers Federation (Österreichischer Bauernbund).

Since the 1950s, co-operation among interest groups has been institutionalized on the basis of voluntary agreements. The most important body is the Paritätische Kommission für Lohn- und Preisfragen which consists of representatives of the three chambers and the ÖGB. Government is represented by two members who, however, have only advisory status. The Paritätische completely controls collective bargaining on wages and sets about 20 per cent of consumer prices – another quarter being administered by government – and 50 per cent of producer prices (Marin, 1981, p. 149). Interest organizations have an important influence on legislative and administrative processes too. Chambers and associations are entitled to give their opinion on all administrative decrees before enactment and on all government bills before they are submitted to parliament.

The party system is intimately geared to this system of interest organization, which is also kept in balance by the pervading principle of parity. Many influential leaders of interest organizations sit in parliament and hold important party functions. On the other hand, leading positions in nationalized industry are nearly always occupied by partisans, with both 'parts of the Empire' (the two 'Reichshälften' as conservatives and socialists are commonly called) represented on a par.

To get an idea of the impact of partisanship on the intercorporate network the party affiliation of all 57 big linkers, those holding at least four directorships, was ascertained. Only six directors were either non-partisan or their partisanship was unknown. Seventeen were affiliated with the socialist party (SPÖ), two with the liberals (FPÖ) and 32 with the Austrian People's Party (ÖVP). The latter two were grouped together and are refered to as 'conservatives' as both parties follow very similar economic policies. Though partisan big linkers constituted a tiny fraction of just two per cent of all 2,550 directors, they held ten per cent of all 3,133 positions and created 74 per cent of all 1,489 interlocks. Among the big linkers there were not only more conservatives than socialists, but the former held slightly more positions on the average (6.3 compared with 6) and created many more interlocks than the latter (24 compared with 16.5 on the average).

At least one partisan big linker sat on either board of 111 out of the 165 interlocked corporations.[9] Both executive and supervisory boards were classified according to the partisanship of their members: having only directors whose partisanship was unknown, socialists, conservatives or directors of both political groups. Cross-tabulating the partisanship of both boards revealed a very neat pattern: among those 88 corporations which had at least one partisan big linker on both boards, 80 showed the same type of composition in supervisory and executive board. Not a single case was found in which one board was dominated by one political group and the other by the opposite party. Six companies had a one-party executive board while both political groups were represented on the supervisory board, indicating perhaps an effort to co-opt members of the political opponent. There were only two corporations with a somewhat implausible constellation: while both political groups were represented on their executive board, directors from one party only were found on their supervisory board. However, some of those directors whose partisanship was not checked might actually have been affiliated with the political opponent.

Table 4.3 shows the distribution of partisanship among all 165 interlocked corporations, combining both types of boards. Almost 60 per cent of these companies had conservative directors on their boards, one-third had socialists and one-third had directors whose partisanship was unknown. The latter were especially frequent among co-operatives and firms owned by the provinces or local communities. This reflected of course the fact that these companies had the lowest proportion of big linkers on their boards and therefore were to be found in the outer margin and on the periphery. The highest proportion of companies with a balanced representation was to be observed in the nationalized sector of industry and banking, which confirms the exceptation stated at the beginning. If the ratio of number of corporations with conservative directors to number with socialists was studied, a clear ranking of ownership categories existed: privately owned firms showed the highest preponderance of conservative directors, foreign-owned ranking second and co-operatives third, having a ratio about equal to the overall one. State-controlled enterprises had an almost balanced ratio, while socialists were more preponderant among companies controlled by the province or local communities and, of course, among union-owned firms.

A final question to be answered was whether conservatives or socialists had a more efficient network of partisan interlocks available to connect those companies in which they were represented. Separate analyses were made for partial subgraphs consisting of those corporations with directors of one political group on their boards and taking into account common directorships by partisans only. Using the pro-

Table 4.3 Distribution of boards' partisanship over categories of ownership in Austria (%)

	Conservatives and socialists	Conservatives	Socialists	Only directors with unknown partisanship	Total number of unisolated corporations
Federal government	61	17	9	13	100 (46)
Bundesländer, local communities	5	19	24	52	100 (21)
Co-operatives	10	24	10	57	100 (21)
Trade-unions	50	0	50	0	100 (4)
Private owners	8	53	3	37	100 (38)
Foreign owners	17	49	3	31	100 (35)
Total	25	33	9	33	100 (165)

Note: Absolute number are in parentheses.

portion of pairs of firms at distance 1 or 2 as a measure of effectiveness, the data clearly indicated that the conservatives could rely on a potentially much more efficient network than the socialists, the proportion being 0.65 compared with 0.39. This was even more remarkable as there were many more firms with conservative directors than with socialist ones. The figures indicated a 0.65 chance of two firms (out of 96 having conservative directors on their boards) being either directly connected by a partisan or having their conservative directors meet in a third company, while there was only a 0.39 chance of two firms (out of 57 having socialist directors on their boards) being linked at distance 1 or 2 by partisan interlocks. Even if the comparison is restricted to those 42 enterprises, where directors of both political groups were present, the conservative network was potentially much more efficient than the socialist, the former connecting 74 per cent of all pairs at distance 1 or 2 by partisan interlocks while the latter linked only 43 per cent.

CONCLUSIONS

Austrian industry and banking is characterized by a high level of nationalization. About one-fifth of all companies selected were directly or indirectly majority-owned by federal government and another eight per cent were controlled by provinces (Bundesländer) or local communities. Two-thirds of the nationalized companies were organized into three combines: 12 industrials were under control of the state-owned holding ÖIAG and 21 financial and production corporations were directly or indirectly majority-owned by the two largest nationalized banks. The groups of enterprises around ÖIAG and Creditanstalt were also strongly and densely connected, while Länderbank was only loosely tied to its subsidiaries.

Though not directly linked to one another by any common directorship, these three important institutions together with the largest old-established private bank, Bankhaus Schoeller, formed the kernel of a densely connected centre to which the largest nationalized companies and a few big foreign- and privately owned corporations belonged. This overall centre was therefore clearly dominated by nationalized industry and banking and there was no tendency among foreign- or privately-owned companies to form separate subcentres. However, a small subcentre of co-operatives existed, being located in the outer margin of the total corporate network. Isolated enterprises were mainly privately owned or partnerships, firms under foreign control and companies operating in the retail industry.

Besides the importance of the nationalized sector, the structure of the network reflected another institutional peculiarity. The corporatist form of interest organization has been well developed in Austria, being supported by an intimate symbiosis with the party system. An analysis of the political affiliations of big linkers revealed a high degree of partisanship. As expected, both political camps were represented on a par in the big nationalized corporations. However, conservatives preponderated in the total network, especially in the private sector. They held directorships in more companies and at the same time created a denser partisan network than did big linkers affiliated with the socialist party.

Though the structure of the Austrian intercorporate network was mainly determined by the interlocks of the big nationalized financials and industrials, no split existed between the public and private sectors, at least as far as the largest private corporations were concerned. However, the majority of these interlocks were due to a few big linkers who held or had occupied positions in employers' chambers or federations. It was especially those directors active in the corporatist system of interest mediation who·contributed most to the integration of the corporate network.

NOTES

1   The work reported here is part of a research project supported by the Deutsche Forschungsgemeinschaft under grant Zi 207/2. Data was collected under the direction of Gerhard Reissner. Checking and analysing of data was performed by Donald Bender and Hermann Biehler with the assistance of Margot Ambs-Schulz, Lydia Buck, Anton Kunz, Irmingard Mühlbauer, Karl-Heinz Neumeier and Erika Steinle. Graph-analysis was done by using the packages GRADAP (developed by the Universities of Amsterdam, Groningen and Nijmegen) and GRALIB (developed by Jacques Anthonisse, Mathematisch Centrum Amsterdam). The chapter was written by Rolf Ziegler.
2   In 1975 the third largest nationalized bank, Österreichisches Creditinstitut, became a 100 per cent subsidiary of the Länderbank.
3   These figures are calculated from a publication of Österreichisches Statistisches Zentralamt (1980). They include the co-operative sector which accounts for about five per cent of total GDP but certainly much less in utilities and mining.
4   Two of the three 'deviant' companies were isolated, the third had a single interlock with only one corporation through which it was indirectly tied to its parent's cluster.
5   Semperit is a 100 per cent subsidiary of the Swiss corporation Sempkler, which in turn is a joint venture of Creditanstalt (55 per cent), Michelin (31 per cent), and Schweizerische Kreditanstalt (14 per cent).
6   By mistake Vereinigte Edelstahlwerke (metals) was included in the selection though it should have been classified as dependent because it is a 100 per cent subsidiary of VÖEST. It is interesting to note that it was located in the outer margin though it ranked third in value added among all production corporations.

7   There was another legally independent partnership, Großhandelshaus Gebrüder Schoeller operating in wholesale, with almost identical owners and board of directors, which was therefore condensed into one point for this type of analysis.
8   Because the two Schoeller-companies have been condensed into one point, the number of corporations inside the overall centre is 33 instead of 34.
9   The analysis reported in this section refers to all 259 companies.

5

Industry and Banking in the German Corporate Network

ROLF ZIEGLER, DONALD BENDER and
HERMANN BIEHLER[1]

The efficiency of the German banking system and its close links with industry have often been cited as partial explanations for periods of rapid growth in German economic development. Earlier studies (Jeidels, 1905; Eulenburg, 1906; Riesser, 1910; Hagemann, 1931) have used interlocks, together with other data, as evidence for their argument. However, to our knowledge this is the first to investigate the *structure* of common directorships among financial and non-financial companies on a large scale.

A brief overview of historical development will be followed by an analysis of strongly connected groups of enterprises. General features of the corporate network will then be outlined and regional and sectoral variations explored. The fourth section will concentrate on different types of interlocks and on the career patterns of so-called 'network specialists'. Finally, a closer look at the largest and most central financial corporations will permit distinctions to be made between different aspects of the relationship of the financial to the non-financial sector.

SOME REMARKS ON THE HISTORICAL DEVELOPMENT OF GERMAN INDUSTRY AND BANKING

Compared with other Western European countries, industrial development started rather late in Germany. The first phase began about 1840 – some 50 years later than in England – and ended with the economic crisis of 1873. Economic and political integration and the expansion of transportation made growth possible and self-sustaining. During the second phase, from 1873 until the First World War, gross national product tripled and Germany had overcome its relative economic backwardness. This period saw the emergence of the large, vertically integrated and diversified firm primarily operating in mining, primary metals, mechanical and electrical engineering, chemicals and textiles (Kocka and Siegrist, 1979). The trend towards concentration, the establishing of cartels and syndicates, was closely related to the development of the large corporate banks which were founded during the boom of the 1850s and around the years of the foundation of the Kaiserreich in 1871. By the turn of the century seven large joint stock banks had brought the older private, local and provincial banks under their control and dominated the Berlin stock exchange. They mobilized dispersed capital and channeled it into the large industrial enterprises. This was even more important as there was less capital accumulated from international trade, commercial activities or colonial possessions than in other countries, a historical development which also caused the independent merchants to play a relatively minor role (Kocka, 1980).

The banks took an active part in founding new firms, issued shares and bonds on behalf of industrial enterprises, held financial participations, provided long- and short-term loans and kept close personal connections, especially through representation on the supervisory boards of the joint stock companies which were the dominant legal form among large industrials. It was Jeidels who first collected detailed information on the amount of interlocking: executives of the six largest banks together held 394 seats on the supervisory boards of industrial joint stock companies and there existed another 407 interlocks between these boards and the supervisory boards of the banks themselves (1905, pp. 161ff.). Later studies showed these numbers to be increasing. Riesser (1910, pp. 603 – 24) listed in detail 725 directorships of the eight largest banks' executives and Hagemann (1931, p. 80) reported 1,789 positions on industrials' supervisory boards held by executives of the seven largest banks.

Jeidels and the later authors were very careful to interpret interlocks only in conjunction with other data on financial holdings, credit relations, underwriting, etc. From a detailed historical analysis of the financial development of both banks and industrials Jeidels drew the following conclusions. Though the banks had not caused the trend towards industrial concentration, they reinforced it by their own striving for expansion. This had drawn together industrial and money capital into a unified whole. Nevertheless, he stressed the continuous presence of cleavages between economic sectors which prevented conscious planning and co-ordination of the total economy (Jeidels, 1905, pp. 268 – 71). These ideas are familiar to the model of 'finance capitalism' presented by Hilferding (1910), which is briefly described in chapter 1. However, later studies have shown this trend not to be straightforward. As the rate of self-financing was increasing, enterprises became more independent of the capital market and thus of the banks (Hoffmann, 1959; Tilly, 1974). At least a temporary reduction of the banks' influence was also caused by the differential losses from the galloping inflation of 1923. While the industrials drastically improved their debt – equity ratio between 1913 and 1924 by getting rid of 60 per cent of their debts and at the same time raising their equities by 12 per cent, the banks lost 80 per cent of their equity and 90 per cent of their foreign capital (Hagemann, 1931, pp. 28 and 41). Industrial concentration continued between the two Wars: the most conspicuous instance being the merger of several chemical corporations in 1925 to form the huge combine I.G. Farben, which in 1945 had 214 subsidiaries and some 500 participations abroad.

For a better understanding of the findings on interlocking directorships between the largest enterprises, a brief overview of the economic situation and some of the institutional peculiarities of the Federal Republic of Germany must also be presented. Some consequences of the Second World War have become essential conditions for its economic and social development. As a result of the decisions taken by the Allies in Yalta and Potsdam and the beginning of the Cold War, most of the important structural conditions for later development had already been determined when the Federal Republic was established in May 1949 and the German Democratic Republic a few months later. These conditions were the territorial boundaries based on the Allied partition of the Deutsches Reich, the integration of both countries into the alliances of East and West as well as the basic elements of their political and economic order.

Though war damage to productive facilities was serious, it did not prevent rapid reconstruction. Similarly, dismantling as a means of reparation and production restriction did not equal the dimensions of the corresponding plans. Whereas in March 1946 there had been about 1,800 firms destinated for dismantling, this planned number diminished until February 1949 when it stood at less than 700. The reparations of the Western sectors amounted to a sum of 5,000 million DM (Henning, 1979, p. 189). This development expressed the growing East – West conflict, which, instead of realizing the initial aims of the Allies, little by little resulted in a massive support of German economic development (above all through food imports and transfer of capital by the Marshall plan). Another consequence was that the dissolution and divestiture of German trusts was soon stopped.

With the currency reform of 1948, which favoured the owners of material goods to the disadvantage of savers, an economic boom started, which had its basis in massive, internal suppressed demand. This boom was accompanied by an economic policy favouring employers and investments, and despite several revaluations of the Deutsch

Mark it was reinforced by foreign trade too. About a third of industrial production was sold abroad in 1976, the share of exports in the total gross national product amounting to 25 per cent. The biggest exporting sectors were mechanical engineering, automobiles, electrical engineering, chemicals and steel. The manufacturing sector contributed more than 50 per cent to GNP while services contributed only 45 per cent, less than in other industrialized countries.

To regulate economic concentration an anti-trust law was enacted in 1957. The foundations of this law can be seen in the anti-trust laws introduced by the Allies in 1947 and in the ideas of economic neo-liberalism, which in the beginning of the Federal Republic influenced economic policy (Rittner, 1981, p. 93). Essential parts of the German anti-trust law are the prohibition on cartels, the public control of abuses by market-controlling enterprises and control of mergers. The prohibition on cartels has several times been loosened. The inefficient control of abuses has not become more important in practice, in spite of a supplementary law. Control over mergers may have had mainly preventive effects but there remained the possibility that prohibited mergers could be permitted by the Minister of Industry and Commerce. Furthermore, the law has had only limited effect in agriculture and forestry, public utilities, transport, banking and insurance and therefore is really operative only for the goods-producing industries.

Despite these attempts at regulation, economic growth has been accompanied by increasing economic concentration. From 1954 to 1976 the average share of the ten largest companies in total sales among all industries grew from 31 to 43 per cent (Monopolkommission, 1980, p. 51). The proportion of gross domestic product accounted for by 259 economically independent companies in the present data set was about 28 per cent. Since many minor firms were economically dependent on these companies, the data set includes the heart of the German economy.

GROUPS OF ENTERPRISES

During the selection process many large corporations were found to be subsidiary companies. In addition to the 205 largest, legally independent, production corporations and the 54 largest, legally independent financial institutions, another 58 non-financial and 8 financial corporations were added in a second step. These were selected on the grounds that although they were majority-controlled by one of the 259 corporations, they were all larger than the smallest of these companies. In no other country was such a large number of legally independent but financially controlled companies found. This seems to be due to the way concentration proceeded after the dissolution of the big German trusts by the Allies. Though some of the dissolved corporations remained separate, many of them joined again but remained legally independent.[2]

The initial analysis of multiple lines should provide some first insights into the existence and localization of groups of enterprises. No account is taken of the distinctions between the two types of boards or the positions held. Though a single line between two companies may be the unintended by-product of processes which do not involve a direct relationship between them, a multiple tie is more likely to be the result of a conscious and purposeful act of both companies and so indicates a closer and more permanent relationship. This is also recognized by the German law against restrictions on competition, which takes an overlap between two boards, involving more than a half of their members, as sufficient evidence for collusion.

In the analysis of the set of 325 corporations two criteria will be used in order to determine the components in the network. Those sets of companies, all of which are connected by a series of lines at a certain level of multiplicity, will be included in the same component. Multiplicities of 3 and 4 turn out to be critical values. Figure 5.1 shows the structure of components. Components are represented by circles proportional to size; the level of multiplicity is indicated by the numbers on the circles. Every component is named by its most central company and the number below it gives the size of the component. Concentric circles symbolize the gradual shrinking of clusters with increasing multiplicity, while excentric circles indicate that a less strongly connected subcluster is cut off at a given level of multiplicity. The smaller clusters are placed on the figure so as to approximate their relative closeness at lower multiplicities.

The total network contained – besides two pairs and 61 isolated companies – one big component with 260 companies. The Deutsche Bank as the most central company reached 239 others in at most two steps. At the next level of multiplicity there were 120 isolated companies, ten pairs and two larger components, one being a regional cluster of six state- or community-owned banks and utilities. In the largest component the Deutsche Bank was still the most central of the 179 companies. At multiplicity level 3 clear groupings appeared for the first time. Besides eight groups of enterprises containing three to five companies, there were two larger clusters: a group of 53 predominantly privately owned companies (THYSSEN) and a group of 30 mainly state- or union-owned companies (VEBA). The first cluster contained the subgroups of Thyssen (steel), Mannesmann (steel), Höchst (chemical), Gute-Hoffnungs-Hütte (mechanical engineering) and DAIMLER; the second cluster split up into a subgroup of four

Figure 5.1   Network components of all 325 companies in Germany

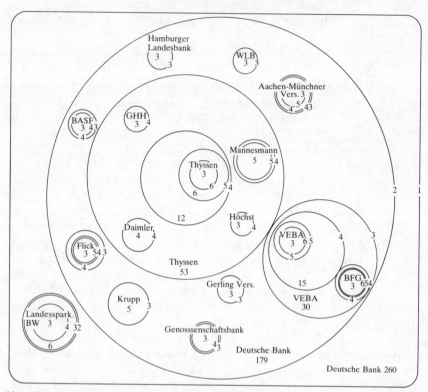

Note: Components are shown as multiplicity levels from 1 to 6 (shown in circles). The size of the components and the most centred corporations are printed inside the circles.

union-owned companies under the leadership of the Bank für Gemein-wirtschaft and a group of enterprises around the state-owned holding company VEBA. The 12 corporations of the component THYSSEN actually formed two subclusters: four insurance companies around the largest German insurance firm, Allianz, which were connected through the largest electrical corporation, Siemens, to the Thyssen combine, which still formed a component at multiplicity level 5. Taking into account lines with lower multiplicity, all these components turned out to be very densely connected. With a single exception (KRUPP), at least two-thirds of the companies in each cluster were directly connected with one another. Though not Konzerne (combines) as defined in German law, these components were definitely formed around combines.

It is important to stress a peculiar feature which may not be obvious when looking at figure 5.1. Whenever banks appeared in these components (at multiplicity level 3 or higher) these tended to be special cases: the union-owned Bank für Gemeinwirtschaft in the centre of other companies controlled by the trades unions, co-operative banks associated with manufacturing co-operatives, and saving-banks and other state- or community-owned financial institutions linked with public utilities. There were only two exceptions: the Bayerische Vereinsbank being located on the edge of the VEBA-cluster and the Deutsche Bank being part of the component DAIMLER because it holds shares in the motor car firm Daimler-Benz. Other big banks (e.g. Dresdner Bank, Commerzbank, Berliner Handels- und Frankfurter Bank) which, as will be seen, played an important role, never appeared among these groups of enterprises. Though banks were important in determining the global structure of the network and its coherence, they did not seem to have been very strongly tied to any specific combine or group of enterprises.

The following analyses are restricted to those 259 companies which were not majority-controlled by any other corporation. The 66 subsidiaries, of which three-quarters actually belonged to the groups of enterprises described so far, were excluded. This selection procedure enhances the comparability of the results with those for other countries, as the internal structure of the combines is no longer biasing our analysis.

GENERAL FEATURES OF THE NETWORK

German corporation law (Aktiengesetz) requires every joint stock company to have two boards: an executive board (Vorstand) with full-time officers and a supervisory board (Aufsichtsrat) with outside directors only; common directorships on these two boards are not allowed. The supervisory board's duties go well beyond the rights of supervision. It appoints and discharges the members of the executive board and may stipulate that certain major decisions on investment and financial transactions should have its prior consent. One person is allowed to be director in at most ten companies, but under special provisions (e.g. directorship in subsidiaries) in at most fifteen. The size of the board of directors varied between 9 and 21, but the highest number was seldom achieved.[3]

There were 15 legal types to be distinguished among the selected corporations which, however, may be grouped together in the following broader categories: 128 joint stock companies, 75 limited liability companies, 27 partnerships and single firms, 24 public corporations representing various legal types under public law and 5 co-operatives. We have tried to classify the boards of these other types of companies (e.g. Verwaltungsräte, Beiräte) as either managing or supervisory. If only one board existed it was always classified as executive.

The total network divides into one large component, consisting of 195 companies, one pair and 62 isolated corporations. The isolates may be classified into four categories: privately owned companies or partnerships, foreign-owned companies (e.g. AGIP, C&A, Renault, Woolworth, Chevron, Dupont, Elf, Ford, IBM, Opel), trading companies with chain stores (especially in the food industry) and missing data (about four cases). Within the large component, 7 per cent of all pairs of firms were directly connected and another 42 per cent had distance 2, i.e. directors of these corporations met each other on the board of a third company. The largest distance was 7, the average 2.57.

The outstanding position of the Deutsche Bank is quite remarkable. It was able to reach 174 of the 194 other corporations in at most two steps, i.e. it was directly linked to 66 companies and connected through these to another 108 corporations. Among the 16 corporations with 37 or more lines, financial institutions were strongly represented. While they comprised 17 per cent of all companies selected, they accounted for 44 per cent of these most central corporations. Besides the three big commercial banks (Deutsche Bank, Dresdner Bank, Commerzbank) there was another commercial bank specializing in industrial credit (Berliner Handels- und Frankfurter Bank) and a state-owned bank providing long-term credit for industrial reconstruction after the War and aid for developing countries and guaranteeing loans in foreign trade (Kreditanstalt für Wiederaufbau). In addition, the largest insurance company (Allianz) and one of its reinsurers (Münchner Rückversicherung) belonged to the group of strongly connected corporations. The nine remaining corporations were production companies belonging to a variety of economic sectors: two to electrical engineering (Siemens, AEG), two to manufacturing of motor vehicles (Daimler, Volkswagen VAG), one to steel production (Thyssen), one to manufacturing of non-ferrous metals (Metallgesellschaft), one conglomerate (VEBA) classified in the chemical sector but also active in mineral oil and mining, one joint venture of mining and steel-producing companies (Ruhrkohle) and one belonging to the transport sector (Hapag).

Within the German centre of 34 corporations, 15 companies were especially important as meeting points for internal communication (as measured by the rush). The composition of this core is given in table 5.1. Five of the most strongly connected corporations noted above did not appear in the core but belonged to the inner margin: Commerzbank, Berliner Handels- und Frankfurter Bank, Münchner Rückversicherung, AEG and Metallgesellschaft. Though connected to more

Table 5.1 Network of the core in Germany

			Number of interlocks within the core															Number of adjacent corporations in			
Name	Sector	Rush	VAG	Deutsche Bank	Allianz	Siemens	Ruhrkohle	Daimler	Hapag	Krupp	RWE	Kreditanstalt	Thyssen	Mannesmann	Dresdner Bank	Karstadt	VEBA	Core	Inner margin	Rest of network	Total
VAG	Motor car	0.045	–	2	1	0	2	0	0	2	2	2	2	1	1	1	1	11	14	18	43
Deutsche Bank	Banking	0.040	2	–	3	3	1	4	2	0	2	2	1	2	1	2	2	12	13	41	66
Allianz	Insurance	0.037	1	3	–	6	1	2	2	1	2	1	2	2	0	2	2	13	12	21	46
Siemens	Electrical	0.027	0	3	6	–	2	2	0	1	0	0	0	2	1	1	1	9	11	24	44
Ruhrkohle	Coal-mining	0.027	2	1	1	2	–	1	1	1	0	0	4	3	1	0	1	13	10	18	41
Daimler	Motor car	0.026	0	4	2	2	1	–	1	2	2	1	2	0	1	1	3	10	11	21	42
Hapag	Transport	0.023	0	2	2	0	1	1	–	1	1	0	2	0	2	0	1	11	12	19	42
Krupp	Primary-steel	0.023	2	0	1	1	1	2	1	–	2	1	0	0	2	2	0	9	12	15	36
RWE	Electrical	0.021	2	2	2	0	0	2	1	2	–	3	3	3	0	0	0	11	10	13	34
Kreditanstalt	Banking	0.019	2	2	1	0	0	1	0	1	3	–	3	1	1	1	0	9	7	24	40
Thyssen	Primary-steel	0.018	2	1	2	0	4	2	2	0	3	3	–	0	1	0	1	12	9	17	38
Mannesmann	Primary-steel	0.016	1	2	2	2	3	0	0	0	3	1	0	–	0	0	0	6	9	13	28
Dresdner Bank	Banking	0.016	1	1	0	1	1	1	2	2	0	1	1	0	–	1	1	11	9	20	40
Karstadt	Retail	0.014	1	2	2	1	0	1	0	2	0	1	0	0	1	–	1	8	8	13	29
VEBA	Chemical	0.013	1	2	2	1	1	3	1	0	0	0	1	0	1	1	–	11	6	22	39

companies in the total network they were not as important meeting points for the centre as the four corporations less often linked: two steel-producing corporations, Mannesmann and Krupp, a public-owned electric utility, RWE, and Karstadt, a company belonging to the retail sector.

The core represented the most important German corporations with two noteworthy exceptions. According to their turnover in 1976 all production companies in the core ranked among the 15 largest except Karstadt (rank 30) and Hapag (rank 79). Their position was entirely due to their strong affiliation with the three big German banks which jointly held the majority of their shares after having rescued them. On the other hand, five of the 20 top-ranking industrial corporations, being foreign-owned, did not belong to the core but to the outer margin (Esso, Shell and BP) or were even isolated (Opel and Ford). As far as foreign ownership is concerned there was only one sizeable holding: the government of Kuwait had a 14 per cent holding in Daimler, though it should be noted that the government of Iran bought 17 per cent of the shares of Krupp in 1977.

As compared with other countries, especially Austria and Italy, the role of the state was rather modest. Two corporations were majority-owned (Kreditanstalt and RWE) and two other companies are generally considered state-controlled as there has been sizeable public minority-ownership (VEBA, 44 per cent; Volkswagen VAG, 40 per cent) with the majority of their shares being dispersed. While there were only some 20 corporations with almost completely dispersed ownership, which could therefore be considered controlled by management, nine were located in the inner margin and four in the core (Deutsche Bank, Dresdner Bank, Allianz and Mannesmann).

The density of lines in the core was extremely high: 74 per cent of all pairs of firms were directly connected. Moreover, 49 per cent of all lines were multiple, as compared with only 19 per cent in the total network. However, the existence of one densely and strongly connected centre did not preclude competition among corporations operating in the same market. No interlocks occured between commercial banks and among competing production companies. Only steel-producing companies were connected with each other. This is not surprising after a long tradition of cartel agreements in this industry; however, none of these connections were primary interlocks. Two other seeming exceptions are easily explained: the three insurance companies in the centre belonged to the same group of enterprises and kept minority-holdings among each other, and the Kreditanstalt is actually not competing with commercial banks but rendering supplementary services. While this tendency to avoid common directorships between competitors holds for the big corporations in the centre, a more detailed analysis of all corporations showed it not to be true for the total network.

It has already been noted that different economic sectors were not equally represented among the centrality groups. Table 5.2 shows a very clear pattern. The first five categories more or less mirror the flow of production from the primary sector, to the manufacturing of basic and investment goods, to the production of consumer goods. The proportion of firms located in the centre declined in that order. On the other hand, companies operating closer to the end of the flow of production were more often found on the periphery or among the isolates. The more polarized distribution of the fourth category may be due to not separating wholesale from retail. Corporations from banking and insurance were quite strongly represented in the centre and were almost never isolated. The last category contains investment

Table 5.2   *Centrality groups and economic sectors in Germany*

| Economic sectors | Centrality groups | | | | | Total number of corporations |
	Core	Inner margin	Outer margin	Peri-phery	Isolates	
Agriculture, mining, utilities[a]	9	14	59	4	14	100 (22)
Basic goods[b]	8	10	52	15	15	100 (48)
Investment goods[c]	7	9	42	13	29	100 (45)
Transport, distribution, communication[d]	4	4	33	12	47	100 (51)
Consumer goods[e]	0	0	40	20	40	100 (25)
Banking, insurance[f]	8	9	58	21	4	100 (52)
Other finance[g]	0	0	50	19	31	100 (16)
Total	6	7	47	15	25	100 (259)

Notes: Absolute numbers are in parentheses.
a   NACE sectors 03, 11, 13, 16 and 21.
b   NACE sectors 14, 22, 23, 24 and 25.
c   NACE sectors 31, 32, 33, 34, 35, 36, 37 and 50
d   NACE sectors 61, 64, 71, 72, 74, 75, 77 and 79.
e   NACE sectors 41, 42, 46, 47 and 48.
f   NACE sectors 81 and 82.
g   NACE sector 83.

Source: Statistical Office of the EEC (1970) *NACE 1970: General Industrial Classification of Economic Activities within the European Communities.* Brussels.

companies and comparatively small holdings of privately owned corporations which were relatively peripheral.

Turning now to regional distribution, the concentration of heavy industry in the Rhein-Ruhr area – due to its natural resources – is of course well known. This area is also the largest of the 24 agglomerations distinguished in the official statistics. Adding West-Berlin, little less than half of the total population of West Germany and West Berlin was living in these 25 agglomerations. Though there was some variation, the distribution of centrality groups over these economic regions was markedly even, indicating that the centre of big German corporations had no pronounced regional base, though these big companies were of course concentrated in the large agglomerations. Among the four largest regions – Rhein-Ruhr (77 companies), Rhein-Main (56), München (24) and Stuttgart (19) – the proportion of firms belonging to the centre varied from 10 to 18 per cent, while corporations from the Hamburg area were underrepresented, with only one out of 34 (three per cent) being part of the centre. On the other hand, companies in and around Stuttgart were much more often peripheral or isolated (69 per cent) than on average (40 per cent). This reflects the peculiar economic structure of the south-western region of the Federal Republic, which is characterized by a very diversified industry and by predominantly medium-sized corporations.

Looking at the densities of common directorships between these regions the first three largest are more densely connected among themselves than the total network, while the other agglomerations are much less densely connected among themselves but a little more with the three main economic regions. This lack of a pronounced regional base of the centre of the network of common directorships among large German corporations seems to reflect the strong federal element in the history of Germany with its polycentric development.

TYPES OF INTERLOCKS

Based on the distinctions made in chapter 2 the contribution of different types of interlocks to the network structure was studied. The primary financial interlocks and especially induced financial interlocks gave cohesion to the centre of the German network. Most row entries of table 5.3 concerning the core and the inner margin show higher percentages in rows 2 and 4 in comparison with row 1. Primary production interlocks were scattered throughout the whole network without a clear concentration in one or the other part of it. Yet the unclassified interlocks were concentrated outside the centre.

Table 5.3   Centrality groups and types of interlocks in Germany (%)

Types of interlocks	Within				Between						Total
	Core	Inner margin	Outer margin	Peri-phery	c–i	c–o	c–p	i–o	i–p	o–p	
All	8	4	24	2	14	22	0	21	1	4	100 (1,628)
Primary											
Financial	12	4	18	4	13	28	0	16	1	4	100 (212)
Production	5	4	19	3	12	25	1	22	2	7	100 (241)
Induced											
Financial	14	5	20	0	22	19	0	19	0	1	100 (327)
Production	6	5	24	0	17	21	0	25	0	1	100 (225)
Unclassified											
All	6	4	30	3	8	20	0	22	1	6	100 (623)
By big linkers	7	6	24	2	12	23	0	24	0	3	100 (378)

Note: Absolute number are in parentheses.

According to German law and widespread practice, chairmen of supervisory boards play an important role in determining a company's policy and are usually informed and consulted by management at least once a month. It turned out that more than half of the unclassified interlocks were carried by chairmen of supervisory boards (who held no executive position in any of the 259 corporations). The residual category could be even further reduced by separating those interlocks carried by multiple directors with at least four positions. Only ten per cent of all common directorships were held neither by executives nor by chairmen of supervisory boards nor by big linkers.

In the German data set there were 46 multiple directors with at least four positions who were not executives but possibly chairmen of supervisory boards. They held 12 common directorships on average. By a study of their biographies (Augustin, 1982) their social background and careers were determined. Median age was 64 years, ranging from 43 to 75. Despite some lack of data there was a clear indication of a predominant but by no means exclusive recruitment from the upper-middle and upper classes. Eight multiple directors were sons (there were no females) of large property owners, 18 of smaller entrepreneurs, higher employees or civil servants, four of other white collar and two of blue collar workers. Twenty-five had been to university and 22 had a PhD.

Of special interest are the careers of these network specialists. Fifteen had been executives in production corporations for many years and had moved into the supervisory board of their home company, nine were former executives of financial institutions now sitting on the supervisory board of their base corporation, eight were politicians holding directorships predominantly in publicly controlled corporations, five were officers in employers' associations, four were trades unionists and five had mixed careers. This indicates the institutional basis in the past or present position of a person for becoming a multiple director.

The careers of these network specialists were searched for 'intersections' in three institutional areas: (1) sitting on the executive or supervisory board of the same corporation; (2) common membership on the board or committee of the employers or trades associations or of the trades unions; and (3) minister or high-ranking civil servant in the same federal or state government. Each of these common memberships had to have lasted for an extended period to be counted as an intersection of careers.

There was a clear separation of careers between trades unions, government and private business, i.e. with a single exception careers of multiple directors intersected only within these institutional fields. Within private business 25 persons formed a (connected) network of intersecting careers. During their careers 17 per cent of all 300 pairs of these 25 multiple directors have met for an extended period on the same boards of corporations, employers and/or trades associations. Two other tendencies in these careers should be noted. First, the intersections tended to be confined within industries. There were two strongly connected career networks among multiple directors active in the chemical industry on the one side and steel or mechanical engineering on the other. Second, careers of directors from different industries were either intersecting within trades associations or on the board of the Deutsche Bank.

From this analysis we may draw the following conclusions. Multiple directors were predominantly recruited from the upper strata. The vast majority had a strong institutional basis in one of the big corporations, having been an executive and moved into the supervisory board or representing ownership interests. This partly explains the position of trades unionists, politicians and higher civil servants. Besides, there surely is an element of personal reputation which has been acquired by a long career in private business. The majority of these network specialists knew each other personally, not only by their present common directorships but by extended contact during their former institutional careers. (Of course there may have been other opportunities for getting to know each other.) Those who worked on boards where interests from different industries meet (i.e. employers and trades associations or big banks, especially the Deutsche Bank) were very likely to have an extended circle of acquaintances.

THE ROLE OF THE BANKING SYSTEM

The important role banks played in the early economic development of Germany was noted at the beginning. Also, in the network of common directorships the very central position of the big German banks has been confirmed. Before exploring this position in more detail, some institutional peculiarities of the German banking system must be presented. German banks are predominantly so-called Universalbanken, i.e. they are not only taking deposits and lending short- and long-term credit but also underwriting and trading securities, financing foreign trade, mortgaging and providing other services like investment-consulting (Wagner, 1970, p. 3). Though many banks concentrate their business, the largest especially do not restrict their activities to any special field or region. During past decades even savings banks have reorganized themselves above the local or regional level and gone beyond their traditional business of taking deposits and lending money.

Another peculiarity of German banks is the extent to which they hold shares in non-financial corporations. Though there are some legal restrictions, these have remained relatively unimportant as the notion of financial participation is still unclear. In practiĉe only holdings in other credit-giving institutions are subsumed under this rule (Immenga, 1978, pp. 23ff.). In 1976, 7.5 per cent of the total stock at nominal value of all German joint stock companies was owned by banks, these holdings being concentrated in certain industries, e.g. brewing, cement manufacturing, building, insurance and retail (Immenga, 1978, p. 34). Another report shows 30 per cent of the financial holdings of banks to constitute majority ownership and another 40 per cent to be qualified minority holdings. Again the three big banks dominate: together they hold 17 per cent of all participations and 38 per cent of the total stock value (Bundesministerium der Finanzen, 1979, pp. 483 and 501).

An important instrument for exercising influence, which has been hotly debated is the 'Vollmachtstimmrecht', permitting banks to vote on behalf of the shares put on deposit. Formerly this was possible by general authorization (then called Depotstimmrecht) but now the proxy has to be renewed after 15 months and the banks have to ask the shareholders for specific orders before each meeting. There are no complete data available on the extent of proxy-voting but the following examples may illustrate its importance. In 1975 the banks exercised proxy-voting in 56 of the 100 largest joint stock companies. One should stress again the dominating position of the three big banks (Deutsche Bank, Dresdner Bank, Commerzbank). While all 360 banks studied jointly commanded about 57 per cent of total votes of the 56 corporations (seven per cent due to owned shares and 50 per cent due to proxy-voting), on the average about 51 per cent of these votes were cast by the three big banks (Monopolkommission, 1978, pp. 294ff.). These banks were founded during the years 1870-72 and first grew mainly by establishing branches. After the First World War, together with seven other big banks, they bought 279 smaller banks. After several mergers, in 1932 only these three big banks remained. Though having been separated into 30 institutions by the Allies after the Second World War, by 1956 they had managed step by step to reaffiliate.

If we now look at the primary interlocks, which more clearly indicate relations of control and co-optation, a very clear picture emerges (figure 5.2). There seems to be a hierarchical structure: executives of the three big banks sat on the supervisory boards of production companies, while the reverse occured much less frequently.[4] However, one should be cautious in interpreting this as an indication of 'bank control'. This structure may well be the result of

*Figure 5.2   Primary interlocks of financial corporations in the
core and inner margin in Germany*

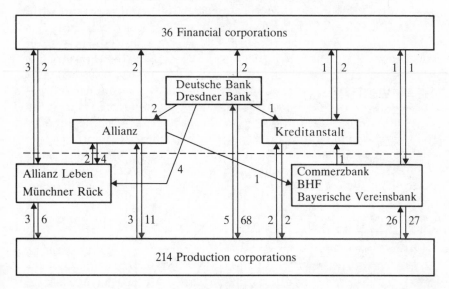

co-optive efforts from the side of production companies rather than of the banks' attempts at control. Without further information, no attempt should be made to impute a one-sided influence to these relationships. However, one reason for the important role of German banks should be noted. After having declined during the past decade, in 1976 equity capital of German industrial corporations amounted to 35 per cent of their total assets, while with American companies this proportion was 59 percent and with British corporations 47 per cent. Large German corporations had even lower ratios around 23 per cent (Bundesministerium der Finanzen, 1979, pp. 432 and 473). It has several times been pointed out in the literature that this relatively low rate of share capital makes German companies more dependent on banks for long-term credit.

The three insurance companies have formed a unified group. Allianz and Münchner Rückversicherung hold 25 per cent of each others shares and together hold 92 per cent of the shares of Allianz Leben. They were closely tied both to other financials and to production companies, though less exclusively than banks oriented towards industry. Kreditanstalt, whose specialized functions have been described in the third section, belonged to the core because it was an important meeting-place not of executives (there were only nine primary interlocks) but of directors of supervisory boards who created another 57 interlocks. Executives of the three big banks held 97

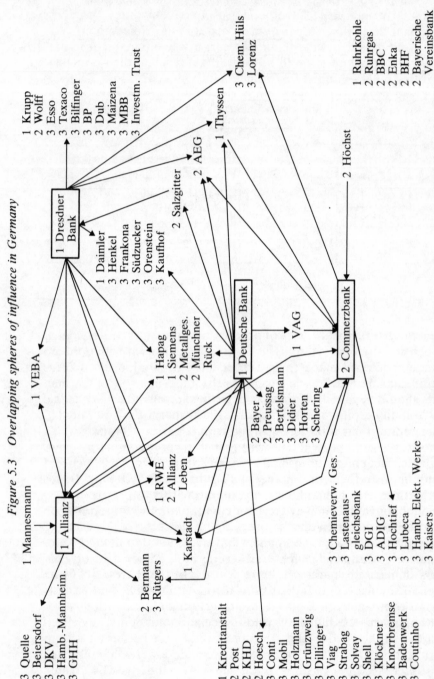

Figure 5.3   Overlapping spheres of influence in Germany

Note: Arrows indicate executives (tail) sitting on supervisory board (head). Numbers refer to centrality groups (1 = core; 2 = inner margin; 3 = outer margin; 4 = periphery). The six corporations on the lower right are in the centre but not connected by primary interlocks with the big four financials.

positions on supervisory boards of 64 corporations, i.e. they were represented in one-third of all other non-isolated companies. Together with Allianz they ranked top in number of outgoing primary interlocks and may be considered the financial heart of the German corporate network. The final question to be answered is whether their domains constituted separate spheres of influence.

Figure 5.3 contains all companies where executives of these four financials are represented as well as all incoming primary interlocks from corporations in the centre.[5] Structurally equivalent companies are put together. The picture looks rather complicated especially if compared with the much simpler structure of the corresponding Austrian network (compare figure 4.2). There was a high degree of overlap among the domains, predominantly on a pair-wise basis. About one-third of the corporations had executives from more than one bank on their supervisory boards. These definitely were economically more important with their average value added amounting to 2,500 million DM while those within an exclusive domain averaged only 1,100 million DM.[6] Size seems to be a decisive factor in attracting the most important bankers. There is an interesting difference even among the three big banks. While the average size of companies sending or receiving executives from Deutsche Bank and Dresdner Bank was about equal, the smaller Commerzbank showed a different pattern of primary interlocks. It tended to recruit executives of very large corporations into its own board and to send its executives to the boards of smaller companies.[7]

An effort was made to determine whether segregation of domains extended to lower levels. If one looks at the primary interlocks among the corporations in the domains (these lines are not shown in figure 5.3) there at first seems to be a tendency to confine primary interlocks to companies belonging to the same sphere of influence, as average density between them was merely half of that inside domains. However, this was only due to those companies exclusively belonging to a single domain. While these were less densely connected with companies outside, those belonging to overlapping spheres were even more often interlocked with large corporations from another domain than with smaller firms inside.

To summarize, separated spheres of influence were typically composed of 'smaller' companies, while larger corporations were able to attract the two biggest banks and did not restrict their primary interlocks to firms which belonged to the same domains.

E

CONCLUSIONS

The German network showed a densely connected centre to which the largest commercial banks, the biggest insurance companies and the most important domestic production corporations (predominantly active in the capital-intensive basic and investment goods industries) belonged. The centre had no pronounced regional base, though of course its firms concentrated in the main economic regions Rhein-Ruhr-Main. The very central position of the three big banks confirms their continuing importance, which has been documented since the turn of the century. The spheres of influence, formed by bank executives sitting on industrial boards, covered one-third of the non-isolated firms but overlapped to a high degree. In these common domains mainly large corporations were located which did not confine their interlocks to other companies within the same spheres. This does not seem to indicate one-sided bank control but more likely a coalescence of major interests from both the financial and non-financial sectors. Banks act more like integrators cross-connecting industrials from various economic sectors and other fractional interests. They even seem to avoid too close a relationship with any particular group of enterprises.

The high level of cohesion of the total network was partly due to a few dozen multiple directors who had accumulated quite a number of positions. Most of them had a firm institutional basis in business but gradually made a career to become something like the elder statesmen of the business world. Those who formerly acted as directors of big banks or officers in trades associations had acquired an extended circle of acquaintances from various sectors facilitating their key role in linking different fractions and interests of the corporate system.

NOTES

1   The work reported here is part of a research project supported by the Deutsche Forschungsgemeinschaft under grant Zi 207/2. Data was collected under the direction of Gerhard Reissner. Checking and analysing of data was performed by Donald Bender and Hermann Biehler with the assistance of Margot Ambs-Schulz, Lydia Buck, Anton Kunz, Irmingard Mühlbauer, Karl-Heinz Neumeier and Erika Steinle. Graph-analysis was done by using the packages GRADAP (developed by the Universities of Amsterdam, Groningen and Nijmegen) and GRALIB (developed by Jacques Anthonisse, Mathematisch Centrum Amsterdam). The chapter was written by Rolf Ziegler.
2   The successors of the chemical combine I.G. Farben provide an interesting example. While two executives of Bayer, which held indirectly 50 per cent of the shares of Agfa and Chemische Werke Hüls, sat on the supervisory boards of these two companies, there were no interlocks (not even induced ones) with and among the other successors in our selection: BASF, Höchst and Dynamit Nobel.

3   The composition of the supervisory board has been regulated by co-determination laws. After the War the trades unions and all the big parties called for extensive co-determination by shareholders and workers. In 1951 the Montanmitbestim-mungsgesetz was enacted. It required that all companies producing mainly in coal-mining or steel have the same number of positions in the supervisory board for representatives of both the owners and the employees. Moreover, both sides together were to nominate one member of the executive board, the Arbeits-direktor. Already in 1952, and against the opposition of the trades unions, the Betriebsverfassungsgesetz for large corporations outside coal-mining and steel was enacted, which required a third of the positions in the supervisory board for representatives of the employees. Since mid 1976, and becoming fully effective in mid 1978, i.e. after the period to which this research relates, there has been a new law of co-determination which led to a long and fierce quarrel and could not satisfy any of the rivals. Though it raises the quota of workers' representatives to 50 per cent, two requirements tip the balance in favour of the shareholders. First, among the representatives of the workers there must be one delegated by senior managers (who are not members of the executive board). Second, in case of a stalemate the vote of the chairman, who normally will be a shareholders' representative, becomes pivotal.
    Our total selection of 325 corporations included 187 co-determined companies of which 30 belonged to the centre and another 41 were subsidiaries.

4   Considering the three commercial banks of the inner margin together masks an interesting difference. While Commerzbank and Bayerische Vereinsbank (one of the largest regional banks) were more often sending than receiving primary interlocks, Berliner Handels- und Frankfurter Bank (BHF, founded in 1854-56 and specializing in industrial credit) obviously followed a strategy of inviting businessmen to become members of its board. Eighteen of the 26 incoming primary interlocks went to this bank while none of its executives sat on supervisory boards of industrial corporations. It might be interesting to study the reasons for these different strategies.

5   There were only seven companies outside the centre, all privately owned, which were represented on the supervisory boards of Deutsche Bank (Bosch, Flick, Klöckner & Co., Varta), Commerzbank (Flick, Voith, Werhahn) and Allianz (Bosch, Quelle). Their average value added amounted to 1,300 million DM.

6   This figure excludes the atypical PTT; if value added of Deutsche Bundespost is included, the average raises to 1,700 million DM.

7   Average value added was 1,700 million DM both of sending and receiving production corporations of Deutsche Bank or Dresdner Bank. Companies to which Commerzbank sent its executives averaged 1,500 million DM but those which were represented on its board had an average value added of 4,700 million DM. Balance sheet total for Deutsche Bank, Dresdner Bank and Commerzbank was 67,000, 54,000 and 42,000 million DM respectively.

6

The Dutch Network: Types of Interlocks and Network Structure

FRANS N. STOKMAN, FRANS W. WASSEUR and DONALD ELSAS[1]

THE CORPORATIONS

Of particular interest for comparison with the other national networks is the position of the commercial banks in the Dutch network. In contrast with the surrounding countries, particularly Germany and (until 1934) Belgium, the Dutch commercial banks were never engaged in large-scale financial participations in Dutch industry. Until the 1960s even the provision of long-term credit to industry was not of any significance for them. Besides acting as issuing houses, their activities were confined to the provision of short-term credit on current accounts.

In 1976 the Dutch banking sector was dominated by four major banks (Bosman, 1973; de Roos, 1982). The ABN bank was the result of a merger in 1964 between the Nederlandse Handel Maatschappij and the Twentsche Bank. The first was founded in 1824 to strengthen trade relations between the Netherlands and its colonies but developed after 1880 into a fully fledged bank with a strong international orientation, although the Dutch East Indies remained its most important area of activity. The Twentsche Bank was founded in 1861, particularly to provide credit to the textile industry of the Twente region. After 1964 several other medium-sized banks were taken over by ABN, most importantly the Hollandsche Bank Unie and the Mees & Hope Bank. ABN is still the most internationally oriented bank in the Netherlands with a large network of offices abroad. The AMRO bank, on the contrary, has always had a strong orientation towards Dutch industry. Like ABN, it resulted from a merger in 1964, this time between the Amsterdamsche Bank and the Rotterdamsche Bank. In its early history the Amsterdamsche Bank (founded in 1871) was involved in financial participations in Dutch colonial industry and it remained very active as an issuing house. The Rotterdamsche Bank, founded in

1863, has always been strongly oriented towards Dutch industry and to trade with Germany. After 1964 AMRO took over medium-sized banks such as Pierson, Heldring en Pierson. The third major bank is the RABO, which resulted from the 1972 merger of two co-operative banks: the Centrale Raiffeisen-Bank and the Cooperatieve Centrale Boerenleenbank. Both the central and the local banks are co-operatives and they have always been strongly oriented towards the agricultural sector but since the 1970s the policy of the RABO bank has been aimed at its development into a fully fledged commercial bank. The fourth large bank is the NMB, founded in 1927 to create more opportunities for the provision of credit to the retail sector and medium-sized industry. The Dutch state has a 23 per cent participation in NMB.

In terms of size, a large gap is observed between these four large banks and the other banks. In 1976 only four middle to large banks were left that were sizeable enough to be selected. The other ten selected commercial banks were subsidiaries of foreign banks. Because of the restricted policy of the Dutch commercial banks with respect to direct financial participation and to the provision of long-term credit, the great demand for these forms of capital provision after the Second World War led to the creation in 1945 of a special joint venture owned by the state (50 per cent of the shares), commercial banks, savings banks and insurance companies. This joint venture has operated since 1963 under the name of the Nationale Investeringsbank or NIB. A large part of its credits are given as postponed loans guaranteed by the government. In 1948 the predecessor of the NIB and a large number of banks and insurance companies created a new joint venture for direct financial participation, the Nationale Participatie Maatschappij or NPM. Although the commercial banks have extended their activities to the provision of long-term credit and other activities that were previously reserved for savings banks, the main providers of long-term credit remain the insurance companies, savings banks and pension funds. Of the latter, it was possible to include only the pension fund of the civil servants.

The fact that the Dutch banks never developed into investment banks is a consequence of the orientation of the Dutch economy towards international trade and commercial activities, particularly those related to the Dutch colonies. Colonial capital is one of the main sources of present-day large corporations. The most important one is the Koninklijke Nederlandse Petroleum Maatschapij (Royal Dutch Petroleum) and the name it had until 1949 – Royal Dutch Company for the Working of Petroleum Wells in the Netherlands Indies – clearly shows this colonial origin (see Gerretson, 1958). Other examples are the conglomerate OGEM, the Overseas Gas and Electricity Company, and Internatio-Müller, which was a merger of a Dutch Indies trade company (Internatio) with a shipping company (Müller). As was the case with ABN, these corporations still had a strong international orientation. Of course, this is particularly the case with the Royal Dutch, which created in 1906 the international Shell group with 'Shell' Transport and Trading of Britain. In this way the complementary activities of the two corporations could be combined and integrated. Shell was the first Anglo-Dutch bi-national corporation.

Traditionally, agriculture has been the second most important sector of the Dutch economy. One of the most decisive structural changes in the Dutch economy in the twentieth century, however, has been the growing importance of industry and services at the expense of agriculture (de Vries, 1978). In 1976 the contribution of agriculture and fishing to the national product had declined to only five per cent. Nevertheless, 28 of the 200 selected corporations in the present study had their main activities in agricultural products. The most important was Unilever, the second Anglo-Dutch, bi-national corporation, created 23 years later than Shell by a Dutch group of corporations known as the Margarine Unie and the British group, Lever Brothers (soap). Whereas in the Unilever group the Dutch and British partners were equally important, the Dutch interest in Shell was 60 per cent. The history of Unilever shows how Dutch corporations were forced to enter the international capital market because of the restricted role of the Dutch banks in direct investments and the provision of long-term credit (Wilson, 1954). Most of the other selected corporations in the agricultural sector were co-operatives of moderate size.

The Dutch industrial sector developed rather late, not earlier than 1890, but is now the second most important sector in the Dutch economy. Whereas the service sector contributed about 45 per cent of the Dutch national product in 1976, the contribution of industry (including energy and building) was about 36 per cent. The three major industrial corporations represent three different paths of industrial development in the Netherlands: Philips was the prototype of a family enterprise, AKZO resulted from a number of very large mergers, whereas Hoogovens (steel) was initiated by a coalition of the Dutch business elite and the state. Dutch industrial capital had rather strong links with German industrial capital, in contrast with the heavy British orientation of the international trade sector that originated from colonial capital. These connections resulted in the creation of two German-Dutch bi-national corporations according to the Shell and Unilever models: Estel by Hoogovens and Hoechst (steel) and VFW-Fokker by VFW and Fokker (aircraft construction). Both bi-nationals have since been dissolved (see chapter 14). Other examples of close connections were AKZO, which produced synthetic fibres, in the

German-Dutch operating company Enka-Glanzstoffe and the strong German links of the Dutch conglomerate SHV (Steenkolen Handels Vereniging). Baudet and Fennema (1983) show how, after 1945, the two business orientations merged into a larger Atlantic orientation due to Marshall aid and the development of the Dutch East Indies towards independence. Shell, Unilever, C&A[2], Philips and AKZO comprise the five largest Dutch corporations in terms of most size criteria.

THE OVERALL STRUCTURE OF THE DUTCH NETWORK

The characteristics of the Dutch network of interlocking directorships are not completely unknown. The first study of interlocks in the Netherlands was done by Wibaut (1913) who followed, on a smaller scale, the research of Jeidels' study of the German banks (Jeidels, 1905). Wibaut found 300 firms interlocked with the nine largest banking institutions (Wibaut, 1913, p. 342). While his study focused on the interlocks between banks and production corporations, the first major study on the whole network of interlocking directorships was the study *Graven naar Macht* (Helmers et al., 1975). This book reported the results of several studies, conducted by students under the direction of Mokken and Stokman, concerning the network of interlocks among the largest 86 Dutch corporations of 1969, its stability over the 1960s, its association with financial participations and joint ventures and the personal interlocks with governmental agencies and committees. This study was followed by a similar study in 1972 (Mokken and Stokman, 1978 and 1979) as well as a number of more specific studies related to such policy areas as arts (Boon, 1975), nuclear energy (Zijlstra, 1979, 1982) and oil (Eggen and Neijens, 1979). Long term developments in the Dutch network of interlocking directorships have been studied by Baudet and Fennema (1983), who focused on the disintegration of the colonial network in the Dutch East Indies before and after independence. Work in progress includes Schijf (1978, 1984), who is studying the development of the Dutch network between 1886 and 1902. Directly related to the present study in 1976 is a study by Beekenkamp (1982, 1984) of the careers of the 250 president executives of the selected corporations. His results can be compared with an earlier study of the sociological aspects of the corporate elite in the Netherlands by Vinke (1961).

The 1969 and 1972 studies of the 70 largest corporations revealed a network of interlocking directorships with a very centralized structure. Moreover, all analyses indicated that the network of interlocks derived its structure mainly from the interlocks of financial corporations and institutions, particularly from those of commercial banks and insurance companies. Therefore, a major conclusion of these studies was that interlocking directorships should be seen primarily as channels of information and control for the aggregation and provision of credit and capital. This interpretation was confirmed by a very strong positive correlation between financial participations and interlocking directorships (Helmers et al., 1975, pp. 266 ff.), by the stability of the lines between production and financial corporations (Helmers et al., 1975, pp. 249 ff.), and the disintegration of the network between production corporations after the elimination of persons with one or more positions in financial corporations (Helmers et al., 1975, pp. 220 ff.).

The overall structure of the 1976 network among the 250 corporations seems to be well in line with these conclusions from the smaller 1969 and 1972 studies. After a short overview of this structure in the remainder of this section, the main focus of this chapter will be oriented towards the question of whether a closer look at different aspects of the network gives rise to a more differentiated interpretation of the network. The 1969 and 1972 studies failed to do this because they did not investigate the contribution of different types of interlocks to their overall structure of the network. This resulted in an over-emphasis on the finance-capital model, without due recognition of the fact that important parts of the network might better be interpreted in terms of other models (see chapter 1).

The 1976 network among the 250 corporations contained three components of directly or indirectly connected corporations. The largest component consisted of 190 corporations, the two other components consisting of two corporations each. The remaining 56 corporations were isolated. Of the 60 corporations outside the largest component about half of the corporations belonged to the wholesale and retail distribution sector (NACE sectors 61, 63 and 64), although they constituted only 20 per cent of all selected corporations. Of the total group of 48 wholesale and retail distribution companies 28 were isolated. Most other corporations outside the large component were either subsidiaries of foreign enterprises, particularly in the oil refining, chemical and banking sectors, or regionally oriented corporations, mainly in energy distribution and the food industry. Two commercial banks, ABN and AMRO, were directly connected with extremely high numbers of corporations, 56 and 54 respectively. The next corporations, the insurance corporation AGO and the chemical corporation AKZO were directly connected with 35 corporations. Among the 13 corporations with 26 or more lines, financial corporations were very strongly represented: two commercial banks (ABN and AMRO), the National Bank (NB), two joint ventures (NPM and NIB) and three insurance companies (AGO, the Nationale Nederlanden and

Table 6.1 Network of the core in the Netherlands

Number of interlocks within core

Name	Sector	Rush	ABN	AMRO	ENNIA	NS	Buhrmann-T	AGO	AKZO	NB	SHV	FGH	Heineken	Philips	Nat. Ned.	OGEM	RSV	NSU	Core	Inner margin	Rest of network	Total
ABN	Banking	0.092	–	0	0	1	2	1	2	1	2	1	1	2	1	4	0	3	11	16	29	56
AMRO	Banking	0.065	0	–	3	2	1	2	1	2	2	1	3	1	2	1	2	0	12	13	29	54
ENNIA	Insurance	0.031	0	3	–	3	1	1	1	1	1	0	0	0	1	0	0	0	7	10	15	32
NS	Railways	0.026	1	2	3	–	3	0	1	1	2	0	1	0	0	0	1	1	9	9	14	32
Buhrmann-T	Paper	0.025	2	1	1	3	–	0	1	0	0	0	0	0	1	1	0	0	6	9	9	24
AGO	Insurance	0.021	1	2	1	0	0	–	0	2	2	0	1	1	0	0	0	3	7	9	19	35
AKZO	Chemical	0.021	2	1	1	1	1	0	–	1	1	1	1	0	0	2	0	0	11	5	19	35
NB	National Banking	0.019	1	2	1	1	0	2	1	–	1	0	1	0	0	1	1	1	10	6	11	27
SHV	Wholesale	0.019	2	2	1	2	0	2	1	1	–	1	0	0	1	1	0	1	10	7	12	29
FGH	Mortgage	0.019	1	1	0	0	0	0	1	0	1	–	0	1	0	0	0	0	5	9	9	23
Heineken	Beer	0.018	1	3	0	1	0	1	1	1	0	0	–	0	1	0	1	0	7	7	9	23
Philips	Electronic	0.018	2	1	0	0	0	1	0	0	0	1	0	–	0	1	1	0	9	6	8	23
Nat. Ned.	Insurance	0.018	1	2	1	0	1	0	0	0	1	0	1	0	–	0	0	2	8	8	16	32
OGEM	Engineering	0.017	4	1	0	0	1	0	2	1	1	0	0	1	0	–	1	0	6	8	9	23
RSV	Shipbuilding	0.016	0	2	0	1	0	0	0	1	0	0	1	1	0	1	–	1	9	5	10	24
NSU	Shipping	0.016	3	0	0	1	0	3	0	1	1	0	0	0	2	0	1	–	7	7	12	26

Number of adjacent corporations in: Core, Inner margin network, Rest of network, Total.

ENNIA). The five remaining corporations were production corporations. Three belonged to the transport sector (the Dutch railway corporation, NS, and two sea-transport corporations, HAL and NSU), one to the chemical sector (AKZO) and one was a conglomerate (SHV) classified in the wholesale distribution sector. The 26 corporations with only one or two lines belonged predominantly to the same categories as the 60 corporations outside the large component: production and distribution of energy (eight corporations), food, drink and tobacco (nine), wholesale and retail distribution (six), subsidiaries of foreign corporations (six) and seven other corporations.

In chapter 2 the size of the Dutch centre and core were given and compared with those of other countries. The composition of the core is given in table 6.1. If the composition of the core is compared with the 16 most central companies (as measured by their adjacency), the two financial joint ventures NPM and NIB and the sea-transport corporation HAL are seen to have been replaced by Heineken, Philips and OGEM. The remaining 13 corporations belonged to the 16 most central corporations according to both criteria. The density of the core was high: 56 per cent of all pairs of corporations had direct access to one another's highest boards of decision-making. No separate clusters can be observed in the core, showing that there was no more than one centre in the network as a whole. Moreover, 21 of the 67 lines in the core had multiplicity 2 or higher. This is a considerably higher percentage than for the network as a whole and indicates that a high number of lines in the core should be considered as strong lines. Nevertheless, it should be realized that the two commercial banks, ABN and AMRO, had no interlock with one another. The same holds for the three insurance companies in the core. The existence of one dense centre in the Dutch network does not preclude competition between corporations operating in the same market and it implies that these competing financial corporations were not oriented to different segments of the Dutch economy (which was the case with a number of less central financial companies).

Although the structure of the Dutch network can be considered still to have been centralized, the 1976 network was both less dense and less centralized than that of 1969. Comparing the network of 86 corporations in 1969 (at the end of a long period of economic expansion) with the 1972 and 1976 networks (in the middle of a period of economic stagnation), it can be observed that between 1969 and 1972 the number of lines was considerably reduced without many consequences for the centralized structure of the network as a whole. With the prolongation of the economic crisis into 1976, the network became less centralized without any further reduction in the total number of lines in the network. Mokken and Stokman (1979, p. 11) attributed the possibly temporary looser structure of the network of interlocks to fundamental changes in financial relations among the largest corporations as a consequence of the prolonged economic crisis.

For the bi-nationals Shell, Unilever, Estel and VFW-Fokker, the boards of the bi-national corporations were selected according to the general selection criteria. Shell was isolated, Unilever belonged to the periphery, VFW-Fokker to the outer margin and Estel to the inner margin. If the Dutch parts of the corporations had been selected, it would have resulted in a more central position for both Royal Dutch Shell (just below the inner margin) and Hoogovens (in the core). Royal Dutch was connected with 17 Dutch corporations, among which were ABN and AKZO, both with double interlocks. The positions of Unilever and Fokker would have been unaffected.

Production corporations in the centre tended to be large (in terms of wage-bills). This confirms the correlation between size and number of interlocks that has been reported in a large number of studies (see Allen, 1974; Pennings, 1980). Moreover, they tended to have a low ratio between turnover and assets, which indicates that industrial corporations tended to be more central in the network than trade and service corporations. Finally, production corporations in the centre tended to have a low ratio between liabilities and total assets as well as a high ratio between current liabilities and total liabilities. This indicates that central corporations tended to be solvent corporations which were nevertheless rather dependent on short-term credit. These results from a discriminant analysis, in which the economic characteristics of production corporations were used to predict their location in the centre, outer margin or periphery of the network, corroborate the interpretation of the overall structure of the network in terms of the finance-capital model. With the above variables it was possible to predict the location of 66 per cent of the corporations correctly. None of the corporations in the centre were predicted as belonging to the periphery or vice versa.[3] More detailed analyses of the network structure in the remainder of this chapter will demonstrate, however, that the finance-capital model is unable to explain all major aspects of the Dutch network and that other models need to be introduced for a better understanding of the network structure.

TYPES OF INTERLOCKS AND NETWORK STRUCTURE

As has been explained in chapter 2, interlocks always have a personal basis but sometimes an institutional basis as well. In chapter 2 it has been argued that the combination of positions in an interlock can be used as an indirect method of determining the importance of different types of interlocks as indicators of institutional links between corporations. In particular, primary financial interlocks, carried by executives of financial corporations, might be interpreted in terms of the finance-capital model. Primary production interlocks, carried by executives of production corporations, can also be interpreted in terms of this model, in so far as they serve as connections between production and financial corporations or coincide with financial participations. In this section the structure that is formed by these interlocks will be investigated. Moreover, the role of other types of interlocks in strengthening this structure will be examined. This will give an indication of whether these other types can be interpreted in terms of the finance-capital model or have a completely different structure and so have to be interpreted in terms of other models. An investigation of the contribution of the different types of interlocks to the network structure can therefore be seen as a first step towards an analysis of the importance of different models for the network as a whole.

The most important aspect of the structure of the whole network is its centralized nature, the existence of a densely connected core around which the main part of the rest of the network is built. For this reason the investigation will begin with the relative importance of the different types of interlocks within and between the four centrality groups: core, inner margin, outer margin and periphery. The first row of table 6.2 gives the distribution of all interlocks over the different groups. This row has been given as a yardstick against which the concentration of the various types of interlock in certain parts of the network can be judged. It can be seen that certain definite patterns existed. Primary financial interlocks had special relevance for the core, both for its inside connections and for its connections with the rest of the network: all columns of table 6.2 concerning the core show higher percentages that are found in row 1 for all interlocks. This was not the case for primary production interlocks, which were somewhat underrepresented in all columns concerning the core and somewhat overrepresented in the connections between inner margin, outer margin and periphery. Induced financial and production interlocks contribute particularly to the density within the outer margin. This is in sharp contrast with the unclassified interlocks. Unclassified interlocks were concentrated within the centre: core, inner margin and the bipartite network between core and inner margin show considerably higher percentages. This is even more the case for the unclassified interlocks that are carried by persons with four or more positions. They show a very strong bias towards the centre.

To summarize, the primary financial interlocks and the unclassified interlocks by persons with four or more positions contributed particularly to the *overall* structure of the network. The unclassified

Table 6.2 *Centrality groups and types of interlocks in the Netherlands* (%)

| Types of interlocks | Centrality groups | | | | | | | | | | | Total |
| | Within | | | Between | | | | | | | |
	Core	Inner margin	Outer margin	Peri-phery	c–i	c–o	c–p	i–o	i–p	o–p		
All	8	5	20	3	14	22	0	23	0	4		100 (1,171)
Primary												
Financial	10	3	6	0	20	37	0	24	0	0		100 (125)
Production	4	2	22	5	13	20	0	25	1	7		100 (161)
Induced												
Financial	7	6	30	0	8	19	0	30	0	0		100 (156)
Production	6	2	32	1	4	33	0	22	0	1		100 (104)
Unclassified												
All	10	7	19	4	17	18	0	21	0	5		100 (625)
By big linkers	14	10	10	0	22	20	0	23	0	0		100 (380)

Note: Absolute numbers are in parentheses.

interlocks made a very significant contribution to the high density of the centre of the network, whereas the primary financial interlocks connected the core with the rest of the network. To a large extent, the outer margin was co-ordinated by the core through the primary financial interlocks, as the concentration of induced financial inter-locks in the outer margin shows. Primary production interlocks were scattered throughout the whole network without a clear concentration in one or another part of the network. No clear co-ordination centre existed, in which the bulk of these interlocks came together, as was the case with the primary financial interlocks but such co-ordination as does occur takes place mainly in the outer margin. This implies that, whatever the significance and meaning of unclassifed interlocks may be, they were generated by a completely different mechanism than the induced financial and production interlocks.

THE NETWORK OF PRIMARY INTERLOCKS

Figure 6.1 gives a more detailed picture of the way in which primary interlocks contributed to the centrality of the two commercial banks, the three insurance companies and the two joint ventures NPM and NIB. With one exception, all the primary financial interlocks of ABN and AMRO were outgoing interlocks, i.e. interlocks carried by their own executives. These outgoing interlocks connected these banks with other financial corporations (particularly insurance companies and NPM and NIB) as well as with production corporations. The main difference between AMRO and ABN was that AMRO had outgoing interlocks to six insurance companies and 28 production corporations, as against one insurance company and 12 production corporations for ABN. The primary financial interlocks of the three insurance compan-ies originated from incoming interlocks from the commercial banks and outgoing interlocks to other financial corporations (particularly the joint ventures NPM and NIB) as well as to production corpor-ations. With only two exceptions, all the primary financial interlocks of NPM and NIB were due to incoming interlocks from the parent financial corporations and outgoing interlocks to production corpor-ations. The primary interlocks give, therefore, a very clear hierarchical structure between three groups of central financial corporations. The highest hierarchical level consisted of the two largest commercial banks, ABN and AMRO, which had outgoing interlocks both to financial corporations at lower hierarchical levels and to production corporations. They were the main co-ordinators in the network and no other corporation was permitted to co-ordinate the policies of these two banks by primary interlocks to both banks. The second hierarchical level consisted of three insurance companies that had incoming interlocks from the two commercial banks and outgoing interlocks both to financial corporations at the lowest hierarchical level and to production corporations. They did not object to commercial-bank executives being directors in several insurance companies, with all the possibilities of co-ordination that result from such a situation. The third hierarchical level consisted of the two financial joint ventures, which were co-ordinated by the financial corporations at the higher hierarchical levels and themselves co-ordinated policies in a large number of production corporations. The importance of these seven financial corporations is revealed in the fact that figure 6.1 contained 98 of all 125 primary financial interlocks that existed in the whole network. Two other financial corporations in the core did not fit this picture: the mortgage bank FGH which had no incoming interlocks and five of its six outgoing interlocks going to production corporations, and the Dutch national bank which had outgoing interlocks to state financial institutions and corporations only.

On the basis of primary interlocks, no other large clusters were discovered. Fifty-seven of the 161 primary production interlocks generated 50 lines between production and financial corporations and strengthened the dominant structure of the network that was determined by the primary financial interlocks. The remaining 104 primary production interlocks generated 95 lines between production corporations. Thirteen coincided with financial participations among production corporations. Of the remaining 82 lines, 34 could be explained by the fact that the production corporations produced complementary products. These lines played an important role in the dairy industry and in the chemical sector but other examples could be found in the steel, electro-technical, building and shipping sectors. Forty-eight lines could not be accounted for in this way as they connected production corporations having no horizontal or vertical market relations.

Between co-operatives a large number of institutional relations were maintained at the level of the governing boards and these directorships were considered as intermediate positions. If these interlocks are included together with the primary interlocks, a second cluster outside the overall centre of the network is revealed around RABO, the third major bank in the Netherlands. RABO is a commercial bank, strongly oriented towards the agricultural segment of the Dutch economy (see the first section) and had no incoming lines from the centre. It had two outgoing lines to the centre, to NPM and NIB, in which it participated. Figure 6.2 shows that RABO was the nucleus of a 2-clique of 11 corporations, of which several corporations in their turn were nuclei of 2-cliques of five or more corporations. In figure 6.2 these nuclei are placed into boxes. Only three of the corporations in the main RABO

Figure 6.1   Primary interlocks of central financial corporations in the Netherlands

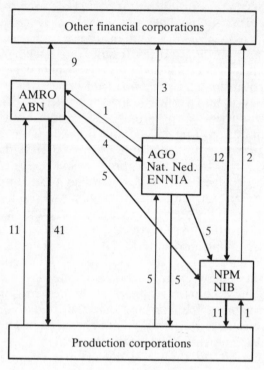

clique had incoming lines from the centre: the insurance compan͏̥ AMEV, a cultivation company Grontmij, and the 100 per cent subsidiary of NIB (the National Investment Bank for Developing Nations). With the exception of the IJssel Centrale, an electricity distribution company, all remaining corporations in the clique were agriculturally oriented. The RABO clique should, therefore, be considered as a local centre outside the network centre. The most interesting 2-clique in figure 6.2, besides the main RABO clique, is the CEBECO clique which connected the main cliques with two other agricultural cliques located almost entirely in Friesland (one of the Northern provinces of the Netherlands). CEBECO was a co-operative that was active in all kinds of agricultural products.

The positions of the three largest banks in the network can be summarized: the AMRO bank and the ABN bank in the heart of the core and the RABO bank as the nucleus of a local agricultural oriented cluster. The fourth large bank was the Dutch shopkeepers bank NMB, partly owned by the state (23 per cent) and by two insurance companies

Figure 6.2 Local centre outside the overall centre in the Netherlands

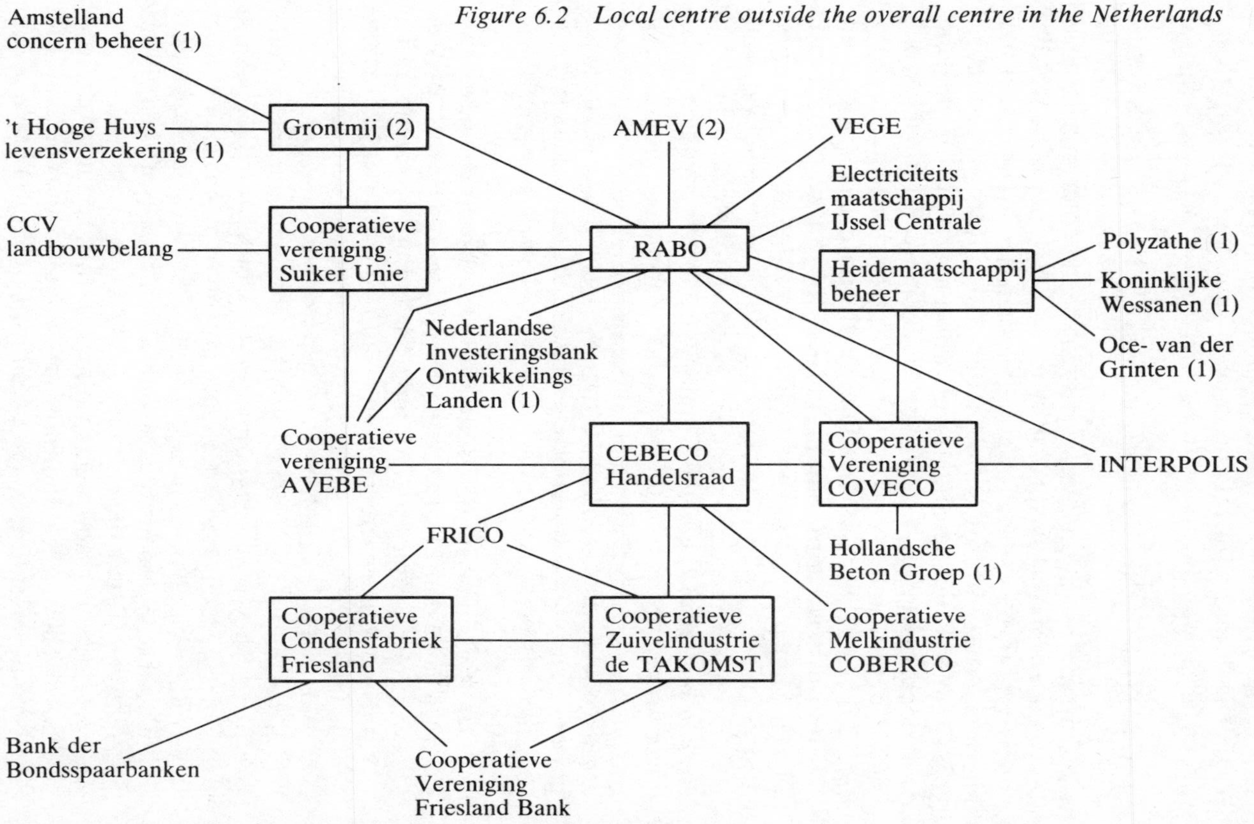

Note: The number of incoming primary lines from the overall centre is in parentheses.

(ENNIA and AMEV, with five per cent each). The NMB belongs to the outer margin, as was the case with the RABO. On the basis of primary interlocks, the NMB had only one outgoing line, to the NPM in which it participated, and no incoming lines. It cannot be considered as a local cluster, as was the case with RABO.

THE NETWORK OF UNCLASSIFIED INTERLOCKS

For all central corporations, unclassified interlocks contributed considerably to their centrality. With only two exceptions (AMRO and NPM) the number of these interlocks was higher than that for any other type of interlock. The centrality of Buhrmann Tetterode (paper) was based almost completely on these interlocks. Considering only the unclassified interlocks carried by persons with four or more directorships, only a small reduction in their significance took place. The reduction is due mainly to the fact that a number of lines with production corporations and with financial corporations outside the centre were due to interlocks carried by persons with three or two positions. The large contribution to centrality of unclassified interlocks carried by persons with four or more directorships makes a further investigation into their meaning a matter of the highest importance for an adequate understanding of the structure of the network as a whole.

The 380 unclassified interlocks carried by big linkers were due to just 34 persons. Through a study of their biographies[4] it was possible to classify these 34 persons into the following categories.

(1)   The main past appointment of 18 persons was chief executive in a large Dutch production corporation. These 18 persons were responsible for 236 interlocks. With two exceptions their age was somewhere between 60 and 70 years (the ages of five people were unknown); the two exceptions were 56 and 59 years old respectively.

(2)   Six persons had national politics as their main institutional basis. They were responsible for 48 interlocks.

(3)   Three persons had been chief executive in one of the main commercial banks (two persons in ABN and one in RABO). They were responsible for only 22 interlocks and they were between 60 and 70 years old.

(4)   Two persons had foreign politics as their main institutional basis. They were responsible for 36 interlocks. One had since become president of the executive board of Wereldhave, a subsidiary of ROBECO which is an investment bank with international reputation.

(5) Two persons had their main institutional basis in local politics. They were responsible for 12 interlocks.
(6) Two persons had special legal qualifications and were responsible for 16 interlocks.
(7) One person's main past institutional basis was the Christian Employers Association. With his 5 directorships in 1976 he was responsible for 10 interlocks.

It can be concluded that the unclassified interlocks of persons with four or more positions were mainly due to people who had been chief executives in large Dutch production corporations. These interlocks were even more concentrated in the centre of the network than the unclassified interlocks of persons with four or more positions in general: more than half of them connected corporations within the centre with one another. These interlocks were, therefore, very important for the centralized structure of the network: they formed the central corporations in the network into a strongly connected centre.

How should these interlocks be interpreted? One possibility is to treat them as primary production interlocks. With only a few exceptions these multiple directors were members of the boards of directors in the corporation of which they had been executives and, as such, they may have remained responsible for certain institutional links between their home corporation and other corporations. This is likely because they accumulated the bulk of their directorships before retirement from their executive positions. As all these multiple directors were directors in at least one financial corporation, they confirmed the legitimacy of interpreting the network structure according to the finance-capital model. Seven of the former executives were members of the board of directors of ABN, three of AMRO and the remaining eight were members of the board of at least one other financial corporation in the centre. The contribution of unclassified interlocks of persons with four or more positions to the dominant structure of the network appears even more strongly if multiple links between the home corporation and financial corporations are considered as well as institutional links. Such multiple interlocks indicate at least a shared system of co-optation, indicating definite possibilities of policy co-ordination and shared information. It seems that ABN in particular used this way of building up its central position in the Dutch network, whereas AMRO relied more on its own executives. Within the Dutch centre, ABN was connected with seven other corporations through two or more of these interlocks against two such contacts for AMRO. AMRO, on the other hand, was connected with 17 corporations in the centre through primary interlocks, as against 11 for ABN. Combining the two gives an equally strong position for both banks. The difference in strategy between the two banks might well be attributed to the difference between the stronger international orientation of ABN and the more marked orientation towards Duch industry of AMRO (see the first section).

Besides these institutional aspects, the interlocks of former executives must have had an important personal aspect too. These multiple directors should be considered as network specialists, persons who know what is going on in business and have experience in managing a large corporation. An important aspect of these interlocks is that the *personal* qualifications of the director serve as the common orientation to the corporations on whose board he or she sits. In so far as the lines between the corporations are induced by such personal qualifications, the interlocks cannot be directly interpreted as primary dyadic communication or control channels between corporations. Their prime function lies in their importance at the level of the network as a whole, knitting the centre together and making it possible for information to flow through the network – particularly around its central area. In the same way, it is likely that at least certain interlocks of non-retired executives of large financial and production corporations with many other positions also had a personal basis. It can be assumed that, particularly above a certain threshold of acquired positions, executives are offered new positions because of their broad experience in different sectors of the economy. Having a number of directorships enhances their opportunities for accumulating even more. In other words, certain executives become network specialists well before their retirement. This may hold particularly for executives of financial corporations, as business scanning is one of the main prerequisites for such corporations to pursue an adaptive strategy. From their home base, certain executives can, therefore, be seen to develop gradually into network specialists. During this process the home basis becomes gradually less important as an institutional base for the acquisition of new positions. This process accelerates after retirement, when the home corporation itself continues to profit from the person's business scanning by offering him or her an outside position on its own board of directors. The retired executive may, at the same time, remain responsible for certain institutional links. It should, therefore, be stressed that the division between primary interlocks and unclassified interlocks is gradual and not an abrupt split in which all primary interlocks can be interpreted as institutional links and all the unclassified as personal ones. For the assessment of the relative importance of personal and institutional bases of interlocks, the present data can give only indirect evidence. One may also doubt whether interviews give valid data on this matter and for this reason

Rutges (1983, 1984) has elaborated the two bases of interlocks into two simulation models. In this way it its hoped to assess which of the two models generate networks that are most similar to observed ones.

If the interlocks of former executives with four or more positions are compared with those of the non-retired executives with four or more directorships a fundamental difference is observed. The interlocks of the former executives knitted the centre together; the interlocks of those still in office were more important in connecting the centre with the rest of the network. The difference is particularly striking between executives and retired executives of production corporations. Two alternative explanations can be given. The first draws on the personal careers of network specialists: non-retired executives had not yet developed into fully fledged network specialists, their directorships were more strongly linked with their home base and a larger proportion of their interlocks were used to link the production corporations with complementary companies. The second explanation has to do with fundamental changes in institutional arrangements as a consequence of the economic crisis. While the former executives may maintain a number of directorships in the old affiliations of their company, perhaps until their ultimate retirement or death, the executives still in office take on the new affiliations. In this case the differential location of their interlocks in the network has to do with the present stage of transition of the network in a period of economic crisis. Further changes can be expected, as the interlocks of the former executives exhibit a time-lag factor. The smaller size of the centre and the lower density of the core in 1976 in comparison with 1969 and 1972 fit remarkably well with this explanation. Only a longitudinal study of long-term changes in the network could differentiate between these two explanations, a study that is at present being carried out (Van der Knoop et al., 1984).

CONCLUSIONS

Most studies of interlocking directorships have emphasized one overall explanation for the pattern of links. This was also the case with former Dutch studies, in which the role of finance capital was emphasized to explain the overall structure. The contribution of the finance-capital model to the overall network structure can be studied most directly by an analysis of primary financial interlocks. These interlocks revealed a hierarchical structure among the financial corporations, with ABN and AMRO at the top and a separate local centre around the third main bank, RABO. Primary production interlocks to financial corporations and multiple unclassified interlocks strengthened this structure, particularly the position of ABN.

It has been shown that former executives of production corporations played an important role in the network, as their interlocks knitted the centre of the network together. These interlocks can partly be interpreted as institutional links of their home corporation. But their main importance seems to lie in the possibility created for business scanning by persons with a broad range of experience in the Dutch economy: the network specialists. Of course, executives with many positions, particularly those in financial corporations, perform this function as well, but it is assumed that their home base plays a more important role for the acquisition of new positions than is the case for retired executives: the personal development to network specialists is seen as a gradual process in which the significance of the home base diminishes over time. These unclassified interlocks can therefore be interpreted, at least in part, in terms of the hegemony model, while they at the same time strengthen the dominant overall structure of the network as a centralized one around a number of financial corporations.

Finally, it was possible to relate a significant number of primary production interlocks to institutional links between complementary corporations. These interlocks should be interpreted in terms of the resource-dependence model: they were scattered around the whole network, linking complementary corporations irrespective of their centrality in the overall network.

NOTES

1   The data for the Dutch network of interlocking directorships were partly collected by project groups of students at the University of Groningen under the direction of Frans N.Stokman. Data collection was completed by John Buissink, Rob Mos and Eric van Sonderen. Jos van der Werf wrote an extensive coding instruction for the economic variables of the corporations. Final checking of all data was performed by Frans N.Stokman. Gerbert Beekenkamp gave valuable suggestions for sources where the desirable biographical data could be obtained. Rob Mos investigated the careers of network specialists.

2   C&A was not selected because of lack of data. It would, however, have appeared as an isolate in the network owing to the closed family nature of the concern.

3   Due to the missing values, the discriminant analysis could be applied to only 135 production corporations. The four multinational corporations Shell, Unilever, Philips and AKZO were eliminated from the analysis because of their very large size. Their outlier positions would seriously disturb the results of the discriminant analysis.

4   The following biographical sources were used: the biographical documentation service of the Dutch Press Agency ANP (their information is mainly based on questionnaires); the European Financial Almanac; and the biographical documentation of one of the leading Dutch newspapers (NRC-Handelsblad).

7

The Banks in the Centre: Integration in Decentralized Switzerland

PETER RUSTERHOLZ

Switzerland belongs to the front runners of industrialization. The process of industrialization took off at about the same time as in the United Kingdom, – in the early nineteenth century. The resulting technological advantages were favourable for entry into foreign markets. On this basis, Switzerland was able to safeguard its chances of improving its position in the international system. Because Switzerland possesses few raw materials, this development was of great importance for the Swiss economy. A number of other important points are relevant to Swiss penetration of markets abroad. Cultural variety and central geographical location, for example, were both favourable pre-conditions for entrance into many markets (Höpflinger, 1974, pp. 53 ff.). This penetration of foreign markets, however, made Swiss industry extremely dependent on foreign policy; a fact which it has come to realize, especially in times of protectionism. As a reaction, Swiss industry entered overseas economies very early and negotiations on privileges in tarifs have been carried on continuously. In this way Swiss industrialists acquired a world-wide orientation and experience in negotiations. At the same time, the political structure was affected: the international orientation of Swiss industry has always been a strong argument for a liberal outlook in Swiss foreign economic policy (Schaffner, 1970, p. 8), including the principle of neutrality. A flexible economy was subsequently regarded as a pre-condition for international competition. This, together with the federal political structure, very much favoured the autonomy of the Swiss economy and the consequent practice of the Subsidiaritätsprinzip in business affairs. Even the famous Friedensabkommen (Agreement of Peace)[1] is strongly related to the foreign dependence of the Swiss economy, because strikes and expulsion would weaken Swiss industries in international competition and would be of disadvantage for both capitalists and workers.

In the literature the decentralized structure of Swiss industry is always mentioned. Indeed, Switzerland, in comparison with other countries, has a low degree of centralization and concentration – spatially as well as on the level of firms (Clark, 1979; Höpflinger, 1974, pp. 59 ff.; Schaffner, 1970, p. 7; Schweizerische Kartellkommission, 1979, pp. 236-40). According to Schaffner, state executives have always been the last to join teams of negotiators abroad (Schaffner, 1970, p. 8). But if industrialists are able to negotiate without the help of the state, institutions where economic strategies could be traced out by industrialists were required for economic administration. Probably the most important institutions for this purpose are the business-interest associations, where common economic interests are co-ordinated. The Swiss business-interest organizations have a rather centralized structure.[2] The most important organization with respect to economic policy, particularly for industrial interests, is the Vorort. Because of its important position within the policy-making process (Zimmermann, 1980), industrial undertakings will generally seek personal representation within this organization or will invite one of its members onto their supervisory boards. The same is true (with some modifications and restrictions) for the sub-units of the SHIV, the cantonal chambers of commerce (Handelskammern) and/or sectoral associations. Because of the intensity of foreign competition relative to internal competition, it might be expected that this will be reflected in business-interest associations and in interlocking directorships.

Swiss finance, in particular the big banks, might be expected to be of great importance for interlocking directorships. In the early stages of industrialization the most important function of Swiss banks was the transfer of capital abroad. Small businesses and industrial pioneers were not interested in credit at all. However, growth and mechanization of production required more and more capital investments. The leading participation of industrialists from Winterthur and Zurich in the establishment of Schweizerische Bankgesellschaft (SBG) is, therefore, not very surprising. Schweizerische Kreditanstalt (SKA) was founded some years earlier. Again, the industrialists of Zurich financed its establishment but, contrary to the SBG, the SKA was set up to finance one giant undertaking: the first Swiss railways. Thus, the financially powerful Zurich industrialists found a promising investment for their capital. The Schweizerischer Bankverein (SBV) was initiated by the private bankers of Basel. Although its relations to regional industry, especially chemicals, have always been very close, the SBV maintains a greater distance from industry than the other two large banks.

These three banks, which make up the 'big three' of today (the so-called Drei Großen), differ in size and in foreign activities from all the other banks, even from the other two larger ones that together with the big three are officially called Großbanken (large banks). The assets of the smallest one of the big three are four times as large as those of the next smaller bank. According to a study of the Schweizerische Kartellkommission (1979, p. 61), the large banks actually see themselves more and more as financial combines. Indeed, the five largest banks, were found by the Kartellkommission to control together 17 financial corporations and a trust company with accounting and advisory activities in more or less all of the important Swiss companies. According to the report of the Kartellkommission, the banks sought not to enter traditional activities but to open up new possibilities (Schweizerische Kartellkommission, 1979, p. 62). There is no doubt about the strength of their surge toward non-financial activities.

In short, there are substantial relationships between the largest banks and industry. This is due mainly to historical reasons (SBV is an exception) but also to financial ties and banking services. The expectation of a high level of interlocking between the largest banks and industry is also supported by some empirical findings of the Kartellkommission. Within their sample of 88 outside boards there were 113 positions on 72 boards held by the five largest banks. This contrasts with private banks, which only held 31 positions on 26 boards, and the cantonal banks with only seven positions on five boards (Schweizerische Kartellkommission, 1979, p. 84). Banks can be supposed to be turntables in the system of enterprises: the corporations related to the former founders of the big three influence the policies of the banks which, in turn, are financially and personally interlocked with an enormous number of other non-financial corporations. However, a difference might be supposed to exist between the interlocks of the SBV and the other two.

The following analysis will try to give a more detailed insight into interlocking directorships. The questions to be answered are whether these interlocks are distributed at random or whether a specific structure can be observed. Because of the high autonomy of the Swiss economy and the position of the three top banks and their related corporations just described, it is assumed that the network will show a strongly centralized structure.

Within the 250 largest corporations selected for study there were 74 corporations from the trade and services sector. Given the international orientation of Swiss industry, this large number is not very surprising. Of the remaining 127 industrial undertakings, there were 20 in food and 18 in machinery and equipment. Chemicals, electronics, paper and publication, precision mechanics and optics, metal working, construction and textiles each had between eight and 12 companies. The 49 financial undertakings comprised 34 banks and 15 insurance companies.

All of the selected enterprises had a board of directors and a supervisory board. The auditing board, which has no executive or supervisory responsibilities, was not analysed. Although members of this board can be of great importance as channels of information, they were not analysed for two reasons: (1) the auditing board has neither executive nor supervisory functions; and (2) its importance as a channel of information varies greatly from corporation to corporation and its functions are often devolved to a trust-company. Some companies also had an international advisory board and this was included in the analysis. The meaning of being a member of the supervisory board varies not only with the legal status of a corporation but also with other criteria, such as directness of involvement in day-to-day activities, that are only partly associated with membership of a specific board. Although a distinction between 'inside' and 'outside' positions has been used, not all directors could be classified in this way and a third group of 'intermediate positions' has also been considered.

OVERALL STRUCTURE OF THE NETWORK

One large component contained 206 corporations. There are only three countries which had more corporations in the largest component of their network: France, Finland and the USA. Both France and the USA had a lower level of centralization than that found for Switzerland, while network densities were similar. Switzerland was one of the countries with a centralized network structure which also had a very large main component. The same holds for Germany. The large component in Switzerland contained 1,002 lines and had a density of 0.05 and a diameter of 6. Including indirect relationships of length 2, of all possible relationships 39 per cent were realized.

Further information on the structure of the network can be obtained by splitting the component into its different segments. The core of the component included 12 corporations and showed a density of 0.79, the inner margin with 16 corporations had a density of 0.23 and the outer margin with 137 corporations had a density of 0.03. The periphery, with 41 corporations, had the smallest density at .01 (see table 2.6). The fact that Switzerland had a high density within the core and a low density within the inner margin strongly supports the hypothesis of a centralized structure.

As is shown in table 7.1, the Nationalbank and the largest three banks (SBV, SBG and SKA) were located in the core of the network. The core also contained the very important air-transport company Swissair, the largest enterprise in metallurgy (Alusuisse), the two most important corporations in machinery and equipment (Sulzer and

BBC), the largest combine in watch production (ASUAG), the giant Nestlé food processing combine, the half-Swiss rubber-processing company Societé International Pirelli and the gigantic chemicals combine Ciba-Geigy. The peak position of the Nationalbank (as measured by the rush) is not accidental but corresponds to the government policy aimed at Swiss economic autonomy. Within the Bankrat[3] of the Nationalbank were found representatives of all segments of the economy, corresponding to the rules for nominating board members.[4] The rest of the corporations belonging to the core had two characteristics in common: they were amongst the largest corporations and they were very multinational.

The corporations of the inner margin were very different from those of the core. There were no banks within the inner margin, but six firms within this circle (about 40 per cent of corporations in the inner margin) were insurance companies, three firms were engaged in electricity and cables (Cableries-Trefileries Cossonay, Grande Dixence and Centralschweizerische Kraftwerke), Wild produced precision instruments, Schindler was well known for its elevators, moving staircases, etc., SIBRA was the result of the merger of various drink producers, Bally was the largest producer of shoes in Switzerland and the BLS (Berner Alpenbahn Gesellschaft) was the most important railway corporation after the national SBB. Overall, the production corporations in the inner margin were more export oriented than multinational, some were even more nationally oriented (railway, electricity, beverages). Apart from the insurance corporations, Schindler was the only significant exception to this pattern.

The activities abroad of the insurance companies were different. There seem to be some regularities in that life-insurance companies had lower portions of premiums abroad than did companies concerned with damage and accidents. A very high proportion (over 90 per cent) of premiums were earned abroad in reinsurance. There was, for historical reasons, a relationship between the three big banks and the insurance companies. The insurance company Winterthur-Versicherungen was founded by the circle of the Bankverein Winterthur (the predecessor of SBG), the Rentenanstalt by the SKA[5] and the insurance companies of Basel were closely related to the private bankers of Basel and the SBV, which had shares in the Basel insurance companies through the merger with the Basler Handelsbank (Holliger, 1977, p. 159). Furthermore, the SKA gave significant financial support to the Zürich Versicherungsanstalt (Holliger, 1977, p. 43), thus securing a significant share of the voting rights of this insurance company for itself. The Mobiliar Versicherungsgesellschaft seems to be an exception in this respect because it was founded by the Gemeinnützige Gesellschaft (Stucki, 1968, p. 170). Even the Schweizer

Table 7.1 Corporations in the centre in Switzerland

Corporations	Rush	Adjacency	Turnover (million SFr)	Domestic turnover (%)	Domestic work-force (%)	Assets (million SFr)	Domestic premium (%)
Core							
Nationalbank	0.1132	23	—	—	—	39,324	—
SBV	0.0586	19	—	—	—	52,757	—
Swissair	0.0472	16	2,184	na	na	—	—
Alusuisse	0.0396	19	4,834	30	24	—	—
SBG	0.0358	16	—	—	—	52,651	—
Sulzer	0.0268	21	3,529	64	58	—	—
BBC (Brown Boveri & Company AG)	0.0255	19	8,431	25	21	—	—
SKA	0.0241	17	—	—	—	41,664	—
ASUAG	0.0179	12	1,041	79	84	—	—
Nestlé	0.0176	18	19,063	3	5	—	—
Soc. International Pirelli S.A.	0.0159	18	2,579	na	na	—	—
Ciba-Geigy	0.0145	17	9,488	37	29	—	—
Inner margin							
Winterthur Schweiz. Unfallvers.	0.0098	15	—	—	—	3,612	43
Bâloise-Holding	0.0069	12	—	—	—	a	b

Table 7.1 *(continued)*

Schweiz. Lebensvers.-u Rentenanstalt	0.0067	9	—	—	—	10,007	68
Schweiz. Mobiliar (Versicherungsges.)	0.0060	11	—	—	97	558	89
Von Roll AG	0.0048	12	641	93	97	—	—
S.A. des Cableries-Trefileries Cos.	0.0045	14	410	75	60	—	7
Schweiz. Rückversicherungsges.	0.0045	12	—	—	—	5,838	7
Wild	0.0038	12	326	na	76	—	—
Schindler	0.0030	8	1,180	39	31	—	—
Sibra-Holding AG	0.0030	11	227	97	91	—	—
C.F. Bally AG, Holdingges.	0.0024	10	701	33	38	—	—
Cellulose Attisholz AG	0.0017	11	160	100	100	—	—
Grande Dixence S.A.	0.0016	7	128	100	100	—	—
Centralschweizerische Kraftwerke AG	0.0014	11	507	na	100	—	—
Zürich Versicherungen	0.0006	11	—	—	—	5,117	21
Berner Alpenbahngesellschaft (BLS)	0.0000	4	145	100	100	—	—

Sources: Höpflinger, 1980; SBG, 1977; SHZ, 1977; business reports; own calculations.

Notes:

a The assets of this holding company are not comparable. The holding includes three corporations. The assets of the largest of them amount to 3,402 million SFr.

b Basler Leben: 17%, Basler Schaden u. Unfall: 31%.

Rückversicherungsgesellschaft, properly an insurance company from and for insurance companies, was not independent from banks and was close to SKA.

Assuming that the number of interlocks relating two corporations to each other is indicative of the strength of the relationship, further insight into the overall structure of interlocks can be gained by differentiating the component according to the multiplicity of lines. The corporations with intensive interlocks could be described as sub-components based on the multiplicity of lines. Figure 7.1 shows that the 206 corporations of the component included a very closely interlocked group of corporations (BBC, Alusuisse, Ciba-Geigy and SKA) which was connected to other corporations of the component by lines of multiplicity 3 or 4. Within the three subcomponents defined by multiplicities 3, 4 and 5 can be found almost all corporations belonging to the core and the inner margin.[6] This analysis underlines once more the notion of a centralized structure with banks and some of the most important multinational corporations in the core. But this gives no information on the direction of the relationships. In the following section an attempt will be made to classify interlocks so as to extract information on dependence relations.

TYPES OF INTERLOCKS AND NETWORK STRUCTURE

As defined in chapter 2, primary interlocks are seen as being associated with institutional links, whereas secondary interlocks may correspond to personal links. The distinction between primary and secondary interlocks is based on the positions a person holds on the boards of two adjacent corporations. Within the large component, 405 multiple directors held 1,087 positions and created 1,314 interlocks. About 15 per cent (117) of the positions were inside positions, 16 per cent (177) were intermediate and 68 per cent (739) were outside positions. Classifying interlocks according to these positions results in 281 (21 per cent) primary interlocks and 1,033 (79 per cent) secondary interlocks, of which 209 (16 per cent of all interlocks) were induced and 824 (63 per cent) were unclassified interlocks. According to these proportions, the distinction between primary and secondary interlocks is very important in the Swiss network because only 21 per cent of all interlocks had an institutional base.

The large number of unclassified interlocks was due to the relatively large number of multiple directors holding intermediate but no inside positions. For the definition of interlocks, the intermediate positions were counted with the outside positions. Although the financial corporations made up one-fifth of the corporations studied, 63 per cent

Figure 7.1 Hierarchial structures based on multiplicity of lines in Switzerland

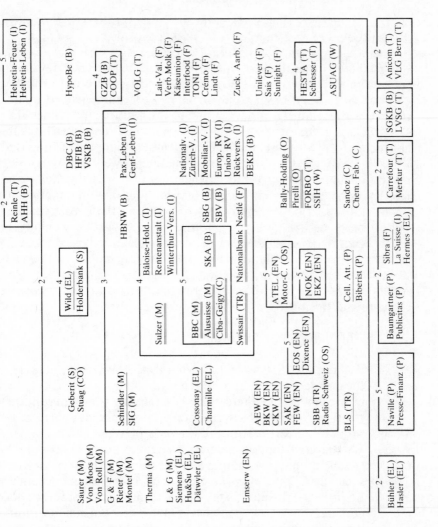

Note: Corporations within boxes with numbers as limits are weak components. Multiplicity level is indicated by the limiting numbers. The weak components based on lines at multiplicity 1 is not within the figure. Corporations belonging to the core are understood twice, those belonging to the inner margin once. Activity of corporation is indicated in parentheses (B=bank; C=chemistry; CO=construction; EL=electrical apparatus; EN=generation, transmission and distribution of energy; F=food; I=insurance; M=machinery, metallurgy; O=other production; OS=other services; P=paper production, printing, publishing; S=state extraction and manufacture; T=trade; TR=transport; W=watches).

of the primary interlocks involved an inside position in a financial corporation. Only seven interlocks involved inside positions in both a financial and production corporation and these were added to the financial interlocks. The distribution of primary interlocks relative to sector (finance and production) and to the different segments of the component (core, inner margin, outer margin and periphery) shows the great importance of primary financial interlocks for the relationships between the core and the outer margin (see table 7.2). The consequence is, of course, a disproportionate number of interlocks which were induced by those primary financial interlocks in the outer margin. Primary production interlocks were overrepresented in the relationships between the outer margin and the periphery. The unclassified interlocks were overrepresented in the core and in the relationships between the core and the inner margin. As can be seen from the last row of table 7.2, most of the unclassified interlocks were created by persons without inside positions but holding more than three directorships. Furthermore, these network specialists were highly overrepresented within the core and the relationships between the core and the inner margin.

From this analysis the following conclusions can be drawn.

(1)   A large proportion of the primary financial interlocks were located between the core and the outer margin. Therefore it can be assumed that there were comparably many dependency relations between the financial corporations of the core and the production corporations in the outer margin.

(2)   The relationships within the core as well as those between the core and the inner margin were generally carried by network specialists. The network of the centre was largely dependent upon network specialists. It can be supposed that interlocks carried by network specialists are more or less symmetric and so, if there is indeed a hierarchical structure from the centre to the periphery, the structure can be described as having a small elite at its very top. As shown in table 2.1, only 14 per cent of the multiple directors (57 persons) held more than three positions.

(3)   Overall, there was a rather symmetric network in the centre, where a lot of information, co-optation and co-operation channels existed for each single corporation.

The banks in the core again show evidence of a turntable function. The production companies within the core were connected to the banks with a relatively small number of primary production interlocks and

Table 7.2 *Centrality groups and types of interlocks in Switzerland* (%)

| | Centrality groups | | | | | | | | | | Total |
| | Within | | | | Between | | | | | | |
Types of interlocks	Core	Inner margin	Outer margin	Peri-phery	c–i	c–o	c–p	i–o	i–p	o–p	
All	10	2	25	1	13	25	0	17	0	6	100 (1,314)
Primary											
Financial	3	0	21	0	7	48	1	14	3	3	100 (112)
Production	5	1	29	2	7	27	0	17	0	12	100 (169)
Induced											
Financial	5	1	47	0	6	24	1	16	0	1	100 (106)
Production	10	1	26	2	15	26	1	17	0	3	100 (103)
Unclassified											
All	13	3	21	1	17	21	0	18	0	6	100 (824)
By big linkers	18	4	15	0	21	23	0	17	0	0	100 (514)

Note: Absolute numbers are in parentheses.

F

through the primary financial interlocks of the banks were indirectly linked to the non-financials in the outer margin. The latter, in turn, had primary production interlocks with peripheral companies.

THE THREE LARGEST BANKS
AND HIERARCHICAL STRUCTURES

This section is concerned with the hierarchical structure in relation to the three large banks. Hierarchies in the network structure were due to asymmetric relationships, where primary interlocks consist of an inside position on one corporation and an intermediate or an outside position on the other corporation. Such interlocks are assumed to be directed from inside to outside positions and those companies in which the inside positions were located are assumed to be in the upper part of the hierarchy. The first question will, therefore, be to discover which corporations had most of their contacts by outgoing primary inter- locks. The corresponding figures are presented in table 7.3. Corpor- ations have been ranked according to the number of corporations to which they had outgoing interlocks (the outdegree in a directed graph). The striking finding is the extremely high outdegree of two of the big banks, SBG and SKA. The corporation in fourth rank turns out to be SBV, having about half of the outdegree of the second ranking SKA. From this rank on there was no other breaking point in the outdegree rank ordering.

Comparing the results in table 7.1 with those in table 7.3, the following differences can be seen.

(1)   Measured on the basis of directed lines, the Nationalbank was no longer in the centre. There was only one directed line from the Nationalbank to a corporation outside of the centre. The discrepancy between its rank in table 7.1 and its inferior position in this component reflects the particular nature of its Bankrat (its supervisory board) as an information channel and the exclusion of the Nationalbank from most of the main business of banks: credits, mortgage and, to a great extent, securities.

(2)   The SBG ranks first, as compared to the fifth rank it had in the overall network.

(3)   Within the top ranks in table 7.3 can be found the largest insurance corporations. It is very interesting that only one of the six insurance corporations in the inner margin appears in table 7.3 (Zürich Versicherungen) but two from the outer margin did appear.

Table 7.3 Corporations ranked by outdegree in Switzerland

Corporations	Outdegree	Outneighbourhood at distance 2[a]	Centrality group
SBG	21	30	Core
SKA	17	26	Core
Zürich Versicherungsanstalt	9	37	Inner margin
SBV	9	14	Core
National-Versicherungen	8	39	Outer margin
Union-Rückversicherungen	8	39	Outer margin
Alusuisse	8	27	Core
Spengler	7	41	Outer margin
UHAG	6	33	Outer margin
Rieter	6	31	Outer margin
Schweiz. Volksbank	6	8	Outer margin
Globus	6	7	Outer margin
BBC	5	45	Core
Ciba-Geigy	5	32	Core
Zürcher Ziegeleien	5	32	Outer margin
Holderbank	5	27	Outer margin
Wild	5	27	Outer margin
VOLG	5	12	Outer margin
Kantonalbank Kt. SG	5	6	Outer margin

Note:
a The outneighbourhood at distance 2 is defined as the number of corporations that can be reached by the given corporation in at most two steps, taking into account the direction of the lines.

(4) Some of the prominent production corporations in the core also had an outdegree smaller than 5 (Swissair, Sulzer, ASUAG, Nestlé and Pirelli) but only ASUAG had an outdegree of 0.

(5) With the exceptions of Wild and the Zürich-Versicherungsgesellschaft (already mentioned above) there was no corporation from the inner margin with an outdegree of 5 or more.

The earlier results already gave evidence of the centrality of the three largest banks. They not only had top rankings according to their adjacency based on all interlocks but even on the basis of their outdegree. This held in particular for SBG and SKA and, to a lesser extent, for SBV too. But were the most central corporations by adjacency really on the top of the hierarchy in the network? In the former section a turntable function was assumed for these banks. If so, some corporations will at least belong to the same stratum of the

Table 7.4 Network of the core (directed lines) in Switzerland

	Outdegree to																	
													Core	Inner Margin		Rest of network		Total
	Nationalbank	SBV	Swissair	Alusuisse	SBG	Sulzer	BBC	SKA	ASUAG	Nestlé	Pirelli	Ciba-Geigy		Finance corporations	Production corporations	Finance corporations	Production corporations	
Core																		
Nationalbank													0				1	1
SBV									1				1	2			6	9
Swissair	1												1			1	2	4
Alusuisse	1												1	1	2		4	8
SBG		1											1		1	3	16	21
Sulzer													0			3		3
BBC	1	1						1					3				2	5
SKA			1										1			1	15	17
ASUAG													0					0
Nestlé	1							1					2			1		3
Pirelli													0		1			1
Ciba-Geigy						1		1					2		1		2	5

Table 7.4 (continued)

Indegree from																		
Core	1	3	2	0	1	1	0	3	1	0	0	0	12	1	7	11	46	77
Inner margin finance corporations	1	0	0	0	1	0	0	2	0	1	0	0	5	0	0	5	6	16
Inner margin production corporations	1	1	1	0	1	0	1	1	0	0	0	0	6	1	0	1	7	15
Rest of finance corporations	2	0	0	3	2	1	3	0	2	0	0	0	13	2	5	17	14	51
Rest of production corporations	5	3	1	1	6	2	4	4	1	1	0		29	6	10	21	48	113
Total	10	7	4	4	11	4	8	10	4	2	1	0	65	10	22	55	121	273

network as the three banks. Some evidence on this aspect of the structure has already been given in table 7.3. Looking at the neighbourhood at distance 2 it can be seen that the variance is larger here than for the outdegree. Whereas BBC had 45 connections at distance 1 or 2 (40 were indirect, resulting from the five outgoing interlocks), the cantonal bank of canton St. Gallen had only six connections at distance 2 on the basis of the same outdegree. The high number of connections of BBC at distance 2 was a consequence of the fact that it was the only corporation with primary interlocks to all three big banks. The primary interlocks within the upper stratum of the hierarchy meant that the largest banks were meeting-points and policy-making forums for the corporations which constituted the upper stratum. Table 7.4 contains more detailed information. It gives an overview of the indegrees and outdegrees of the individual corporations of the core, the inner margin and the rest, each divided into finance corporations and production corporations. As in table 7.3, the figures represent lines and not interlocks. By comparison with the other corporations, the banks of the core had a very high indegree not only from the corporations of the core but also from the production corporations outside the centre. Within the core, more than half of the lines went to the banks. Of the directed lines to the core from the production corporations outside the centre, 45 per cent went to the three largest banks. These production corporations belonged to the leading corporations of Switzerland, namely Rieter, Sandoz, Saurer, Holderbank, Lindt & Spruengli, UHAG (world trade) and Volkart-Holding. It is indeed remarkable that with only very few exceptions the largest corporations according to turnover had directed lines to one or more of the three largest banks. The prominent exception was the chemical firm Hoffmann-Laroche, whose own financial base was so large that it was in no way dependent upon any bank.[7] Not only the indegree of the banks but also their outdegree was exceptionally high. Eighty-one per cent of the lines running from the core came from the three banks. However, looking only at their outdegree within the core and within the centre, these values are not particularly high.

SUMMARY AND CONCLUSIONS

The introductory section of this chapter postulated a high level of interorganizational relations based on economic structure. The structure resulting from this network was assumed to be centralized. Furthermore, differences in the tightness of the relations of SBV and the other two large banks, SBG and SKA, with the rest of the corporations was postulated. This analysis has given some empirical support to these postulates. However, compared with other countries, the Swiss network was neither especially dense nor particularly centralized but its largest component contained a larger proportion of companies than usual. It can be concluded that, contrary to regional and operational dispersion and decentralization, Switzerland had a dense and centralized network of interlocking directorships.

In addition, the analysis gives a picture of the position of the largest banks in the network. Directed lines were concentrated around the three largest banks, in particular SBG and SKA. The third bank, SBV, ranked fourth by outdegree, but there was a large gap between the second and the fourth rank. This contrasted with ranking according to adjacency based on all interlocks. SBV had, therefore, more interlocks, but looser ones. The reason for this is historical: the formation of SBG and SKA was mainly initiated by industrialists, whereas SBV was formed by bankers. The separation of directed lines illustrated the turntable function of the largest three banks. Only a few, but in particular the largest, production corporations had outgoing interlocks to these banks, whereas the outgoing interlocks from these big banks established relationships to the important, more nationally oriented corporations of Switzerland. This underlines the centralized structure of the Swiss network.

NOTES

1   This agreement has always been regarded as very progressive and decisive for the Swiss economy. See Holliger (1977, p. 237)
2   However, there is a separation of business and professional from industrial interests. So within the two peak associations, Schweizerischer Handels- und Industrieverband and Schweizerischer Gewerbeverband, there are different, sometimes conflicting interests organized.
3   The boards of the Nationalbank are the general meeting of share-holders, the authorities of the bank (Bankbehörden) and the executive board. Within the authorities there are the Bankrat, the committee of the bank, the committee of revision and local committees (Schweizerische Nationalbank n.d., pp. 330ff.).
4   The bank board consists of 40 members and there are precise rules governing their recruitment. See Schweizerische Nationalbank (n.d., p. 333).
5   This relationship was cut off in 1879 by official decree and in 1882 the Rentenanstalt was changed into a co-operative.
6   The exception from the core is ASUAG and the exceptions from the inner margin are Von Roll, Wild, Cellulose Attisholz and SIBRA.
7   Nevertheless Hoffmann-La Roche has very close relations with the SBG as manifested by regular recruitment of former executives of SBG. See Hollinger (1977, p. 164).

8

Financial Groups in the Belgian Network of Interlocking Directorships

LUDO CUYVERS and WIM MEEUSEN

The predominant place of the holding companies in the Belgian economy is a specific institutional and historical datum and renders this country particularly suited for a case-study on the delimitation of family- and manager-control in an intercorporate network. Such is the subject of the present chapter. In the first section a few introductory remarks are made on the Belgian holding-company phenomenon. The following section discusses some general characteristics of the network and clears the ground for a more thorough study of the place of the holding companies in the network with regard to their centrality (third and fourth sections) and to the type of interlocks they carry (fifth section). The last section sets out the major conclusions.

INTRODUCTORY REMARKS ON THE
BELGIAN HOLDING COMPANIES

The Belgian intercorporate structure shows peculiar characteristics when compared with other European countries and the USA, largely due to the dominant position of holding companies in Belgium. This institutional datum is indeed not found in most other countries and it is therefore necessary to give some explanation for it. Some, but not all, dominant Belgian holding companies have their roots in wealthy families: one category of holding companies is therefore related to industrial tycoons or bankers of the nineteenth century and their descendents today. Another category was established quite differently. The first category can best be called the category of the 'family-controlled' holding companies. Control in the second category is much less in the hands of a family, although ownership control exists. It has been argued that the second category is 'managerially controlled' (ABVV, 1956, pp. 140-1; CRISP, 1962, p. 65). It seems safer however to call the latter category 'non-family controlled', since it confronts us with the somewhat surprising situation of *managerialism within finance capitalism*, i.e. the systematic presence of professional managers in boards of directors of companies, who are tied to the group by ownership, either directly or indirectly (De Vroey, 1973, pp. 156-7, 185).

Typical examples of family-controlled holding companies are Compagnie Bruxelles-Lambert (controlled by the Lambert family and the de Launoit family), Compagnie Coppée de Développement Industriel (the Coppée family) and Electrorail (the Empain family). As an example of a non-family-controlled holding company the Société Générale de Belgique can be mentioned, the most important Belgian holding company. In 1975, the main shareholders of the Société Générale were the companies of the insurance groups A.G. and Royal Belge and the insurance company Assubel, all of which were in turn controlled by the Société.[1] As a result of these cross-participations, the main shareholders of Société Générale de Belgique are at the same time controlled by the Société and their representatives on its board of directors are representing a board dominated by the Société. Hence, the directors of the Société Générale and of the insurance companies which are the main shareholders of the Société are continually co-opting each other (CRISP, 1962, pp. 67-9; ABVV, 1956, pp. 140-1). Other non-family-controlled holding companies, apart from those within the Société Générale group (e.g. Sofina, Traction et Electricité, Finoutremer and Sibeka) are Almanij and Cobepa. However, in quite a number of holding companies in Belgium different interest groups, family and non-family alike, meet. This is for instance the case with Electrobel, Electrafina, Sofina, Glaverbel-Mécaniver and Financière du Ruau.

The main holding companies were established in the mid 1930s when, due to the economic crisis and the immobilization of short-term liabilities in long-term loans and participations, some important mixed banks went bankrupt. By the law of 22 August 1934, banks were compelled to give up all permanent industrial participations (cf. the Glass-Steagull Act of 1933 in the USA). Consequently, most mixed merchant banks immediately adopted a policy of splitting themselves into a holding and a banking company. Among the most notable metamorphoses of that time was the Société Générale de Belgique which yielded its banking activities to the Banque de la Société Générale de Belgique (today the Société Générale de Banque). Also prominent was the case of the Banque de Bruxelles which became a holding company but changed its name to Brufina (today part of Compagnie Bruxelles-Lambert) and yielded its banking activities to a newly founded company under the old name of Banque de Bruxelles.

An explanation for the existence and persistence of the former Belgian mixed banks and the present-day holding companies must be largely institutional.[2] In the first half of the nineteenth century, there was a considerable need for long-term financial resources to be invested in the industrialization of the southern part of Belgium. This need was much greater than could ever be met by the entrepreneurs. On the other hand, the wealth of the propertied classes was immobilized in land and the land-owners were rather reluctant to invest in risky industrial projects. A similar situation existed in neighbouring countries but there, as a result of the greater need for capital for the financing of commercial transactions with the colonies, international banking houses had already emerged spontaneously (e.g. the Rothschilds).

In Belgium, nothing of the sort had happened. Only family-sized preindustrial banking enterprises were active with a limited commercial activity mainly oriented towards the class of wealthy land-owners (SGB, 1972, pp. 14–16). Therefore, the foundation in 1822 by the King of the Netherlands of what later became the Société Générale de Belgique was of the utmost importance. The task of the Société was to attract financial resources by radiating trustworthiness and to channel these resources to the emerging industrial companies. As a result of its creation, a thin but dominant layer of captains of finance developed before the wealth of the captains of industry could possibly have accumulated. In a later period, industrialization outside the sphere of influence of the Société Générale de Belgique – and still later and to a lesser extent of the Lamberts, representatives of the Rothschilds in Belgium since the 1840s – laid the foundations of industrial empires such as those of the Boëls, the Solvays and the Empains.

The existence of a powerful mixed bank controlling important industrial and commercial enterprises influenced the way in which the rising industrialists managed their capital and exercised their control over companies. The financial institutions specializing in shareholding and corporate control constituted an example to be copied and recopied by the nouveaux riches. The mere existence of a few of these institutions created newcomers. An expanding industrial concern, in the face of the overwhelming financial power of the Société in a limited market such as Belgium, would be continuously under threat of financial dependence, if not takeover, if it did not fight back with the same weapons: for example, to channel resources into a holding company and to adopt techniques such as cross-participations and multiplication of subholdings for the sake of corporate control. These techniques are very efficient for economizing on the use of scarce family capital per unit of productive investment. In this way the family fortunes were in a position to control a maximum number of companies and to remain in control for a considerable time.

The historical priority of the holding companies of the 'bankers' over those of the 'industrialists' probably established policy priorities such as corporate control and risk minimization rather than contributing to the creation of efficient structures of supply, production and marketing. As Daems (1978, p. 5) rightly emphasizes, the 'transition from holding company to grand enterprises took place only when the holding company was used to control an *intra*-market multicompany system and/or when anti-trust legislation threatened the survival of the combine.' It will therefore be clear that in many instances corporate control by the holding companies and their policy of asset diversification has hampered a thorough vertical integration of the group (SGB, 1972, pp. 55–64, 74). At the same time the non-emergence of large vertically integrated corporations has kept the holding company up to the present in a virtually unchallenged position as the centre of the group.[3]

Detailed and systematic evidence on the Belgian holding companies and the financial-industrial groups they dominate, was gathered by the authors of the pioneering CRISP study (CRISP, 1962). On the whole, their main conclusions about the Belgian holding companies, although formulated more than 20 years ago, are still highly relevant today.

(1)   The Belgian holding companies are financial powers, not specialized industrial conglomerates. They do not normally interfere in the technical and commercial decisions of the companies of their group. By and large, the scope of interest of the Belgian holding companies is limited to a sufficient return and the stability of their participations. This explains, at least in part, why as a rule the production technology used by the companies at issue is limping behind and why the interests of the group are mainly confined to 'traditional' sectors (CRISP, 1962, p. 404).[4]

(2)   The participations of the Belgian holding companies are mainly concentrated in the financial sector, heavy industry and energy. There has been an apparent bias towards semi-manufactured articles (e.g. rolled steel, cement, non-ferrous metals, etc.) (CRISP, 1962, pp. 407–10).

(3)   As a result of the many reorganizations and mergers in traditional sectors, communal interests of different holding companies have increased considerably. New ventures are often financed jointly by the holding companies (e.g. in the oil industry, nuclear energy, aluminium production, etc.) (CRISP, 1962, p. 401).

SOME QUANTITATIVE EVIDENCE ON THE IMPORTANCE OF HOLDING COMPANIES IN THE BELGIAN INTERCORPORATE NETWORK

The dominant position of holding companies in the Belgian system of interlocking directorships can best be illustrated by constructing an input–output type matrix, which depicts the total number of interlocks within and between industrial sectors. Table 8.1 is such a matrix.

Table 8.1   Interlocks within and between economic sectors in Belgium

		0	1	2	3	4	5	6	7	8	H	1976 share in GDP (%)[a]
Agriculture	0	0	0	0	0	0	0	0	0	4	1	3.2
Extraction and energy	1		135	81	60	19	14	14	1	39	180	4.0
Iron and steel, chemical industry	2			140	125	20	32	43	13	54	220	5.4
Metals and mechanical engineering	3				66	13	33	15	30	50	144	9.5
Food, textile, paper, rubber, plastics	4					9	1	1	4	7	25	9.7
Building and civil engineering	5						1	2	9	11	33	7.5
Distribution	6							6	1	26	28	9.6
Transport	7								2	18	20	6.1
Banking, insurance	8									82	110	4.6
Holding companies	H										107	—
Total											2,049	59.6

Sources for GDP: Institut National de Statistique: *Bulletin de statistique,* September, 1981 (9), 476. Eurostat: *National Accounts ESA, Detailed Tables by Branch 1970–1979.* The sector classification is that of the Statistical Office of the EEC (1970) *NACE 1970: General Industrial Classification of Economic Activities within the European Economic Communities,* Brussels.

Note:
a Post, harbours, real estate and other services, which account for 37 per cent of GDP, are not included in the table.

It can easily be calculated, using the sum of the tenth column of table 8.1 (labelled H), that the interlocks of the 250 largest industrial, financial and commercial companies in Belgium[5] with the 20 largest holding companies, together forming the corporations selected, represented 37 per cent of all interlocks of the former companies. Together with the interlocks within the set of 20 holding companies (107), the share of interlocks of holding companies was 42 per cent. The interlocks of the holding companies essentially were concentrated in heavy industry, energy, metal industry and mechanical engineering and to a lesser extent in the financial sector, which might indicate that the conclusions of CRISP (1962) about the 'industrial conservatism' of the Belgian holding companies still largely hold good.

These findings, by and large, also confirm the pattern of intra-and intersectoral control linkages in the Belgian economy in 1967, evidenced by Daems (1978, p. 82), who distinguishes 24 industrial sectors and finds that in 23 the number of interlocks with the holding companies is most or second-most important. Whereas table 8.1 shows that the corporations of each sector were more interlocked with holding companies than with companies of the same sector, Daems' calculations show that seven of the 24 industrial sectors (utilities, mining, glass, textiles, sugar, distribution) had more interlocks within the sector than with holding companies. The difference between Daems' and the present results is probably due partly to the differing levels of aggregation of industrial sectors and the composition of the sets of corporations studied but most of all to the important mergers which have taken place in these sectors since then.

It may be interesting at this point to focus attention on the relationship between the accumulation of directorships and the positions of the persons involved as top managers or family representatives in one or more holding companies. Among the 12 directors with ten or more directorships, three were clearly family representatives, one of a family going back to an industrial 'tycoon' of the nineteenth century. The nine others were directors of the Société Générale. There was no clear evidence of vested family interests in their case (no homonyms in the boards of other corporations in 1976 or in earlier years). This illustrates the exceptional character of the holding companies which are part of the Société Générale group (the Société Générale itself, the A.G. group, Traction et Electricité and Finoutremer among those which were in our data set): in contradistinction to the other Belgian holding companies (of which Compagnie Bruxelles-Lambert was the most important) they were manager-controlled instead of family-controlled, as shall be confirmed later on. Nevertheless, apart from the aspect of direct control, there is, as will be seen, evidence of family interests in the Société group also. Whether or not interlocks with holding companies are also important in qualitative, rather than purely quantitative terms, will be investigated in Sections 3 and 4.

COMPONENTS IN THE BELGIAN NETWORK AND THE CENTRAL POSITION OF THE HOLDING COMPANIES

The network of interlocks between the 270 companies of the Belgian data set contained five components. Four of these each consisted of two firms connected by one line and controlled either by foreign capital (Unilever and a Soviet multinational) or by small independent Belgian groups (Vandemoortele, the food group, and L.Delhaize, the retail group). The fifth component contained 182 companies and 1,215 lines and had a density of 0.07. Of the 182 companies of the large component, 54 (30 per cent) were multinational companies or branches of multinationals and in another ten companies foreign multinationals had an important minority share.

The remaining 80 companies in the network were isolated points, of which 54 (68 per cent) were branches of multinationals. An overwhelming majority (36) of these multinationals had their parent company in the USA. In the main component however, France ranked before the USA according to the number of subsidiaries. As might be expected, the number of branches of companies from other EEC countries was much higher in the main component (35 of the 54 foreign branches) than among the isolates (13 of 54 foreign isolates). It should be noted that the isolates in the network of interlocking directorships were not necessarily isolated in the structure of ownership and control. A striking example was GTE Sylvania, a 100 per cent subsidiary of General Telephone and Electronics Corporation of USA, which was an isolate in the interlock network, whereas another 100 per cent subdidiary, GTE ATEA, was in the main component. The latter had an interlock with the aliuminium producer SIDAL, which in turn had an interlock with two other companies that were members of the main component.

A comparison of component structure and economic sector showed that companies outside the main component were more frequently to be found in mineral-oil refining, manufacturing of motor vehicles, food, drink and tobacco, and retail distribution, whereas companies belonging to the main component were relatively more engaged in production and distribution of energy, production and preliminary processing of metals and, of course, in holding activities. The main Belgian financial groups were highly interlinked and, apart from energy production and distribution, were mainly engaged in rather traditional economic activities. These results thus seem again to corroborate the above mentioned conclusions of CRISP (1962).

It will be clear, indeed, that the behaviour of holding companies as outlined in CRISP (1962), given their dominance, should produce an industrial composition of companies in the main component similar to that discovered here. Some differences, however, await explanation.

(1) The oil industry, though mentioned by CRISP (1962) as a sector which was financed jointly by the holding companies, accounted for just 4 per cent of the companies in the main component. However, if the 'oil refiners' are added to the 'petrochemicals' of the chemical and plastics industry, this percentage increases to 8 per cent. Most of the petrochemicals thus added were linked to foreign companies.

(2) Companies belonging to the main component and active in electrical engineering accounted for 6 per cent. This share, together with the share of the chemical industry, exclusive of petrochemicals, implies that the industrial activity of the Belgian groups might well have shifted somewhat to relatively new sectors. But, as for the petrochemical industry, a great majority of the companies active in electrical engineering and belonging to the main component were linked to foreign rather than to Belgian capital.

The network of interlocks, as long as the direction of the interlocks is neglected, can be analysed further by drawing contour lines for different levels of line multiplicity. A line multiplicity threshold of 1 leads to the 80 isolates, the main component of 182 corporations, and the four isolated pairs already mentioned. At higher levels of line multiplicity, other small components separated off from the largest original component. At multiplicity threshold 2 new components affiliated with the South African Rembrandt Tobacco group, the French EMC group, the Dutch Philips group and British Petroleum, as well as with small Belgian groups (Boerenbond, Kreglinger), were found. At multiplicity threshold 3, two important Belgian insurance groups could be discerned (the A.G. group and the Royal Belge group) in addition to two other Belgian subgroups (Eternit and the ship-building group Van Damme).

In figure 8.1 the remaining main component of the graph with lines of multiplicity 5 or more is depicted. In the centre of the structure was the Société Générale de Belgique. Its central position is very clear as it was strongly connected with and, at that level of multiplicity of lines, had direct access to a lot of other corporations, many of which had no such intensive direct access to each other. The Belgian branch of the Paribas group is depicted at the top left of the figure (consisting mainly of Cobepa, Banque de Paris et des Pays-Bas and Financière du Ruau). Figure 8.1 also illustrates the peculiar situation of Electrobel as a meeting-place of different financial interests in Belgium.[6] This energy

Figure 8.1   Main component at multiplicity level 5 in Belgium

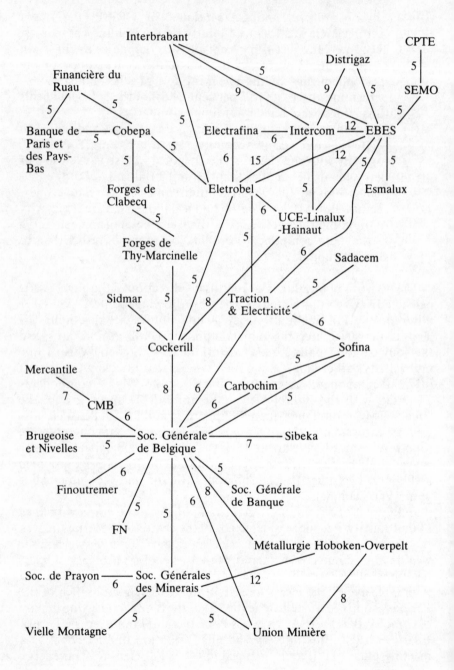

holding company was tied with lines of multiplicity greater than or equal to 5 to the Société Générale group and the Paribas group and with the cluster of electricity producers and distributors (Intercom, EBES, Interbrabant, UCE-Linalux-Hainaut[7]). At least two other remarkable results should be stressed. The A.G. group was one of the main shareholders of the Société Générale. The directors of both had important common interests and were co-opting each other. However, the A.G. group, although interlinked at multiplicity level 5, was not heavily linked to the Société Générale. On the other hand, the Bruxelles-Lambert group consisted of Banque Bruxelles-Lambert and the Compagnie Bruxelles-Lambert and was not connected to the main component at multiplicity level 5.

The high multiplicity of director lines in the Société Générale group, as compared with the Bruxelles-Lambert group, is the result of a different mechanism for selecting and co-opting directors. In the Bruxelles-Lambert group the controlling families are directly represented on the board of directors of the holding company and at the same time sit on the board of a number of companies in which the holding company participates.[8] In the Société Générale group, however, the family representatives and owners are concentrated in the board of 'commissaires', the board of directors consisting of managers. These managers started their careers somewhere in the group and climbed the pyramid accumulating directorships. When they were finally co-opted into the general staff of the group, each of them became mainly responsible for controlling the economic sector from which he originated (see De Vroey, 1973, pp. 141–2). Consequently, each sits on a large number of boards of companies in 'his' sector, not to speak of the positions in the boards of companies which perform the function of nodal points in the system of control, e.g. subholding companies and sectoral holding companies. Hence, the co-optation mechanism in the Société Générale group involves an extraordinary accumulation of directorships as compared to the family-controlled groups such as Bruxelles-Lambert.

INDUSTRIAL COMPOSITION OF CENTRALITY GROUPS WITHIN THE MAIN COMPONENT

If the frequency distribution of distances in the main component is considered, then the pairs of companies at distance 1 or 2 represent 44 per cent of the total number of pairs (compared with the density 0.07, i.e. the proportion of pairs at distance 1). The greatest distance was 8: each company in the main component could be reached from each other company of this component in at most eight steps. Cockerill-

Ougrée-Providence, the largest Belgian steel producer, had the highest number of contacts (64) at distance 1 with the rest of the main component; the Société Générale de Belgique ranked second with 62 contacts. However, at distance 2 the Société ranked highest as it was able to reach 152 companies out of 182 in two steps or less. Cockerill ranked fourth at distance 2 (149 contacts), after the electricity holding company Electrobel (150 contacts at distance 2) and UCE-Linalux-Hainaut, a producer and distributor of electricity. Moreover, it appears that 82 of the corporations in the main component (45 per cent) had direct access (distance 1) to more than ten other companies and 33 corporations (18 per cent) to more than 25 others.

It is important to focus attention on the industrial structure of the core, the inner margin, the outer margin and the periphery.[9] If the industrial structure of the set of companies belonging to the main component of the network of interlocks is compared with that of its centre, i.e. core and inner margin, the following conclusions can be drawn, which by and large confirm the results of the foregoing section.

(1)   Corporations operating in the energy sector, in the production and preliminary processing of metals and in the manufacturing of metal articles, as well as holding companies were clearly much more central in the main component than others. Out of the 20 holding companies selected, 12 were in the centre of the main component. The same proportion can be observed for the nine energy producers or distributors. There were no holding companies outside the main component. Moreover, the share of the holding companies in the main component was 11 per cent and increased the more the central parts of this component were approached – 22 per cent of the companies belonging to the inner margin, but 29 per cent of those belonging to the core.

(2)   The number of banks and financial institutions, and to a lesser extent corporations belonging to the chemical industry, increased rapidly in the less central parts of the network. For instance, the share of banking and other financial corporations in the main component was 16 per cent, but was just 5 per cent in the core of that component and 11 per cent in the inner margin. Moreover, one-third of all commercial and savings banks (14 out of 43) and of all corporations operating in the chemical industry (nine out of 27) were outside the main component; this was no doubt due to the heavy penetration of foreign capital in both sectors and to the 'division of labour' within the groups between banks and holding companies.

(3)   Companies active in building and civil engineering were evenly spread over the central and less central parts of the network.

The share of building and civil engineering in the set of 270 Belgian companies was comparable to the share of this sector in the main component of the network.

The most important feature of this pattern of sectoral representation in the different centrality groups of the network is, in our view, the relatively reduced centrality of banks (see also table 8.1). This might signify that in those countries where holding companies are present and where the simultaneous performance of banking and holding activities is prohibited by law, the original finance-capital model of Hilferding regains some relevance *vis-à-vis* its more popularized version, which stresses the role of banking, as such, in the hierarchy of economic power and, in particular, the role of banks as suppliers of credit. The Belgian case seems to indicate that if finance capital is important at all in the network, it is in the first place because of the links of ownership and financial participation that it implies rather than because of the decisive weight of creditor-debtor ties.

WHICH TYPES OF INTERLOCKS ARE PREDOMINANTLY USED BY HOLDING COMPANIES?

Let us first pave the way and consider the different kinds of board positions which can be held. The Belgian sociétés anonymes (limited companies) have a Latin type two-board system, i.e. a board of administrateurs and a board of commissaires.[10] The board of administrateurs is entitled to act for the company in all respects whereas commissaires have only an unlimited right of supervision of the business of the company. Both administrateurs and commissaires are appointed by the general assembly of shareholders. One or more of the administrateurs may be delegated to conduct the day-to-day management, i.e. the day-to-day acts taken to insure the good course of business, with due regard to the guide-lines issued by the board. The director thus delegated is called 'administrateur délégué'. In many cases, the commissaires are accountants but the Belgian financial and industrial groups tend to recruit also representatives of the main shareholders or shareholding families, as well as representatives of minority groups. The commissaires play no role at all in the management. They take no strategic decisions as administrateurs do; their power is purely supervisory and for what follows the commissaire functions are ignored (see also Daems, 1978, p. 75).

The administrateurs délégués or the members of the 'comité de direction' who sit on the board of directors are considered inside directors, whereas the chairmen and the vice-chairmen of the boards of administrateurs, unless they are 'delegated', can best be thought of as having a function 'intermediate' between inside and outside director. Outside directors are the ordinary administrateurs. In the Belgian situation, a director may often combine several positions as administrateur délégué or as member of the comité de direction. Hence, a Belgian inside director is not always strictly comparable with an inside director in other countries, as he or she may not perform a full-time role in any one corporation.

An interesting question which arises immediately is, What types of interlocks are predominantly used by holding companies to link with other companies? This question can be answered by analysing the distribution of primary interlocks, i.e. the use of interlocks where the person concerned has an inside position in at least one of the two corporations. Different types of primary interlocks can be distinguished according to the type of corporation on the board of which the inside position is held. Unlike primary interlocks, induced interlocks between boards of directors are generated by a person having an outside function in the companies concerned but at least one inside function elsewhere. (Chapter 2 gave a detailed description and discussion of these different sorts of interlocks.) On the basis of three assumptions it was stated that inside directors are used to maintain institutional links. These assumptions hold only if the few inside directors in a board are viewed by their fellow directors as true representatives of the interests of the corporation. This, in turn, is the case only when there are no conflicting interests between directors on the same board. It will be remembered, however, that the boards of directors of the main Belgian holding companies were often meeting-places of family representatives of financial empires. As a consequence, the struggle between these empires for control via the boards of directors can be very intense. The administrateur délégué who is a representative of family A, might well be supported by the representatives of the other families only if family A allows family B a vice-chairmanship in the board or an inside function on another company which is controlled by the first. The latter possibility implies that directing the personal interlock from inside function to outside function as is conventionally done, might be contrary to the 'true' direction of influence between the two companies involved.

There is another way by which the conventional direction of interlocks from inside to outside might be misleading. This is when, in an effort to economize as much as possible on the controlling power of the representatives of a holding company, people sit on the board of the parent company as ordinary (outside) directors but are posted on the boards of the controlled companies as executives (inside directors). In these circumstances, also, the notion of an induced interlock becomes

Table 8.2 Types of interlocks and number of directorships in Belgium (%)

Types of interlocks	Number of directorships of multiple director					Total as percentage of overall interlocks
	2	3	4	5 or more	Total	
Primary financial interlocks	33	21	18	28	100 (78)	4
Primary production interlocks	15	15	10	60	100 (261)	13
Primary holding interlocks	11	16	8	66	100 (120)	6
Holding and financial interlocks combined	*20*	*18*	*12*	*51*	*100 (198)*	*10*
Primary financial–production interlocks	—	—	—	—	— (—)	—
Primary financial–holding interlocks	15	46	39	—	100 (13)	1
Primary production–holding interlocks	1	—	—	99	100 (269)	13
Primary financial–production– interlocks	—	—	100	—	100 (6)	0
Induced financial interlocks	—	7	14	79	100 (70)	3
Induced production interlocks	—	6	7	87	100 (304)	15
Induced holding interlocks	—	4	5	92	100 (201)	10
Other induced interlocks	—	—	0	100	100 (222)	11
Induced production–holding interlocks	*—*	*—*	*—*	*100*	*100 (221)*	*11*
Not classified interlocks	26	21	18	36	100 (505)	25
Not classified when intermediate is inside	*31*	*26*	*17*	*26*	*100 (312)*	*15*
All interlocks	10	11	9	70	100 (2,049)	100

Notes:
Absolute numbers are in parentheses. Administrateurs only and intermediate position considered as outside.

dubious. If, then, the directing of interlocks is meant as a means of directing the network in terms of influence or dominance, a number of preliminary tests should be performed.

Let us, however, first look at the distribution of interlocks over types of interlocks and over number of positions of the directors concerned (table 8.2). Among the administrateurs, 25 per cent of all interlocks could not be classified as either primary or induced. In addition, the category of unclassified interlocks is partly due to missing data on who are the inside and outside directors on a board[11], and its share is very sensitive to changes in the way intermediate directors are treated: if intermediate directors are considered as insiders the proportion of unclassified interlocks falls to 15 per cent. Primary and induced interlocks had an almost equal share in the total number of interlocks (36 and 39 per cent respectively). This is, however, due to the deliberate grouping of intermediate directors with outside directors; if inter-mediate directors are not considered to be outsiders, 59 per cent of all interlocks were primary, and only 26 per cent induced.

Closer study of the percentages of table 8.2 reveals:

(1)   13 per cent of all interlocks were primary production–holding interlocks or, in other words, interlocks generated by persons with inside functions in both holding and production com-panies:

(2)   only 6 per cent of all interlocks were simply primary holding interlocks; and

(3)   11 per cent were induced production–holding interlocks.

These percentages shed some light on the role of directors with inside positions in both a holding company and a dependent industrial corporation, as compared with that of directors of which only the position in the holding company was an inside function. Although there can be no doubt that the industrial corporation was dominated by the holding company, inside directors of the holding company showed no clear tendency to be outside directors in the dependent industrial corporation but in many cases were insiders in the industrial corporation as well. This conclusion is not dependent on considering intermediate directors as outsiders; on the contrary, when intermediate directors are considered as insiders the conclusion is strengthened.[12]

Further inspection shows that the primary financial interlocks accounted for only some four per cent of all interlocks and that the respective shares of the primary and induced financial–holding and financial–production–holding interlocks were negligible. As might be expected, this showed that the contribution to interlocks made by banks and insurance companies was of little importance in relation to the contribution of the holding companies. This, no doubt, reflects the 'division of labour' between holding companies on the one hand, and banks, etc., on the other, which was brought about in the middle of the 1930s as a result of the 1934–5 bank-regulation laws.[13]

The conclusion on the importance of primary and induced interlocks in the overall structure of the network and the significant role in it played by the holding companies is obvious, but it is still necessary to examine how the (undirected) lines of the corresponding graph are transformed into (directed) arrows. In order to try to clear up this matter a Pearson correlation coefficient was computed. This was calculated between the financial participation rate between two corporations on the one hand and the difference between the number of inside–outside and outside–inside interlocks on the corresponding line in the interlock network on the other hand.[14] The hypothesis underlying the conventional drawing of arrows from inside to outside would be confirmed if this correlation was significantly positive. Actually, it is not: for the 266 interlocks considered, the correlation is positive (0.05) but not significantly ($p = 0.78$). If the analysis is repeated separately for interlocks where the underlying participation emanates from a holding, financial or industrial corporation respectively, the significance levels still do not reach acceptable levels. It is interesting to note, however, that the least indefinite result was obtained for interlocks carried by financial corporations (commercial banks, savings banks and insurance companies): the correlation was negative (-0.27, $p = 0.89$, $n = 23$). It should be remembered however, that financial participations by banks are, by law, confined to their own sector. A test performed on the relation between the financial participation rate and the *intensity*[15] of the corresponding line in the interlock network was, as might be expected, much more conclusive: a Spearman rank-order correlation of 0.43 was obtained and was significant with a probability of 99 per cent ($p=0,01; n=1,271$).

As was already noted in the previous section, Belgium seems to obey the predictions of some variant of the finance-capital model. Unlike the situation in several other countries, including the Netherlands, where an important role can be assigned to the unclassified interlocks generated by the so-called network specialists, in Belgium only 25 per cent of all interlocks were unclassified. Nearly 47 per cent of these interlocks were carried by persons with three or fewer positions and 36 per cent by persons with five or more positions. This looks like a mirror image of what has been reported for the Netherlands, where 48 per cent of the unclassified interlocks were carried by persons with five or more positions and just 39 per cent by persons holding three or fewer positions.[16] Again, taking intermediate directors as insiders strengthens this conclusion, as the distribution over number of positions of the unclassified interlocks in this case reveals (see table 8.2, last row).

The evidence suggests that the unclassified interlocks in Belgium, as compared with the situation in the Netherlands, tended to be associated with those with few directorships and the primary production interlocks as well as the primary production–holding interlocks were associated with those with many (see share of multiple directors with four or more positions in table 8.2). This leads to the conclusion that what has been called elsewhere the network specialists, i.e. persons who know what is going on in business and have considerable experience in running a large corporation, were in Belgium insiders of the main holding companies or held intermediate functions in their board of directors. They were definitely not outsiders having no inside function in the intercorporate structure.

CONCLUSION

Although some of the results of the foregoing study could no doubt be reached by other and, perhaps more straightforward, means, the analysis of the network of interlocking directorships has proven, in the case of Belgium, to be a powerful tool. A relatively large number of salient features of the Belgium economy indeed emerge at the same time.

(1) Belgium followed by and large the finance-capital model, with the holding companies as nodes of the structure.

(2) The centrality of the network was greater than in the neighbouring countries. One could say in this respect that the holding companies acted as a kind of 'glue'.

(3) The so-called network specialists were identified as the representatives of the holding companies. They usually accumulated a large number of positions among which were several inside functions.

(4) The sectoral composition of the different centrality subsets in the network confirms the long-standing impression of a certain lack of vitality on the part of the holding companies: their control (in terms of the network of interlocking directorships) was confined to the traditional sectors of the economy. The corporations in newly developing industries were mostly to be found at the fringes of the network. The corporations concerned were for the most part multinationals.

NOTES

1   With a minor proviso for Assubel in which the Société is interested with other groups.
2   Cf. the argument of Daems, which is more flavoured by main-stream economic theory (Daems, 1978, p. 25–8).
3   Other more specifically economic reasons can be listed as incentives to integrate vertically. See Cuyvers and Meeusen (1982, pp. 10–11).
4   See also SGB (1972, p. 194), where this bias is explained for the period between the end of the Second World War and 1959 by the high customs tariffs abroad for finished products. Other historical reasons are provided in CRISP (1962, pp. 406, 423).
5   For a discussion of the selection procedure see Cuyvers and Meeusen (1981).
6   For the peculiar situation of this holding company as a meeting-place of the different financial interests in Belgium, see Cuyvers and Meeusen (1976, p. 66).
7   Interbrabant and UCE-Linalux-Hainaut disappeared in the course of the year 1976 as a result of a 'reorganization' of the industry of production and distribution of electrical energy. The former merged into a newly created corporation Unerg, the latter was absorbed by Intercom.
8   There seems to have been an agreement between the Lambert family and the de Launoit family involving the family interests after the merger of Brufina and Compagnie Lambert in 1972.
9   See chapter 2 for definitions and densities within and between the centrality groups.
10   For co-operatives and partnership firms similar regulations are in use as for limited companies.
11   Although some 15 per cent of all directorships are unclassified due to missing data, they account for only four per cent of all interlocks.
12   When intermediate directors are considered as insiders the share of primary production–holding interlocks is 33 per cent and that of primary holding interlocks 4 per cent.
13   This division of labour is also clearly revealed by the low number of primary financial, primary financial–production, primary financial–holding and primary financial–production–holding interlocks, the more so as the primary interlocks in Belgium of holding companies and financial institutions combined show a distribution over the number of functions which is remarkably close to the distribution of the primary financial interlocks in the Netherlands.
14   The test was carried out only for those pairs of corporations where a financial participation was involved. Conventionally the pairs were ordered such that the participating corporation came first and inside–outside and outside–inside interlocks were discriminated accordingly. Also, participation rates were normalized with respect to the total value of the shares not distributed among the public.
15   By intensity of a line is meant a weighted sum of the number of interlocks of different types, an inside–inside interlock carrying the heaviest weight and an outside–outside interlock the lightest weight.
16   Information received from the Dutch team.

9

Finnish Interlocking Directorships: Institutional Groups and Their Evolving Integration

ILKKA HEISKANEN and ERKKI JOHANSON

This analysis of the Finnish interlocking directorships in 1976 will focus on one major theme: the new integration of the traditional institutional groups. An attempt is made to find out whether recent economic developments – especially the internationalization of Finnish economy via free-trade agreements and the related greater actual and anticipated susceptibility to turbulence in the international economy – has induced new 'superstructures', i.e. new modes of communication and co-operation between the business firms and the institutional groups they may form. On the empirical level this theme breaks down into three interconnected tasks. First, to find out if there are grounds for expecting new kinds of co-operation and integration, deciding where to look for them and finding a way to identify them empirically. Second, to identify the 'traditional' types of communication and co-operation between the business firms, i.e. the historical institutional groups of the Finnish economy, if there still are any. Third, to investigate the consequences of the role that the state has played in the Finnish economy, both traditionally (in terms of public enterprises) and via modern economic policies. One can expect that these policies would be reflected in the institutional structure of the Finnish economy on at least two levels: in the position of state-owned industrial firms within the economy and in the status and role of public financial institutions. The empirical investigation and the interpretation of the research results must pay special attention to these two areas.[1]

Initially some facts on the overall and institutional development of the Finnish economy will be given. This provides a background for understanding and interpreting the empirical findings and suggests some clues as to why changes in Finnish institutional economic structure are to be expected and where to look for them.

THE FINNISH ECONOMY: SPECIFIC DEVELOPMENTAL FEATURES AND INSTITUTIONAL BASIS

Finland is a relative newcomer to the family of Western industrialized nations and its entrance to this family was short and intense. Between 1950 and 1980 the proportion of the labour force in primary production fell from 46 per cent to 11 per cent and the proportion of those employed in secondary production and tertiary production rose from 27 per cent to 35 per cent and 26 per cent to 54 per cent respectively. The average annual growth rate of the GDP was 5.1 per cent between 1950 and 1969 and 4.3 per cent between 1970 and 1981. This development raised Finland to the top 20 in international income per capita comparisons and was fed by the internationalization of the Finnish economy. The landmarks in this area are: the liberalization of trade in 1957, the free-trade agreement with EFTA in 1961, membership in OECD in 1969 and free-trade agreements with the EEC and CMEA (Comecon) in 1974.

The above development has taken place in a geographical and historical context which has given it some peculiar national features which no doubt are also reflected in the institutional structure of the economy. First, Finland is a small peripheral northern country with limited and one-sided natural resources (mainly wood, water energy and, to a lesser extent, minerals) and small home markets. The development costs of industrial infrastructure and primary industries are high and require government participation and regulation, both financially and in terms of its own entrepreneurship. This is especially true as regards the exploitation and protection of the natural resources of the remote northern region of Lapland. The home markets cannot support several big firms in a given industrial sector and the few which have room to operate must – especially in the new free-trade environment – become internationally oriented and prove their competitive edge. The limited home markets and the fear of monopolistic pricing and cartels in purchasing the raw materials from primary production have given rise to strong consumers' and producers' co-operative movements. The financial markets are underdeveloped. The small number of large business firms and the legislation regulating the foreign ownership of stocks makes it difficult to raise risk capital from abroad, through share issues or through stock markets in general. And this, in turn, enhances the role of private and public financial institutions. Second, Finland is not only in the periphery but is in a peculiar double periphery between the East and the West. It has learned a nationalistic strategy of both defending its own national interests and exploiting its position. This is reflected in the legislation regulating foreign ownership of Finnish business and in Finland's present avant-garde position in East–West trade.

The above special features are reflected directly in the ownership structure of the Finnish economy. The government has a prominent role as an owner. The share of the public enterprises – organized as state-owned joint stock companies – is about 20 per cent of the value added of the Finnish manufacturing industries.[2] Due to the above legislation, foreign firms play only a minor role within the Finnish economy. The agricultural producers' and general consumers' co-operatives have a prominent role in the economy. The former own or regulate via their input most of the food-processing industries and similarly control to a large extent the acquisition of raw materials for the wood-processing industries. The consumers' co-operatives control a prominent part of the wholesale and retail-sales business. Both have also expanded in several other industries (wood processing, textiles, furniture, construction, metals, hotels and restaurants). The co-operative spirit is also reflected in banking: co-operative banks and savings banks have been important in gathering savings and have lately developed an increasingly important role in financing. The same spirit is also reflected in the insurance sector where mutual insurance companies play an important role. In the financial sector, the major units are the private commercial banks, savings banks, co-operative banks and insurance companies. The national central bank (Bank of Finland) is directly subject to parliament and regulates, jointly with the government, the monetary and investment policies. The other central public financial institutions include the Mortgage Bank of Finland (a subsidiary of the Bank of Finland), the Postal Savings Bank, the National Pensions Institute and the Regional Development Fund. The government has several financial arrangements within the system of public administration to subsidize small and middle-sized firms and export firms and, as will be seen later, it also co-operates with private financial institutions and business firms in these areas of financing. A new centre of financial power is the complex private sector employment pension scheme controlled to a large extent by the organizations of collective bargaining.

Ownership information has been used in some journalistic analyses to identify the major institutional groups in the Finnish economy and to assess their relative sizes (*Veckans affärer*, 1975). Some interlocking directorship analyses have substantiated these analyses to a certain extent (Heiskanen 1977). All these studies indicate that the major institutional groups centre around two major private commercial banks. Furthermore, the studies are unanimous that there are two major co-operative groups: a bourgeois group where the agricultural producers play a central role and a Leftist group where the workers and their organizations (trades unions, Leftist political parties) play a central role. The government financial and non-financial companies are considered to form a fifth group and it is assumed that a sixth minor group centres around the commercial bank owned and patronized by the Swedish-speaking minority. All the past analyses of institutional groups are, however, rather inconclusive in terms of consequences. They use rather loosely such terms as 'control' and 'economic power' and the criteria used to delineate the groups are left unspecified. Similarly, the composition and the hierarchical structure of the groups has not been thoroughly investigated. In the following empirical analysis of the institutional structure stringent criteria are used to identify the basic structure of the institutional groups and their mutual relations. The analysis is not, however, only an exercise in group identification. An attempt will be made to connect the results with the themes of new co-operation and integration mentioned at the beginning of this chapter.

THE FINNISH INTERLOCK NETWORK IN 1976

The selection of the corporations for the Finnish study was carried out according to the general instructions agreed upon by the international project group. The breakdown of the Finnish data set according to type of ownership and two-digit NACE-categories are given in tables 9.1 and 9.2. As regards the 24 financial institutions, the following more detailed breakdown can be given:

(1) five joint stock commercial banks; two of them are, however, umbrella organizations for co-operative banks and for savings banks respectively;
(2) one private and one public mortgage bank;
(3) one private joint stock insurance company;
(4) seven mutual insurance companies;
(5) two regional savings banks;
(6) six public financial institutions; and
(7) one pension loan-guarantee centre (Central Pension Security Institute).

The number of financial institutions was low because of the high concentration in Finnish banking. One can also notice the strong representation of consumers'/producers' co-operatives and wholesale and retail firms. These two features are interrelated, because two of the four major Finnish groups of wholesale/retail businesses were organized on the basis of consumers' co-operatives. Wholesale and retail firms were overrepresented in the data because of the use of an unweighted turnover criterion. For the same reason, import/export agencies were overrepresented.

Table 9.1   Ownership of corporations in Finland

Ownership	%	N
Private joint stock companies	63	149
Public joint stock companies[a]	8	20
Consumers'/producers' co-operatives	19	45
Mutual insurance companies	3	6
Governmental agencies/boards	2	5
Other	5	12
Total	100	237

Note:
a Public=more than 50 per cent of shares in direct or indirect governmental ownership.

Table 9.2   Sectoral distribution of corporations in Finland

Sector	%	N
Energy and mineral extraction and primary refining (sectors 13, 14, 21, 22, 23)[a]	3	7
Production of energy (sectors 15, 16)	3	7
Mechanical engineering and metallurgy (sectors 31, 32, 35, 36)	5	12
Instruments (sectors 33, 34, 37)	2	5
Wood and paper products (sectors 46–7)	10	23
Building and civil engineering (sector 50)	5	12
Food processing (sectors 41–2)	16	39
Leather and textiles (sectors 43–4)	2	4
Wholesale import/export agencies (sector 61)	20	48
Retail sales (sectors 64–5)	13	31
Transport and communication (sectors 71–7)	3	6
Banking, insurance and social security (sectors 81–3, 91)	10	24
Other sectors	8	19
Total	100	237

Note:
a The sectors refer to the NACE classification.

Source: Statistical Office of the EEC (1970) *NACE 1970: General Industrial Classification of Economic Activities within the European Communities,* Brussels.

The selection of the boards and their members is crucial in interlocking-directorship analyses. Finnish firms have generally adopted the two-board system, although national legislation provides for only one board. Some firms (mainly within co-operative movements) may, however, have a three-board system. Using formal labels only as a rough guide, two boards, 'supervisory' and 'executive', were selected whenever possible. Internal executive groups and external representational bodies were excluded. When coding the members of these boards, their positions were classified as supervisory or as executive. A further distinction was made among those having executive functions. Managing directors, managing vice-directors, chairmen and vice-chairmen of the executive boards were seen as a group of inside executives maintaining primary interlocks. The other executive-board members were seen as maintaining intermediate interlocks and the members of the supervisory boards as maintaining supervisory interlocks.

A total of 3,110 board members held 4,178 positions in the 237 corporations and financial institutions, linking together 210 firms and leaving 27 isolated companies.[3] There were 564 multiple directors holding 1,632 board posts and 2,248 interlocks. The biggest linker had 13 directorships and created 78 interlocks; 344 people had only two posts and 78 persons were big linkers with five or more board posts.

Table 9.3 gives the breakdown of different types of interlocks and multiple directorships. This table gives some validity to the classification of interlocks according to their importance. Most of the big linkers were 'inside' executives. The only real exception in the table – a person having seven board memberships and classified as having only supervisory positions in production companies – was a recently retired executive of a major commercial bank. The prominence of the financial institutions is obvious. There was, however, a relatively high multiplicity of posts among those having intermediate posts in production companies only. This means that the network was by no means organized around financial institutions solely.

FINNISH NETWORK: THE INSTITUTIONAL GROUPS AND THEIR INTEGRATORS

The international comparison indicates that the large component in the Finnish interlocking-directorship network as a whole was dense and concentrated (see chapter 2, table 2.4, figure 2.2). On the other hand, neither the core nor the inner margin were particularly dense. The relative density and centralization in the network of primary interlocks were also at a medium level (table 2.10). This seems to

Table 9.3 Distribution of interlocks in Finland

Directorships	Main position of multiple director									Total	Number of persons holding positions
	Inside			Intermediate			Outside				
	Financial Production	Financial	Production	Financial Production	Financial	Production	Financial Production	Financial	Production		
2	0	5	81	5	19	96	32	12	94	344	344
3	0	30	126	6	6	63	39	6	54	330	110
4	0	6	78	30	12	30	30	0	24	210	35
5	10	50	160	0	10	70	30	0	0	330	33
6	0	45	120	0	15	15	30	0	0	225	15
7	21	42	168	21	0	21	0	0	21	294	14
8	28	0	56	28	0	0	0	0	0	112	4
9	36	36	72	0	0	36	0	0	0	180	5
10	45	0	45	0	0	0	0	0	0	90	2
11	0	55	0	0	0	0	0	0	0	55	1
13	78	0	0	0	0	0	0	0	0	78	1
Total	218	269	906	90	62	331	161	18	193	2248	564

suggest that the Finnish network contained long hierarchical chains (institutional groups) which were mutually rather tightly integrated at the top, i.e. in the centre of the network. The preliminary analyses confirmed this assumption of integration. Even with a stringent line requirement – primary lines only and a multiplicity of 2 or more – there were still 76 firms left for analysis. They formed nine components, one of which contained 52 of the firms. The clique analysis which was used to analyse these components showed no systematic pattern. One should suspect that the network had one or more integrators or forums, where the different business interests met. These maintained the intergroup cohesion and obscured the basic structure of the network. If these integrators can be found and 'bracketed' from further analyses, it is possible to find and interpret the basic structure and then to proceed to analyse also the role of these integrators.

In order to find the integrators, it was first necessary to conceptualize what kind of firms these integrators might be. First of all, they naturally had to belong to the densest part of the network, i.e. the centre. Second, they had to be neutral meeting places (e.g. jointly owned firms or monopolistic firms outside normal business competition and still in the area of such general interest as investments, infrastructure, communication, etc.) where conflicting interests could meet and discuss 'communal matters'. Third, they had to be 'passive' meeting-places, i.e. their own executives should not participate actively via their own interlocks in the structuring of the network. This last condition would prevent the analysis from eliminating firms which were made into forums by their own active executives. In order to identify such integrators all the firms in the centre of the Finnish network were examined. Using the second criterion it was possible to identify six firms which would fulfill this above requirement.[4] They are described in table 9.4.

The activity or passivity of the 'home' executives of these firms were examined. The two industrial firms (SF127 and SF059) had active executives, whereas the executives for the four other organizations did not create interlocks. A closer examination of their boards and managers indicated that they were controlled from outside, even to the extent that one of them (SF236) did not have its own managing director but was taken care of by the managing director of the Finnish Bank Association. We excluded these four organizations (SF242, SF238, SF236 and SF218) from further analysis. Even the exclusion of the forums did not help much in separating the institutional groups on the basis of primary interlocks at multiplicity level 2. There were still 72 firms which formed 12 components and one of these included 40 firms. The clique analysis now, however, gave better and more interpretable results. Searching for cliques at distance 1 (so-called 1-cliques), only

Table 9.4   *Major integrators of the network in Finland*

Name and code	Area of activities	Ownership relations
SF 242 Industrial Fund of Finland	Founded 1954 and since 1962 active as a development credit agency; channels loans mainly to small and medium-sized firms.	Joint stock company, owned by commercial banks and public finance institutions. Some foreign banks and financial institutions are minority shareholders.
SF 218 Central Pensions Security Institute	Founded 1962. Provides credit insurance for private pension foundations and facilities the use of their funds as corporate capital.	Semi-public corporation under supervision of Ministry of Social Affairs and Health. Strong representation of major labour-market organizations on boards.
SF 127 Perus Yhtymä Ltd	Founded 1940 and expanded through mergers in 1968. Specialized originally in infrastructure construction for agriculture and forestry. Now important in construction export, especially to the Soviet Union.	Joint stock company, owned by the state (28.1%), commercial banks, insurance companies, agricultural producers' co-operatives and Federation of Finnish Agricultural Producers.
SF 238 Finnish Export Credit	Founded in 1954 and active as a development credit agency since 1963. Promotes exports by facilitating credit and, to a lesser extent, by direct financing.	Joint stock company, owned by the state (55.6%), commercial banks and some major production corporations.
SF 236 Industrial Bank of Finland	Founded in 1924 as a mortgage bank. Makes bond issues and grants long-term investment credits, mainly to industrial concerns.	Joint stock company, owned by three major commercial banks. Some major corporations are minority shareholders. The Ministry of Finance has had its representative on executive board since 1924 and public finance institutions since 1953.

SF 059 Kemi Ltd	Founded 1893, government ownership participation since 1953. Originally concerned with processing wood resources of Lapland.	Joint stock company owned by the state (24.9%) (via another state-owned company), by forest owners (via their co-operative corporation), banks (via a holding company), insurance companies and some major corporations.

cliques of size 3 were found: 12 in the component of 40 and one in the component of nine. Twelve cliques at distance 2 (2-cliques) were found that had a minimal size of 5. Two of these were found in the component of nine and ten in the component of 40. The latter varied in size between five and ten corporations.

The above cliques, 13 1-cliques and 12 2-cliques, could be used as building blocks for constructing the institutional groups. The 1-cliques, where all the firms were directly connected with each other, could be combined into cores[5] for the institutional groups; and the 2-cliques, where all the firms were indirectly connected with each other, could be combined into the main 'bulks' of the institutional groups. On the basis of this general idea different types of cores (defined in terms of overlapping or single 1-cliques) with different 'bulks' (defined in terms of overlapping or single 2-cliques) were combined. The first core was formed by taking all the firms which formed, together or pair-wise and with a third firm, two or more 1-cliques. There were three such firms which could be considered the core of the first institutional group. This core was connected with its bulk, i.e. with all firms which formed 2-cliques with it, to give the preliminary contours of the first institutional group of size 16. Within this group the firms which formed 1-cliques with the core firms could be considered a kind of 'second layer' around the core and the rest of the firms thus formed a 'third layer'. After the first institutional group was thus delineated the remaining 1-cliques were examined. There were only three 1-cliques left which did not overlap and which could thus be considered independent cores. They could be connected with three of the remaining 2-cliques to form three more institutional groups of sizes 6, 7 and 8. One 2-clique remained without a core of any 1-clique formation and it could be considered a fifth, independent, 'decentralized' group. There were in all, five institutional groups: one with a large core and two layers of firms around it, three with 1-clique cores and one additional layer each and one consisting of a single circle (a 2-clique) without any core. Three of these institutional groups were connected through a joint member firm. The groups are depicted in figure 9.1. The differences in group structure are reflected in the measures of density. Controlling for size and comparing within each group the comparable 2-cliques of approximately the same size (6–8), the density index in the four 'core-centred' groups varied from 0.47 to 0.67, while the index for the one 'coreless' group was only 0.33. The groups can be rather easily labelled in terms of their core organizations and the type of predominant ownership. The relative importance of the core firms – and also firms in the 'coreless' group – can be further assessed by examining the number of their overall connections, i.e. how many firms they could reach with primary lines directly or via another firm.

As figure 9.1 indicates, the largest of the institutional groups centred around three focal firms: a major commercial bank, the largest Finnish insurance company and a wood-processing firm. As to their importance, the bank and the insurance company – which were closely connected through mutual minority ownership, through joint ownership of other firms and through joint lending policies – had the highest contacts to other firms both within the group and also outside the group. They also shared a common ideology: they were founded to counterbalance the economic power of the Swedish-speaking minority. The group can be called the Group of the Nationalistic Commercial Bank. Its second layer contained another insurance company, two major industrial conglomerates, two production firms and one construction firm; and its third layer contained five production firms (one having also wholesale activities), one foreign firm and one oil-distribution company. Four of the firms formed a regional subgroup, i.e. they had their own 'core' of a 1-clique. All these firms were established to exploit the water energy and wood resources of Northern Finland.

One of the remaining institutional groups was linked with the Nationalistic Commercial Bank group via mutual exchange of one of each other's major firms. This institutional group centred also around a core of three firms: an insurance company (closely connected with agricultural producers' interests), a major construction firm (SF127 in table 9.4, it also belongs to the second layer of the first institutional group) and an oil-distribution company (a subsidiary of a large agricultural producers' wholesale firm, obviously a stand-in for its mother company). The second layer of this group contained a commercial bank (an umbrella for the co-operative banking), two production firms and the commercial bank from the core of the previous institutional group. Because of its predominant agrarian orientation this group can be called the Group of Agricultural Finance, Industry and Trade.

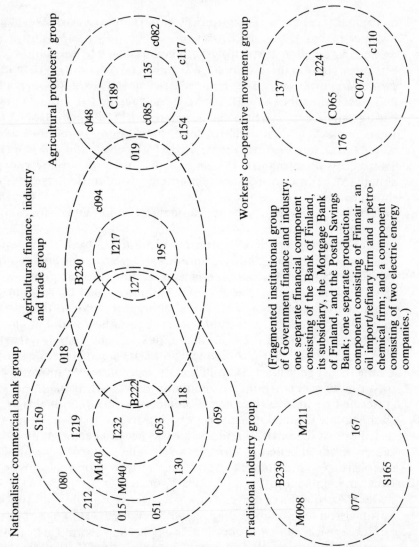

Figure 9.1   Structures of main institutional groups in Finland

Note: The fragmented Government Group is indicated within parentheses. Firms are denoted by code numbers The sector of the firm is indicated with an alphabetic prefix (B=commercial bank; I=insurance company; C=central co-operative organisation; c=consumers'/producers' co-operative; M=major conglomerate [wood machinery, machinery–shipbuilding, wood–machinery– electronics]; S=wholesale/retail sale; no prefix=production). The codes and names of corporations are as follows: 015=Ericsson; 018=E.Oeljyt; 019=Farmos; M040=Huhtamaeki.Yhtymae; c048=Itikka; 051=Joutseno.Pulp; 053= Kajaani; 059=Kemi; C065=Keskusosuusliike.Otk; C074=Kulutusoisuuskuntien.Keskuslitto; 077=Kymi. Kymmene; 080=Lassila. Tikanoja. Yhtymae; c082=Lihakunta; c085=Lounais.Suomen.Osuusteurastao; c094=Metsaeliitto.Yhtymae; M098=Nokia; c110=Osuunsliike.Elanto; c117=Osuusteurastamo. Karjaportti; 118=Oulu; 127= Perusyhtymae; 130=Pohjolan.Voima; 135=Raision.Tehtaat; 137= Rakennuskunta.Haka; M140=Rauma. Repola; S150=Saastamonen.Yhtymae; c154=Satahaemeen. Osuusteurastamo; S165=Stockmann; 167= Sunila; 176=Suomen.Sokeri; C189=Tuottajain.Lihakeskus-kunta; 195=Union.Oeljy; M211=Waertsilae; 212=Yhtyneet.Paperitehtaat; I217=Aurayhtioet; I219= Elaekevakuutusyhtioe.Ilmarinen; B222=Kansallis. Osake.Pankki; I224=Kansa.Yhtioet;B230= Osu-uspankkien.Keskuspankki; I232=Pohjola.Suomi.Salama; B239=Suomen.Yhdyspankki.

The next institutional group centred around a core of two meat-producers' central co-operatives and a major grain and vegetable oil-processing conglomerate owned by the farmers. The second layer of this group contained four meat-producers' co-operatives and a production firm (of medicines, technochemical products and agricultural chemicals) which also linked this group with the previous one. This group can be labelled the Agricultural Producers' Group. The joint members mentioned above linked these three groups into a chain, where the Group of Agricultural Finance, Industry and Trade served as the intermediate link. The links between the groups were single primary interlocks which were supported by induced interlocks produced by the mutual relations within the groups. All in all, these three groups can be said to form the nationalistic agricultural backbone of the Finnish economy.

Looking at the 'coreless' institutional group, its most important firm by far was a commercial bank founded and patronized originally by the Swedish-speaking population and its industrial interests.[6] The group contained, furthermore, two wood-processing firms, two major conglomerates and a major retail firm. This group reflects the spirit of the historically important wood-processing industry and it can be labelled the Group of Traditional Industry. The very fact that it belongs to the same large component as the previous three institutional groups indicates that it has a link of two primary interlocks with at least one of them. Although the interlock data do not show it, it is connected to the Nationalistic Commercial Bank group through a shipping-line owned by firms from both groups.

The last of the institutional groups was again a cohesive one which can be easily labelled. It centred around the core of an insurance company and two workers' central co-operatives. In its second layer were one large regional co-operative, a construction firm owned by the workers' co-operative movement and a sugar refinery. This group can be labelled the Workers' Co-operative Movement Group.

The above results and interpretations tend to support the earlier journalistic descriptions and interlocking directorship analyses of the institutional structure of the Finnish economy. The findings differ from these descriptions and analyses in two respects. First, one can see clearly the hierarchical structures in group formation and second, one can understand the dependence of the group delineation on the criteria used. As regards hierarchical structures, it has been shown that the groups vary as to their concentration and complexity. These variations were, no doubt, due to historical, economic and ideological factors. The 'decentralized' structure of the Traditional Industry Group reflects the unavoidable competition between firms in the traditional wood-processing industry. Co-operation could be at best a joint ownership of a third firm for lumber purchase, for providing semi-products, for paper mills, etc., and even the financial institutions respect confidentiality by splitting their representation and sending different persons to the boards of potentially competitive firms. The rest of the institutional groups reflect more of the co-operative spirit – which results in the formation of rather united cliques of elite business leaders. The complex hierarchical structure can also be seen in the interlinkings between the groups. It was noted that three of the groups formed a nationalistic agricultural backbone of the Finnish economy. This backbone can also been seen as a hierarchical structure where the major institutional group, that of Nationalistic Commercial Bank, has had a dominant position. The development of industrial agriculture and the agricultural industries is, however, slowly changing the relations between the groups and making them more equal. The relative importance and the hierarchical ordering of the institutional groups is also reflected in their linkages to the four integrators which were excluded from the analysis. The Group of the Nationalistic Commercial Bank had 24 primary interlocks with the four integrators, the Group of Agricultural Finance, Industry and Trade had 12, the Agricultural Producers' Group had one, the Traditional Industry Group had eight and the Workers' Co-operatives Group had one.[7]

The dependence of the group delineation on the criteria used is reflected in the fact that fewer institutional groups were found than expected. This was due to the stringent line requirement and to limitations set on the size of the cliques examined. There were, of course, several smaller components and cliques and they may be interlinked if less stringent criteria are used but their further analysis in this context is not very informative. One can, however, comment on the most conspicious 'missing group', that of Government Finance and Industry. As indicated in figure 9.1, the group emerged as three minor components. The most important of these components – in terms of the big linkers and connections to the four forums excluded from the analysis – was the Government Finance Group. It consisted of three financial institutions (the Bank of Finland; its subsidiary, the Mortgage Bank of Finland; and the Postal Savings Bank). The firms of this component (jointly with the Ministry of Finance) represented the state in the ownership of two of the four excluded forums (SF242, SF238) and also participated in controlling the operations of a third (SF236). The other two minor industrial components indicate how the government joint stock companies are concentrated in the area of infrastructure, primary production and provision of energy and transportation.

Even if the line requirements were loosened, e.g. to the level of primary lines and multiplicity of 1, the separate parts of Government

Finance and Industry were not united into a single institutional group. Thus the group was rather fragmented – at least from the perspective of 'pure' business concentration. This, of course, does not exclude the possibility that it was politically or administratively united and controlled. The political and administrative units which may hold the group together were not included in our data set. If, however, the interlocks of the public financial institutions with the four integrators are examined it can be seen that at least in this respect the role of the public sector in the formation of the Finnish network was by no means insignificant. There were nine primary interlocks between the three major public financial institutions (Bank of Finland, Postal Savings Bank and the Mortgage Bank of Finland) and four integrators. This is naturally due to the ownership relations (see table 9.4, last column) and to the very fact that the integrators function in the areas of investment policies and aid to industrial firms.

One could continue the above analysis by slackening the line requirement and by following longer linkage chains: distance longer than 2, bridges which may, for example, connect regionally decentralized firms to the group. By relaxing the criteria along these lines, more than 50 per cent of the studied firms could be assigned to the above and some minor institutional groups. These analyses also indicate that a considerable number (about 30 per cent) of the selected firms were not connected with any larger institutional group but maintained only weak or random interlocks with them, remained isolated or formed small chains with few other firms. The above percentage figures do not, of course, mean anything if the line requirements for belonging to a group are not indicated. One cannot make any conclusions as to how much of the Finnish economy was 'controlled' by the groups if 'control' varies from group to group depending on the internal structure of the group (see for example the more centralized and more decentralized groups in figure 9.1). The group structure must be standardized in some fashion – as happened to a certain degree in figure 9.1 with cores and layers – before one can actually compare the groups and add up how much they control and in what manner.

INTERPRETATIONS AND CONCLUSIONS

The empirical analyses have provided two results: first they identify the integrators which cause the new overall integration of the Finnish network; and second they reveal the contours and nature of the traditional institutional groups. Discussions and interpretations could proceed in two directions: to explicating the factors behind the formation of the institutional groups or to examining the nature of the potential new integration. This section will briefly touch the first of these themes and then focus more on the latter.

The nature of the institutional groups identified in the analysis is, to a large extent, indicated by the above discussion and the labels given to the groups. One can easily infer some of the major factors behind the formation and cohesion of the groups. One can first notice that type of ownership and financial control play an important role in group formation (see also chapter 2, table 2.8). There are, however, in the background still deeper sectoral interests and ideological factors which are reflected in the composition of the groups. Examples are the contrast between agricultural industries and other industrial sectors, the old language cleavage between Finnish- and Swedish-speaking Finns, the co-operative ideologies and the orientation to advance national interests and accept public-sector interference. The regional factors, especially the exploitation of the resources of Lapland, have also shaped the Finnish network. Among these deeper factors one can also add the prominence of family ownership and underdeveloped capital markets. To probe these factors in greater detail would require further data and analyses.[8]

The results concerning the second and main theme can be summarized by examining table 9.4. The nature of the integrators reflects those issues which have brought the traditional institutional groups together and forged new bonds between them. Founding and/or reorganizing firms which function as integrators took place during the 1950s and 1960s. At least two of the integrators were directly instrumental in improving the competitive edge of Finnish industry in hardened international competition. All four which were excluded from the group analysis were instruments for national trade and investment policies. They were established or reorganized to provide credit to export industry and loans for small and medium-sized industry, for safeguarding long-term loans or for lending back pension funds to all firms. The other two firms of table 9.4, which were not excluded from the group analysis, reflect two common concerns of the Finnish economy: the need to exploit geographically remote resources, and Soviet trade.

This 'new' integration should not blur the fact that more traditional co-operation has existed and still exists between the institutional groups. The firms cross the group boundaries to co-operate in such areas as provision of raw material and semi-products, transportation, communication and Soviet trade. Furthermore, many large 'independent' firms which do not belong to institutional groups participate often rather intensely both in the old and new type of integration. Many of those independent firms can also act as 'minor' integrators between the institutional groups. What is, however, important to note is that the institutional groups and their major organizations, together with the state firms and administrative representation, almost completely control the functioning of the 'new' integrators and the policies one can generate using them as instruments. The meeting of the representatives of the institutional groups and of the state interests in the forums provided by the integrators has actually created a kind of 'quasi-government' for those policy areas listed above (Heiskanen, 1982).

The last comment on the quasi-government leads to a reconsideration of the role of the state and the government enterprises as they are reflected in the Finnish network of interlocking directorships. It was indicated above that the government joint stock companies and financial institutions did not form an institutional group of their own but remained fragmented, even if the line requirements were loosened considerably. This fragmentation is naturally partly technical: the data set did not include such government agencies as might have the same functions in the public economic sector as the commercial banks, central co-operatives or holding companies have in the private sector. The political and administrative appointments to the boards of the public enterprises and financial institutions are also necessarily thinly distributed because of political competition and the fact that firms and institutions belong to the jurisdiction of several different ministries. Furthermore, there seems to be a double policy concerning the government industrial joint stock companies. If they do well economically, they are given more freedom and allowed to co-operate more with private business. If they do less well or suffer crises they are taken into closer political and administrative tutelage. This naturally fragments the government group further.

The role of the government enterprises and financial institutions in shaping the new integration of the traditional institutional groups and the economy as a whole should not be underestimated because of the seeming fragmentation. The government has created new forums between public and private sectors by establishing organizations and institutions which distribute government aid or regulate investments and other business activities. Some of these forums – especially when moved from public administration to joint public–private tutelage – will develop new communicative and integrative functions and become general integrators which do not interlink only public and private sectors but which also function as new integrators *within* the private business sector. These integrators will also necessarily influence the relative importance of the different institutions and agencies which take care of the governmental industrial and economic policies. Close contacts and co-operation with private business may enhance the status of some of these institutions and agencies – and also alter their policies. These contacts and present economic depression have probably given enhanced status to the Finnish public financial institutions. To what extent this also has changed their policies is a research problem which demands more research and different data.

A last comment concerns the limits of the present analyses and interpretations. These have dealt only with the bare contours of the institutional structure of the Finnish economic sector in 1976. To give a more comprehensive picture many other issues should be taken up: the role of the independent organizations which do not belong to institutional groups, the different decision-making orientation of the firms within different institutional groups, the joint enterprises of individual private and public firms, etc. The theme and issues focused upon in this chapter have hopefully brought forth some intrinsically Finnish properties of the Finnish interlocking-directorship network and related them to the major issues of the Finnish economy.

NOTES

1 The analyses of this chapter could be related to the theoretical discussions, concerning institutional structural patterns underlying economic policies, of Inoguchi (1979) or to more specific analyses of the interface and 'transmission belt' between the public and private sectors (cf. e.g. Offe and Wiesenthal, 1978).

2 The Finnish government joint stock companies operate either in the infrastructure and primary industries or are monopolies in certain 'strategic branches' (alcohol, oil import and refinery). They are also capital intensive (value added 20 per cent of all Finnish manufacturing and only 13 per cent of all employees in manufacturing).

3 The Finnish isolates – and those firms which had only random links to the other firms – were mainly subsidiaries of foreign firms, regional companies with headquarters outside the capital and family companies in construction, civil engineering and wholesale/retail sales.

4 A more detailed analysis of the cliques the top business leaders form and of the institutional basis of these cliques indicated that there are 'external forums', i.e. business firms other than the own home organizations of the leaders, where they often meet to discuss and decide 'communal matters'. The six firms of table 9.4 were the most frequently used external forums. The analysis is reported in Heiskanen (1982).

5 'Core' is used here to refer to the kernels of institutional groups and not in the sense of the network core.

6 'Importance' in this group was measured by the firm's primary contacts within and outside the group.

7 Two of the joint members of the groups were treated in this analysis as members of those groups to whose core they belonged. The third joint member did not have any interlocks with the integrators.

8 These sectoral and ideological factors will be discussed in greater detail in the final report of the Finnish project.

10

French Interlocking Directorships: Financial and Industrial Groups

DAVID SWARTZ[1]

The May–June 1981 electoral victories of François Mitterrand and the French Socialist Party initiated the most sweeping changes in corporate organization and leadership yet witnessed in any Western capitalist country during the period since the Second World War – the most striking and certainly contested feature being the broad-scale nationalizations of the largest industrial and financial institutions in that country.

State control of major firms is of course nothing new in France; state intervention had already been well established in areas such as mining, transportation, banking and armaments prior to the Second World War. The wave of nationalizations under De Gaulle put coal, gas, electricity, Renault, Air France, SNECMA (aircraft engines), the Banque de France, the four largest savings banks and two-fifths of the insurance sector also under state ownership (Delion and Durupty, 1982, ch.2). But the 1981 nationalizations were the most far-reaching expansion of the public sector: the two largest financial groups (Paribas and Suez), the remaining largest private savings banks and five of the largest industrial groups were fully nationalized and state-majority ownership was established in several other large industrial groups (including foreign ones). Today, this gives the state virtual control over all banking and finance in France and control over one-third of the country's industrial capacity.

The French state has played an interventionist role in radically altering the economic landscape in France during the entire post-war period. The 1958 entry of France into the EEC signalled an end to a long era of economic protectionism by opening up domestic markets to foreign competition. In response, the state, through planning, a variety of advantageous fiscal and tax measures and direct negotiations between large-firm leaders and government officials – frequently of the same social and educational backgrounds – sought to encourage the development of sectoral oligopolies and monopolies ('national champions') in order to meet, through the advantages of economies of scale, the competitive challenge of foreign multinationals and, in particular to resist the *défi Américain*. This perceived 'industrial imperative', promoted by state managers and found acceptable by large-firm leaders, responded to the Gaullist design for international prestige for the Fifth Republic.

Unfettered by the lack of any anti-trust tradition, such as found in the USA, the French state openly and actively encouraged corporate concentration and centralization, thereby contributing to the highest rate of mergers in Europe during the post-war period (Venturini, 1971). The number of mergers and absorptions among large firms in France far surpassed any similar trends in other capitalist countries: an average of 66 per year among the 500 largest firms and 229 per year among the 1,594 largest firms during the 1966–69 period (Jenny and Weber, 1974). Because of a long tradition of debt-, rather than equity-, financing of firm investment, the state was the primary source of French private investment (Dyas and Thanheiser, 1976). Private-firm leaders actively sought government support for investment major plans. An unquestioned article of faith of corporate leaders and state managers at the time was that big business meant unequivocally better business and a better France.

As a result, the number of large firms grew in technologically advanced sectors, such as electronic equipment and computers. They increasingly diversified their product lines and they moved rapidly into mass-consumer markets. New industries appeared on the list of the 100 largest firms in France: six firms that processed or produced petroleum, including Elf-Aquitaine and Compagnie Française des Pétroles, appeared among the top 25; L'Oréal and Roussel-Uclaf, producers of toilet articles and pharmaceuticals, and Céments Lafarge, producer of building materials, also appeared (Lévy-Leboyer, 1980). Furthermore, much of the growth in firm size increased and consolidated the strength of several large financial and industrial holding companies, such as Paribas and Péchiney-Ugine-Kuhlmann.

The study of corporate power structure in France must focus on the large financial and industrial ownership groups that have come to characterize the top end of the firm hierarchy in the country.[2] Characteristic of corporate ownership and organizational patterns throughout the century, these groups were originally created to respond to the relative lack of development of capital markets and banking facilities (Lévy-Leboyer, 1980). But it was only during the 1960s that their development accelerated considerably.[3] By the early 1970s, 18 of the largest industrial groups in France produced 11 per cent of the total value added in manufacturing, employed 11 per cent of the labour force and were responsible for 23 per cent of French exports (De Vannoise, 1977). Some financial groups, such as Paribas, Suez, Crédit Commercial de France and Lazard, concentrated their activities in banking; others, such as Empain-Schneider and Rothschild, had a relatively greater proportion of their activities in industry; and still other groups, such as Rhône-Poulenc, De Wendel and Péchiney-Ugine-Kuhlmann, had their bases in industry rather than in finance (Gilly and Morin, 1981, pp. 47ff.).

The large firms diversified their product lines and in many cases shifted their organizational form from functional to multidivisional units, thereby bringing the structure and strategy of many large French corporations in line with that of other capitalist countries.[4] However, the organizational form favoured by many French ownership groups has remained the holding company, which frequently links large industrial and financial concerns and has historically been the organizational structure adopted to obtain capital and to finance investment in an environment where banking and capital markets were inadequately developed. It has also been an organizational mechanism for owning families to consolidate and retain their vested interests in a rapidly changing economic environment.[5] This has, in many cases, taken the form of complex exchanges of shareholdings between holding companies and their subsidiaries and between different holding companies. Of considerable interest in the study of interlocks is the question of the extent to which shared directorships reflect the ownership patterns of corporate groups.

THE INTERLOCK NETWORK: A SEGMENTED STRUCTURE

Of the 250 large firms (200 industrials and 50 financials) in the 1977 data[6], 220 were tied by a variety of interlock patterns into a single large component. This component contained 1,065 interlocks but its density was only 0.04. The comparative analysis in chapter 2 shows that there was a low level of centralization in the French network, both in terms of all interlocks and primary interlocks. Thirty firms were not tied into the national network and another 39 were without primary interlocks. Half of these 69 companies were smaller, family-owned industrials, though several were foreign subsidiaries and state-owned corporations. They were distributed fairly evenly over more than 15 industrial branches.[7]

A key issue in the study of intercorporate organization is whether there is a core group of firms – the apex of the corporate order – that, because of their close connections, are well positioned to exercise a powerful influence over corporate life. This question was first add-ressed by determining the network centre through selecting the maximal subset of central corporations at distance 2. This procedure yielded a comparatively small centre of 15 corporations with a comparatively low density of 0.45. If the interconnections between the 15 firms are examined, the result is not a network centre but the outline of a corporate-group structure. Confining the analysis to primary interlocks in the centre, the largest financial company in France, Paribas, interlocked with nine of the other 14 firms and in five cases this involved an exchange of inside directors. One other firm from the centre, Crédit du Nord, interlocked with three other firms in the centre but Paribas held majority ownership of this bank through a separate holding company. These findings indicate that although the overall interlock network in France was not highly integrated or centralized, interlocking-directorship patterns were linked to the largest financial group in France. The other major financial centre in France, Suez, also appeared in the network centre but with connections to only one other centre firm, suggesting the possibility that interlock patterns may follow the contours of major ownership group structures. If relatively independent, these might show patterns of integration at the group level rather than at the national level. An analytical strategy for exploring this possibility is provided by the search for N-cliques.

Clique analysis of primary interlocks for the entire sample revealed two large clusters of firms and several smaller clusters (see figure 10.1). There were 25 2-cliques with eight or more corporations and 14 of these cliques formed stars – cliques held together by ties to one central corporation. Table 10.1 shows that two stars were appreciably larger than the rest. The largest star, of 19 firms, was organized around the largest financial holding company in France, Paribas, and the second-largest star, with 16 firms, was organized around Suez, the second-largest financial holding company. Three of the other star centres were also financials, though one of these was the Crédit du Nord bank, which was majority-owned by Paribas. A second bank, Crédit Commercial de France, had diverse ownership interests and the third, Banque Worms, was under family ownership and control. Chargeurs Réunis had substantial financial activities characteristic of financial companies as well as its industrial activities (Bellon, 1980, p. 56). Moreover, it was tied to the Lazard financial group that held 20 per cent of the equity; the Fabre family held another 33 per cent.

Among the star centres were also the key holding companies of some of the largest industrial groups in France, such as Compagnie Générale d'Electricité, Péchiney-Ugine-Kuhlmann and Saint-Gobain Pont-à-Mousson. But there were also a few of the principal industrial subsidiaries of financial groups, such as Merlin Gérin, the producer of

Figure 10.1 Suez and Paribas cliques and star centres in France

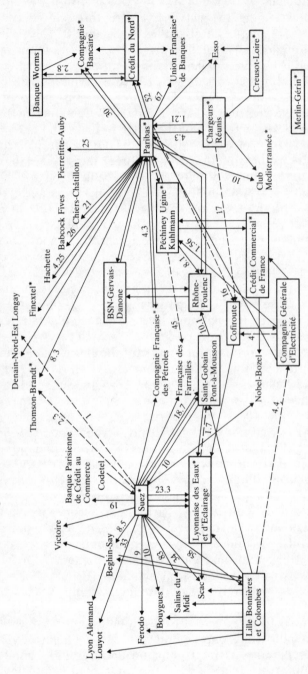

Note: Rectangles indicate forms that are centres of stars with eight or more firms. Asterisks identify firms that are also in the network centre. Arrows indicate direction of primary lines and numbers represent accompanying ownership interest. Broken arrows with numbers represent ownership interests between firms that are not interlocked.

electrical equipment and subsidiary of the Empain-Schneider group, and Lille Bonnières Colombes, an industrial subsidiary of Suez.

Seven of the stars were organized around corporations included in the network centre, yet themselves interlocked very little. Only five out of the 21 possible pairs of these seven firms were interlocked through primary lines and three of these pairs involved interlocks with only Paribas. Most of the firms that were members of the network centre as well as star centres fell within the broad cluster of firms situated around Paribas. More generally, all of the central firms of the 14 cliques that formed stars were only very sparsely interconnected. The second column of table 10.1 shows that while Paribas, Compagnie Générale d'Electricité and Lyonnaise des Eaux et d' Eclairage each interlocked with four other star centres, Merlin Gérin held no such interlocks and Banque Worms and Creusot-Loire each interlocked with only one other star centre. An examination of the 91 possible pairs of the 14 star centres shows that only 17 pairs involved a primary interlock – and seven of these involved either Paribas or Suez. Figure 10.1 shows that the firms that were star centres distributed into two clusters of firms centered around Paribas and Suez. Yet, Paribas and Suez did not interlock, nor were they connected through one of the other star centres.

By taking into account ownership ties as well, the dominant positions of Paribas and Suez were even more striking. Paribas sent two inside directors to the board of Crédit du Nord and at the same time held majority ownership in that bank through an intermediate holding company. Primary interlocks and ownership ties tightly knit Saint-Gobain Pont-à-Mousson, Lyonnaise des Eaux et d'Eclairage and Lille Bonnières Colombes to Suez. Suez owned 58 per cent of the equity of Lille Bonnières Colombes and held a significant minority ownership position in Saint-Gobain Pont-à-Mousson (18.7 per cent), with which it exchanged inside directors. Suez also controlled 22.3 per cent of Lyonnaise des Eaux et d'Eclairage, to which it sent three inside directors. If on the basis of directorship and substantial ownership ties, Lille Bonnières Colombes and Lyonnaise des Eaux et d'Eclairage are considered as key units of the Suez group and Crédit du Nord a key unit of the Paribas group, then only five of the 17 connected pairs of star centres were actually outside of the Paribas and Suez ownership groups. The third column in table 10.1 shows a significant decrease in the number of primary interlocks between star centres if these ownership-group factors are taken into account. Moreover, separate analysis revealed that star members, organized around corporations that were connected to the Paribas and Suez holdings through significant ownership ties, tended not to interlock with other star centres: 75 per cent of the members of the Lille Bonnières Colombes,

*Table 10.1 2-cliques (minimum size 8) of primary interlocks
that form stars in France*

Star nuclei	Size of stars	Number of other star nuclei interlocked with this nucleus	Number of other star nuclei outside of Paribas and Suez groups interlocked with this nucleus[b]	Number of firms in clique without ties to other star nuclei (N=58)
Paribas[a]	19	4	2	7
Suez[a]	16	3	0	4
Credit du Nord[a]	12	2	1	6
Lille Bonnières Colombes	12	3	0	3
Chargeurs Réunies[a]	11	2	1	6
Crédit Commercial de France[ac]	10	2	2	4
Saint-Gobain Pont-à-Mousson	8	3	0	3
Lyonnaise des Eaux et d'Eclairage[a]	8	4	1	1
Companie Générale d'Electricité	8	4	3	2
Péchiney-Ugine-Kuhlmann[a]	8	3	2	2
Creusot-Loire[c]	8	1	1	5
Cofiroute	8	2	1	3
Banque Worms	8	1	0	4
Merlin Gérin[c]	8	0	0	8

Notes:

a In network centre

b Takes into account ownership ties that linked Crédit du Nord to Paribas and Saint-Gobain-Pont-à-Mousson, Lille Bonnières Colombes and Lyonnaise des Eaux et d'Eclairage to Suez.

c Star nuclei that did not hold primary interlocks with the Paribas and Suez ownership groups.

Saint-Gobain Pont-à-Mousson, Lyonnaise des Eaux et d'Eclairage and Crédit du Nord cliques held no ties to other star centres.

A consideration of the overlap between stars emphasizes the segmented character of these network ties. The fourth column of table 10.1 shows that 58 (23 per cent) of all firms in the data set had primary interlocks with only one star centre. The cliques varied, however, in degree of overlap. None of the eight firms in the Merlin Gérin clique interlocked with any of the other star centres, whereas all but one of the eight firms in the Lyonnaise des Eaux et d'Eclairage did. While seven (37 per cent) of the firms in the Paribas clique held no primary interlocks with other star centres, only four (25 per cent) of the firms in the Suez clique held no such ties. Figure 10.1 shows that this difference occurs because virtually all of the firms in the Suez clique that were tied to star centres interlocked with those that were also units of the Suez ownership group.

Some cliques, on the other hand, were situated at the intersection of other cliques. The fourth column of table 10.1 indicates a relatively greater degree of interconnection between members of the stars organized around Compagnie Générale d'Electricité, Péchiney-Ugine-Kuhlmann and Cofiroute. Only two or three members of each of these cliques were without interlocks with other star centres. Chargeurs Réunis, for example, had interlocks with two star centres, Paribas and Creusot-Loire, and these were reinforced by similar interlocks held by two of its clique members. Compagnie Générale d' Electriciié interlocked with four other star centres as did several of its clique members. Some cliques, however, such as those organized around Banque Worms, Creusot-Loire and especially Merlin Gérin, appear to have been relatively isolated from the other clusters and in particular from the Suez group. Creusot-Loire and Merlin Gérin were connected through ownership to the Empain-Schneider financial group.

It is noteworthy that several important financial and industrial groups in France did not appear as pivotal firms in the interlock structure. Several tightly controlled centres of private capital, such as the Rothschild financial group, Dassault aeronautics and Michelin tyres, did not interlock extensively with other groups. Neither Dassault nor Michelin held any primary interlocks with other firms in the sample and the Banque Rothschild held only five.[8]

Emerging from this brief consideration of interlocks and the related ownership ties is an image of intercorporate relations in France that points to a segmented structure in the French interlock system. There were, first of all, two large 2-cliques organized around the two financial holding companies, Paribas and Suez. Second, because of ownership ties and overlapping directorship ties, these two holding companies represented centres of corporate ownership groups. Third, from these two groups, particularly Paribas, radiated larger spheres of influence that involved other large industrial groups, through interlocking shareholdings and especially directorships. And fourth, there were several smaller groups that appeared to be relatively independent of the two principal financial groups.

Underlying these distinctions are the concepts of 'ownership groups' and 'constellations' or 'spheres of influence' that are useful in classifying the patterns of intercorporate relations in France. Owner-ship groups refer to centres of corporate power that aim for control and co-ordination of the various subunits through substantial owner-ship (in many cases majority-control), the selection of directors and top management and the formulation and choice of long-range cor-porate strategy (Herman, 1981; Sweezy, 1953). Constellations or spheres of influence refer to interlocking patterns of ownership and directorships for the purposes of investment and communication ra-ther than control and co-ordination (Scott, 1979, p. 42).[9]

These patterns suggest, therefore, that though France may have been without a unified centre in its corporate interlock network, there was evidence of relatively autonomous clusters of interlocking cor-porations organized around two principal financial centres and around a few smaller financial and industrial ownership groups. The N-clique analysis of primary interlocks reveals several stars that were organized around major financial and industrial holding companies that were widely recognized, both in the business press and research literature, as having been centres of ownership groups and broader constellations of interests (Allard et al., 1978; Bellon, 1980; Bertrand et al., 1981; De Vannoise, 1977; Gilly and Morin, 1981). Moreover, clique analysis brings into relief what was not apparent from the analysis of the network centre; namely, the existence of the Suez group.

These results generate support, therefore, for the idea that corporate ownership groups and their broader spheres of influence, rather than individual firms or aggregate network structures, represent the appro-priate unit of analysis for the study of corporate structure in France. The results also muster some support for a finance-capital theory of intercorporate relations, since the two largest groups, Suez and especially Paribas, were rooted in banking and finance and were joined by three other major financial groups, Crédit Commercial de France, Banque Worms and Empain-Schneider through Merlin Gérin and Creusot-Loire. Within their distinct network clusters, the majority of primary interlocks linked core financial holding companies to indus-trial corporations. Banking and investment companies, therefore, were clearly key organizing pivots for substantial segments of the interlock network. However, this was not the case entirely: several large industrial groups, such as Compagnie Générale d'Electricité and Péchiney-Ugine-Kuhlmann, were also prominent centres of inter-corporate organization through interlocks.

PARIBAS AND SUEZ: TWO CENTRES OF PRIVATE CAPITAL

The Paribas and Suez groups were clearly the two principal centres of interlock and ownership power in France. Both were organized around principal holding companies, both pursued a wide range of activities in banking and finance, both held major investments in industry and both functioned as centres of broader constellations of ownership interest. Differences in historical origins, organizational and control structures and corporate strategy, however, sharply distinguished the two groups and undoubtedly heightened competitive relations between them (Allard et al., 1978; Aron, 1959; Bellon, 1980; Claude, 1969; Morin, 1974; Sagou, 1981).

Founded in 1872, the Banque de Paris et des Pays-Bas quickly established itself as a major commercial bank with broad connections in public as well as private finance and with major ownership interests in industry even prior to the First World War. Reorganization in 1968 placed the locus of ultimate control of the group in the holding company Compagnie Financière de Paribas and assigned to the restructured Banque de Paris et des Pays-Bas and six other intermediate holdings the tasks of co-ordinating the diverse range of financial activities of the group (Sagou, 1981).

The historical antecedents of Suez stem from the building and administration of the Suez Canal. But the origins of Suez as a financial group actually begin in 1956 with the task of recycling capital received from the indemnities paid by Egypt following the nationalization of the canal. As late as 1956 the British Government held 44 per cent of the equity in Suez, though by the mid 1970s this ownership interest dropped to 7.6 per cent when an exchange of shareholdings between Suez and Saint-Gobain Pont-à-Mousson gave the latter a ten per cent ownership interest in the former and shifted the locus of control from London to the principal holding company. In addition, the INA Corporation of the USA held seven per cent. By contrast, Paribas had no dominant shareholders with more than seven per cent of its equity.[10]

These differences in origins and ownership quite likely contributed to the development of a more centralized structure of control within the Suez group than within the Paribas group and to differences in the investment strategies pursued by the two groups (Bellon, 1980; Morin, 1974). In the mid 1970s, the Suez holding employed 200 salaried personnel, whereas the Paribas holding employed only three. Paribas delegated the tasks of control over operations and many of the important investment decisions to its intermediate holding companies. In terms of investment strategy, Suez appeared to pursue one of 'control' by concentrating its investments in specific firms and in selected sectors, whereas Paribas pursued one of 'influence' by diversifying its portfolio across a wide range of firms and sectors. Examination of interlock data shows that these differences in degree of centralization as well as separateness of the two groups were reflected in their respective interlock patterns.

Figure 10.1 shows there was only one firm, Compagnie Française des Pétroles, with which both Suez and Paribas had primary interlocks. The chief executives of both financial centres were on the board of this second-largest industrial firm in France in which the French government held 35 per cent of the equity and Paribas held another 4.3 per cent. Clearly then, these two holding companies were separate in terms of directorship ties. Moreover, this appears to have been largely the case for the affiliated corporations within their respective cliques. Although 12 of the 19 corporations of the Paribas star had primary interlocks with other star centres, only one (Rhône-Poulenc) connected with another corporation (Saint-Gobain-Pont-à-Mousson) that was closely affiliated to Suez. Thus, not only the centres of these two stars but also their members appear to have represented two quite distinct cliques of affiliated corporations.

Both cliques corresponded to the type of network structure that one would expect to find in a finance-capital model of corporate interlocks, since primary interlocks connected key financial companies to industrial firms. But from the standpoint of both the directionality and multiplicity of the primary interlocks, as well as ownership ties, the internal structures of the two cliques appear quite different. Comparison of the *intra*clique interlock patterns in figure 10.1 suggests there was a more centralized structure in the Suez clique than in the Paribas network. The Suez holding tended to send out directors but receive few; it sent 17 inside directors to firms within its clique but received only one. The Paribas holding sent 20 inside directors to firms within its clique but also received six from six different firms. Five of these cases involved director exchanges with large industrial groups, such as Péchiney-Ugine-Kuhlmann, Rhône-Poulenc and Compagnie Française des Pétroles, with which Paribas had only small or no ownership interests. Yet Paribas had played a decisive role in the development and growth of these same groups (Sagou, 1981, p. 58).[11]

Furthermore, multiple-director ties gave the Suez clique a substantially greater degree of integration. Multiple ties closely linked Saint-Gobain Pont-à-Mousson and Lyonnaise des Eaux et d'Eclairage to the Suez holding; moreover, many of the intraclique ties with the principal holding were paralleled by ties stemming from Lille Bonnières Colombes, which was majority owned by Suez and which itself sent out eight inside directors to other firms within the clique but received only two.

The primary interlocks maintained by both financial centres tended to parallel ownership connections, though this appears to have been more the case for Suez than for Paribas. Both centres held majority ownership interests in two corporations and substantial minority interests (over 20 per cent) in four or more of the corporations in their respective stars. The blocks of equity held by Suez tended, however, to be somewhat larger. The median percentage of equity held by Suez in ten firms was 21 per cent, whereas it was only ten per cent for the 13 firms in which Paribas had ownership interests. Paribas exchanged directors with five corporations and had primary interlocks with six additional corporations where it had less than five per cent ownership interests. Suez exchanged directors with only Saint-Gobain-Pont-à-Mousson and had primary ties with only four firms in which it did not also have significant ownership interests.[12] This suggests, as some previous research discovered (Bellon, 1980), that the Paribas group was a more loosely knit network than that of Suez.

The patterns suggest that if the magnitude of ownership ties as well as the direction and multiplicity of interlocks are taken into account, then each of these stars can be subdivided into a small number of corporations. These are centered around a key financial holding, that would appear to be linked by the degree of ownership and leadership control suggested by the concept of an ownership group and, at the same time, a broader array of several corporations that would seem to indicate larger spheres of influence radiating from each of the group centres.

PRIVATE GROUPS AND THE PUBLIC SECTOR

Because of the post-war nationalizations and the interventionist role played by the French state in promoting the concentration and restructuring of the corporate sector, one might expect to find state-owned firms to be well connected to the private financial and industrial groups. The data set included 45 firms with five per cent or more state-ownership, though six were isolated from the national network and 22 had no primary interlocks. Clique analysis revealed no single firm or group of firms from which radiated a significant number of directorship ties. The most interconnected firm, Société Nationale des Chemins de Fer, had only eight lines and only two primary interlocks. Moreover, neither majority- nor minority-ownership control by the state appeared in any of the 14 star centres.

Inspection of the interlocks of the 12 most important nationalized industrials and financials showed there to be only 24 lines and only nine primary interlocks connecting them to the 20 largest private industrial groups in France. Only two primary interlocks existed between the 12 state firms and the star centres.

These patterns suggest that to the extent that the French state has given direction to the French corporate economy, it has not been – at least until the advent of the new Socialist government and the ensuing nationalizations – through communication networks provided by the corporate practice of shared directorships. Rather, influence has, as pointed out by several observers (Dyas and Thanheiser, 1976; McArthur and Scott, 1969; Shonfield, 1965; Suleiman, 1978), been expressed through tax and credit policies and direct negotiation between top firm heads and senior civil servants. The Socialist government's attempt to exercise control in the boardroom, in light of the above evidence, therefore appears to be a novel effort.

CONCLUSION

This investigation of interlock network patterns in France demonstrates that, despite the merger movement and considerable growth in corporate concentration during the 1960s and 1970s, French capital was *not* highly integrated and centralized around a network centre; rather, it was organized around a few ownership interest groups and their corresponding spheres of influence. Since state-owned firms held few ties with these groups, the important role frequently assigned to the French state in directing the course of the French economy during the post-war period must be tempered in view of the organizational capacity of private capital, through ownership and shared directorships, to operate within the private arena.

The analysis in the chapter further shows that the source of much intercorporate interlocking came from private finance, providing some support for a finance-capital interpretation of intercorporate linkages in France. Finally, the analysis emphasizes the considerable scope and complexity of intercorporate shareholding and directorship ties that characterized the largest and most influential financial groups, Paribas and Suez. Thus, there was considerable logic to the strategy of the Left government in France, a strategy that included full nationalization of these two key centres of private financial power.

NOTES

1 I wish to thank all the contributors to this volume for their helpful comments on an earlier version of this chapter. I am especially grateful to Frans Stokman and Frans Wasseur for their patient efforts in introducing me to GRADAP, to Beth Mintz for giving me some key pointers in analysing cliques, to Herlinda Cancino for preparing the graphics in figure 10.1 and to John Scott for his editorial work. Michael P. Allen of Washington State University kindly made available an initial data set of the 230 largest French corporations and their directors. The generous

efforts of Anne de Beauregard and her colleagues at the Commission des Opérations de Bourse proved most helpful in gathering the additional firm data. And conversations with Patrick Allard alerted me to several important sources of ownership connections within the largest financial and industrial groups in France.

2   The exact definition offered by French observers of groups is a little fluid and boundaries, especially the actual degree of control of member firms and impact on firm performance, remain open to debate (Bellon, 1977, 1980). But the general idea of relatively autonomous centres of corporate power that consist of clusters of firms that frequently link financial and industrial capital and are to various degrees co-ordinated by ownership and board-director ties through a focal organization (usually a holding company) has been adequately documented by researchers and resonates in the business press.

3   In 1966 alone, Elf-Aquitaine, the third largest group in France, took form in the public sector; the private sector witnessed the formation of Thomson-Brandt, the absorption of Souchon-Neuvesel by Boussois and several major absorptions and mergers in steel with the largest one leading to the creation of Usinor DNEL. In 1968, the merger of Sidélor and De Wendel placed this enterprise within the ranks of the largest ten corporations in France (Gilly and Morin, 1981; Bertrand et al., 1981).

4   Dyas and Thanheiser (1976, p. 187) found that by 1970, 54 of the 100 largest industrial corporations in France had adopted multidivisional units and 52 had started to pursue diversified strategies. These figures overestimate, however, the extent of this transition since the study did not include state-owned firms or a few of the largest industrial groups, such as Denain-Nord-Est Longway, whose basic activities were seen as ownership or banking rather than industrial production.

5   One study estimates that 222 (44 per cent) of the 500 largest industrial firms in France during the mid 1970s were under family-ownership control, 117 (23 per cent) were foreign-owned, 62 (12 per cent) were owned by the French state, and 79 (16 per cent) were classified as being under 'technocratic' control – a category designating those firms characterized by institutional shareownership (Morin et al., 1977, p. 38).

As in other capitalist countries, intercorporate shareholdings had become increasingly pronounced among the large French firms. Whether substantial interlocking shareholdings among the large firms gave them a purely managerial and technocratic orientation, however, was open to question. Allard et al. (1978, p. 18) argued that the alleged technocratic character of such firms was a myth, since behind an apparent managerial or technocratic ownership structure stood a 'financial oligarchy' represented among top management and on boards. Indeed, in their examination of the composition of the boards of Denain-Nord-Est Longway, Péchiney-Ugine-Kuhlmann and Compagnie Générale d'Electricité – three apparently management-controlled groups – Allard et al. found members of old, established ownership families.

6   The selection of the industrial as well as financial firms was based on assets rather than turnover and for 1977 rather than 1976. Firm names, their sector and their rank were drawn from the November 1978 listing of the largest corporations in France provided by the *Le Nouvel Economiste*. The names of chief executive officers, board chairmen and members were drawn in large part from the *Annuaire Desfossés-SEF* (1978), which lists all the major public companies in France. Some information on firms and directors was gathered directly from annual reports. The ownership data was taken from the following sources: Allard et al.(1978), Morin et al.(1977) and *Les Liaisons Financières en France*.

7   This actually underestimates the number of isolates from the network since several large foreign subsidiaries were not included in the data set because of lack of adequate information for the analysis. Examination of several individual cases of this type of firm shows they tended not to interlock with French firms.

8   Separate analysis of all lines as well as just primary lines between the star centres generated support for the observations.

9   Spheres of influence should not be confused with manangement control since they imply sufficient concentration of shareholdings or dependency on credit and markets that management is constrained by vested interests. Ownership groups, on the other hand, should not be construed to necessarily imply a tightly knit and highly centralized control structure that leaves little latitude for any managerial discretion at the level of the subunits.

10   The French state, through the Caisse des Dépots et Consignations and the Union des Assurances de Paris, held about seven per cent of the equity of each holding, though this ownership interest does not appear to have significantly affected either the structure or the strategy of either group.

11   Figure 10.1 actually underestimates to some extent the number of interlocks within the Suez clique and especially within the Paribas clique, since it does not include several intermediate financial holdings organized around the two principal holding companies. Selection of only firms with the largest assets in France did not lead to the inclusion of these firms. Separate analysis, however, revealed that Indosuez and Suez International for the Suez group and Omnium de Participations Financières de Paris et des Pays-Bas, Banque de Paris et des Pays-Bas, Omnium de Participations Financières et Industrielles and Paribas International were interlocked among themselves and with the principal holding companies and a few other firms in their respective cliques.

12   In this regard, it is noteworthy that in the case of Paribas, two industrial groups, Poliet-Chausson and Société Commerciale de l'Ouest Africain, which on the basis of substantial minority ownership ties (25 per cent or more) should be considered part of the Paribas group, did not appear within the Paribas interlock network.

11

Property, Capital and Network Structure in Italy

ANTONIO M. CHIESI[1]

This chapter presents an analysis of the Italian network and tries to give a theoretical interpretation to the specific characteristics of the Italian case. Although a general description of the network is given, the discussion is mainly focused on the implications of the presence of two different centres in the network. This finding differs from the results found for other countries in the available literature on interlocking directorships (Fennema and Schijf, 1979) and can be explained in terms of the mode of state intervention in the economy.

HISTORICAL BACKGROUND

Modern capitalism has experienced two important changes in the ownership of the means of production: the increasing intervention of the state in the economy and the increasing internationalization of capital. In general, state intervention has been seen either as a powerful tool of economic development in the industrialization of backward economies (Gerschenkron, 1962) or as a modernizing factor capable of overcoming bottle-necks in national industries. In the Italian case, state intervention in economic activities goes back to the birth of the unified kingdom (Cianci, 1977) when the government ran, directly or through specific bodies, economic activities related to war and defence, such as arsenals. With the increasing national organization of the country these activities were added to by state control of the Post Office and the railways. State intervention was also very important in non-monopolistic sectors from the beginning of industrialization at the end of the nineteenth century and became prevalent in credit and in heavy industry during the Fascist period (Holland, 1972; Grifone, 1971). After the Second World War the state progressively increased its control over the energy and communication sectors. This process culminated in the nationalization of the electricity-supply companies. During the 1970s the increase in state intervention has mainly been due to financial operations in order to rescue collapsing firms, confront unemployment or gain political consent (Maraffi, 1980). In 1973, public firms in various sectors accounted for the following percentages of gross output: energy 100 per cent, mining 53 per cent, metals 49 per cent, mechanics 10 per cent, transport 26 per cent, chemical 9 per cent and communications 100 per cent (Martinelli, 1981).

It is hypothesized that the intervention of the state in the economy affects the structure of the network from both a quantitative and a qualitative point of view. If the Italian case is seen as an instance of heavier state intervention, compared with other European economies, it can be supposed that the directorships and the interlocks carried by directors in the public sector are more important than in other nations. An additional hypothesis about the position of the state corporations in the network can be put forward. A central position does not depend only on the importance of the economic sectors run by the state-owned corporations but also on the legal devices that have been applied in order to exert economic control. Two interesting examples in Italy can be quoted as evidence of this hypothesis: the structural consequences at the network level of the nationalization process and the effects of the introduction of the shareholding formula.

The electrical-energy sector is a state monopoly which has important relations with the rest of the economy (i.e. through energy supply to other sectors). When this sector was nationalized in 1962 there was a debate about whether to create a public authority directly dependent on the Ministry of Industry or to control the sector through the already-existing state shareholding formula.[2] The first alternative was chosen and the result was that the once-central private electricity corporations disappeared from the network of interlocking directorships. In fact the 1976 study revealed that nationalization had made a single isolated point (ENEL, *Ente Nazionale per l'Energia Elettrica*) with no interlocks with other boards from a group of highly connected points[3] with extensive connections to the rest of the network.

The state shareholding formula was introduced during the Fascist period in order to confront the general problems in the years after the 1929 crisis. It was apparently a compromise between an economic need for state intervention to resolve the financial problems of the crisis and a political requirement to retain the concept of private property and the free market, for which the regime received the support of the business class. The shareholding formula was 'conceived as a mixture of responsiveness both to the inputs coming from the political system and the stimuli of the market' (Maraffi, 1980, p. 520). The state shareholding formula is hierarchically structured as follows. A public holding company is at the top of the system and is entirely owned by the state; it is controlled directly by the Ministry of Industry and it is subject to public law. The public holding company owns an amount of shares of joint stock companies, not necessarily the majority. This can be done directly or via subholdings that co-ordinate the activities in a specific economic sector. These companies operate in the market according to commercial law, like any kind of privately owned firms (Saraceno, 1956). Moreover, the fact that the state can own different percentages of the total shares fosters the creation of interlocks and joint ventures between private and public sectors.

THE STRUCTURE OF THE ITALIAN NETWORK OF INTERLOCKING DIRECTORSHIPS

Although the Italian network was selected according to the general criteria set up for the project, some modifications had to be made because of the specific features of the Italian economic structure. This was primarily because of the legal devices by which state intervention in the economy is exerted. Ultimate financial control of the state economic sector is always found in the ministries or the government itself but they can exert only little control over the policy of the state-owned companies. For this reason it was decided to take into account the state holding companies and to consider them as having ultimate financial control over state-owned corporations.

In the data set it is possible to distinguish six different legal structures among the firms: 226 joint stock companies, two co-opera-tives, two savings banks, ten public economic institutions, five state holding companies and two departmental agencies. Joint stock companies have mainly the same legal status in Italy as in other European countries and in 1976 in Italy it was still possible for a company to own a limited amount of its own shares and to own shares of the parent company. In the co-operative banks shares are owned by a great number of shareholders, each of which has only one vote no matter how many shares are owned. Savings banks are public institu-tions founded in the nineteenth century in order to aid the growth of savings among the people. Their chairmen and vice-chairmen are appointed by the Ministry of Industry and sometimes also by the Chancellor of the Exchequer. The state holding companies are con-trolled by the Ministry of State Participations, their chairmen are appointed by the government and their aim is to manage joint stock companies under state control. The departmental agencies were for-merly private joint stock companies; they are the State Railways Authority, which depends on the Ministry of Transport, and ENEL, which depends on the Ministry of Industry.

In general these different types of legal structure are based on three types of governing bodies:

(1) the assembly of the shareholders which has legal authority for appointing the two following bodies and for deciding on the proposals of the first board;

(2) the first board (Consiglio d'amministrazione) which is the executive body of the assembly of the shareholders (administrative power belongs jointly to its members but executive power is usually delegated to one or a few of them [delegato]); and

(3) the second board (Collegio sindacale), whose members (sindaci) are also appointed by the assembly of the shareholders and cannot be dismissed during their period of office (their duty is to exercise control and supervision over the management of the company, to monitor the decisions taken by the first board and to take administrative decisions if the first board fails in its duties).

The second board is legally responsible, jointly with the first board, for the decisions taken by the first board itself. The number of the second-board members is set by law and some of them must belong to the special list of the Revisori Ufficiali dei Conti edited by the Ministry of Justice. Although there is a formal structure of two boards in Italy, the board system is different from other two-board systems because the different legal functions carried on by the second board do not coincide with those of the supervisory board in the German system. The sindaci have only to certify the correctness of the accounting practices and they exert a more general and public function than the supervisory-board members in other countries. In practice they are not managers but professional bookkeepers at a high level.

As a result of these particular functions, the analysis of the two boards showed completely different structures.[4] The second boards were formed into a very loose network in which the same number of corporations was connected with fewer interlocks. While the network of the first board had a centre of 21 companies, the network of the second board had no centre at all. Moreover, an examination of companies that had many contacts, showed that only two of the first 15 companies in the first-board network were also in the second-board network. Only ten companies out of the first 30 were common to both networks. As further evidence, it can be seen that the two boards interlocked only in a limited number of cases. Only 184 out of the total 2,082, i.e. (9 per cent) were interboard interlocks.[5] For this reason it would be misleading to make an overall analysis of the whole network. The network of the two boards together would in fact make it impossible to distinguish the separate networks that seldom connect. The network of the first board showed a definite centre and a hierarchical structure, while the network of the second board was not only looser but had no centre. This is due to the limited importance of the second board in the Italian corporate system.

In the first-board network only 322 persons out of 2,358 were multiple directors (14 per cent). Two-hundred-and-three of them held only two positions in different boards. Forty-one of them had five or more positions and only four persons held ten or more positions. These four formed 309 interlocks. The 43 who held five or more positions created 895 interlocks. The multiple directors were a small minority of the total directors and among them a tiny group formed a large number of interlocks. In the second-board network 158 were multiple directors out of 1,047 people (15 per cent), with only 13 of them holding five or more positions. Therefore the proportion of multiple directors in the second-board network tended to be slightly higher, compared with the first board, but the former did not hold many positions. From the data we can see what functions are more likely to interlock. This is important in order to distinguish full-time from part-time directors. In the first board the most frequent position was consigliere (50 per cent of the total 3,410 positions), followed by presidente and vice-presidente. Next are the different delegato functions, i.e. the directors to whom the other board members delegate managing power. Sixty-three directors held two different positions in the same board. They were presidente or vice-presidente and delegato at the same time. All the delegato functions tended to be full time in one corporation only, while the likelihood of a presidente or consigliere being a multiple director was about two times higher. Because the network of the second board did not show a centre, it was decided to concentrate attention on the first-board network.

THE STRUCTURE OF THE NETWORK ACCORDING TO THE TYPE OF PROPERTY

To investigate the hypothesis presented above, the companies were divided into four different groups: 76 state-owned companies (50 per cent plus one share owned by the state), 49 foreign companies (50 per cent plus one share owned by foreign multinationals), 66 private companies (shares owned neither by the state nor by foreign multi-nationals) and 27 so-called 'mixed' companies (various owners, none of which owned the majority of the shares). Twenty-nine companies could not be assigned to one of the above groups because of missing data on ownership and have been omitted from the analysis.

Table 11.1   Density by ownership in Italy

	State	Foreign	Private	Mixed
State	0.120			
Foreign	0.005	0.005		
Private	0.016	0.009	0.049	
Mixed	0.056	0.012	0.034	0.037

The densities in table 11.1 show that state-owned companies, beside being the most numerous, were the most interlocked among themselves. This was mainly due to the fact that state control was mainly exercised by ministries through the state holding companies and the ultimate financial control of most of them was through the Ministry of State Shareholding. The lowest density was found among the foreign companies because they were subsidiaries of multinationals whose headquarters were abroad. The mixed group of companies showed the highest values for bipartite densities, especially with the state companies. One of these companies was a joint venture between state and private corporations (Aeritalia), others (Montedison and Snia Viscosa, both belonging to the chemical sector) had been in the centre of the political debate about the opportunity to balance state control with private property in the chemical sector.

Two different centres can be identified, based on state- and privately owned corporations. The starting point of the analysis is the identification of the overall centre, a centre only for state companies, and a private centre. The state centre consisted of a set of 22 companies. For the private companies a set of 14 points was found. These general results can be seen in figure 11.1 in matrix form. In each column and row are three groups of companies. The companies that belong to the state centre have been divided into state A (companies belonging to the state centre but not to the general centre) and state B (companies that belong both to the state centre and to the general centre). The companies belonging to the general centre have been divided into state B, other (i.e. companies belonging to the general centre but neither to the state nor the private centre) and private A (companies belonging both to the general and private centre). The companies that belong to the private centre have been divided into private A and private B (companies belonging to the private centre but not to the general centre).

Figure 11.1 General, state and private centres in Italy

```
 1. State A                                    State centre
                                               D(12,12)=0.65
 1. Credito Italiano       1
 2. Italcantieri           . 2
 3. Alsaldo Generale       . x 3
 4. Banco di Roma          x . . 4
 5. Terni                  . xx . 5
 6. Dolmine                . xx . x 6
 7. Cantieri Nav. Riun.    . xx . xx 7
 8. Autostrade             x . . x . . . 8
 9. Innocenti S. Eustuchio . xx . xxx . 9
10. Alfa Romeo             xxx . xxx . x 10

                           D(1,1)=0.56

 2. State B

11. Finmeccanica           xxxxxxxxxx   | 11                General Centre
12. Finsider               xxxxxxx . xx | x 12              D(234,234)=0.50
13. Italsider              xxxxxxx . xx | xx 13
14. Italimpianti           . xx . xxxxxx | xxx 14
15. STET                   x . . x . . xx . . | xxxx 15
16. Cementir               xxxxxxxxxx   | xxxx . 16
17. Fincantieri            xxx . xxxxxx | xxxxxx 17
18. SMI                    . . . . . . x . . | xx . xxxx 18
19. Dreda Termomeccanica   . xx . xxx . xx | xxxx . xxx 19
20. SME                    . . . x . . . x . . | x . xxxxxxx 20
21. IMI                    . . . . . . . . . . | . xx . x . . x . . 21
22. Alitalia               . x . x . . xx . x | . . . . x . xx . xx 22

                           D(1,2)=0.62      D(2,2)=0.76

 3. Other

23. Efibanca               . . . . . . . . . . | . . . . . . . . . xx .   23
24. Snia-Viscosa           . . . . . . . . . . | . xx . x . . . . xx .    x 24
25. Imilcable              . . . . . . . x . . | x . . xx . xx . x . x    . . 25
26. Acc. Tubificio Brescia x . . xxx . . x .   | xxxx . x . . . . .       . . . 26

                           D(1,3)=0,15      D(2,3)=0.40      D(3,3)=0,17

 4. Private A

27. Bastogi                . . . . . . . . . . | . x . . x . . . . xx .   xx . .      27       Private Centre
28. Falck                  . . . . . . . . . . | . x . . x . . . . x .    xx . x      x 28     D(45,45)=.66
29. RAS                    . . . . . . . . . . | . . . . . . . . . xxx    xx . .      xx 29
30. Italcementi            . . . . . . . . . . | . . . . . . . . . x . .  xxxx        xxx 30
31. F. Tosi                . . . . . . . . . . | . . . . . . . . . x . .  xxxx        xxxx 31

                           D(1,4)=0          D(2,4)=0.20      D(3,4)                   D(4,4)=1.00
                                                              =0.75

 5. Private B

32. Borletti               . . . . . . . . . . | . . . . . . . . . x . .  . x . .     xxxxx     32
33. IBI                    . . . . . . . . . . | . . . . . . . . . xx .   xxx .       xxxxx     . 33
34. Italmobiliare          . . . . . . . . . . | . . . . . . . . . x . .  xxx .       xxxxx     . x 34
35. Mira Lanza             . . . . . . . . . . | . . . . . . . . . x . .  xx . .      xxxxx     . xx 35
36. C. Gr. Far.            . . . . . . . . . . | . . . . . . . . . . . .  . . . .     xxxxx     xxx . 36
37. Burge                  . . . . . . . . . . | . . . . . . . . . x . .  xx . .      xxxxx     . xx . . 37
38. SMI                    . . . . . . . . . . | . . . . . . . . . . . .  . . . .     . x . . .  x . . . . . 38
39. Naz. Ferro. Net. Car.  . . . . . . . . . . | . . . . . . . . . . . .  . . . x     . x . xx   . . . . . . . 39
40. Celestri.              . . . . . . . . . . | . . . . . . . . . . . .  . . x .     . . . xx   . xx . . . . x 40

                           D(1,5)=0          D(2,5)=0.06      D(3,5)        D(4,5)    D(5,5)=0.36
                                                              =0.36        =0.80

                           D(12,45)=0.06
```

Note: X = direct interlocks; · = no direct interlocks; D (I,J) = density of direct interlock between I and J.

H

Analysis of the general centre (density 0.50) shows that there was only a limited overlap between the private and state centre. The latter also had higher densities of 0.66 and 0.65 respectively. The general centre was composed of 12 state companies (state B), five private companies (private A) and four other companies that belonged neither to the state nor to the private centre. Moreover the latter four companies had a low likelihood of interlocking with themselves (density 0.17), but were highly interlocked with the state centre (density 0.40) and especially with the private centre (density 0.75). So, although the four companies were in the general centre, they were strongly connected with the private centre. On the other hand, while there is a certain overlap between the three centres, state and private centres had only a six per cent chance of interlocking; state B and private A groups had the highest densities, in particular private companies formed a clique of five points. Further evidence is given by the analysis of Snijders H index for the different kind of centres. This index had a value of 0.23 for the large component in the total network but there was a much lower value for the overall centre (0.10) and higher values respectively for state (0.31) and private (0.61) centres.

From these results it can be concluded that the general centre was mainly the outcome of the relations between two different centres that did not interlock frequently. The structure of the network was affected by state intervention and, in particular, by the state shareholding formula. If state intervention in the economic structure took the form of nationalization, the nationalized sector would be isolated from the rest of the network (Chiesi, 1978). The logic of shareholding, in contrast, does not lead to a reduction of the network but to a transformation of its structure. The strength of this transformation depends on the importance of state control in the economy.

CONFIRMATION OF THE ANALYSIS: THE STRUCTURE OF THE DIRECTED GRAPH

As has been shown in chapter 2, the direction of lines in the network can be drawn when an executive is an outside director of another company. Because a certain possibility of control can be imputed from the company in which the person is an executive, it is possible to select different kinds of lines according to the hypothesis that co-ordination, information and control functions are not diffused throughout the network. These are exercised to different degrees according to the position in the network itself and the function carried out by the multiple directors in the different corporations. It has already been shown that the two-board system in Italy is different from the other

Western countries, so the criteria for distinguishing between inside and outside functions are quite different and based on the fact that in the first board some members delegate the executive power to one or a few other members of the board. For that reason it was decided to consider the following positions as inside members: amministratore delegato, consigliere delegato, amministratore unico, direttore generale and procuratore. The presidente and vice-presidente were also considered as insiders, even if they were not delegated by the other members of the board, because they formally hold the most prominent positions, in private companies usually representing the main share holders or owning the corporation itself if it is family-owned. It can be useful to remember that, despite their formal importance, the presidente and vice-presidente very often behave like absentee owners, while this behaviour is impossible for those with delegated authority. Consiglieri and all the positions on the second board were considered outside functions because their behaviour was more supervisory and advisory.

Only 548 (26 per cent) out of the total 2,082 interlocks formed directed lines. In particular, 459 were directed from inside to outside positions (84 per cent) and the remaining 89 were from inside to inside. The latter were considered twice, as pairs of lines joining mutually reachable points. In this way there were 637 directed lines. The network of primary lines had a density of 0.02, contained 75 isolates and a large component of 155 companies. Treating the primary lines as directed from inside to outside makes it possible to analyse strong components. The connectivity of this total network was lower because 135 points were isolated and the biggest component was reduced to 82 points. On the other hand the density in the largest component was 0.07.

It can be concluded that the strong components occupied a more central position in the network and were centred around a group of companies which was close to the centre identified in the analysis of the undirected network. In fact, restricting the analysis to the network of the strong component, but considering only multiplicity 2 or more, 17 components[6] were discovered, the size of the largest one being 22. Eight companies out of the first ten, as measured by the number of companies at distance 1 or 2, belonged to this main component. This very central component reflected the structure outlined in the analysis of the state and private centres (see figure 11.2) and can be partitioned into two subsets. All the companies in private A were part of one of these subsets and four belonged to private B. In the other subset of the component, four companies belonged to state B and two belonged to state A. A state holding company (SME) was an exception because it was found in the private subset and in a peripheral position.[7] Two companies (Snia Viscosa and Acciaieria e Tubificio di Brescia), which

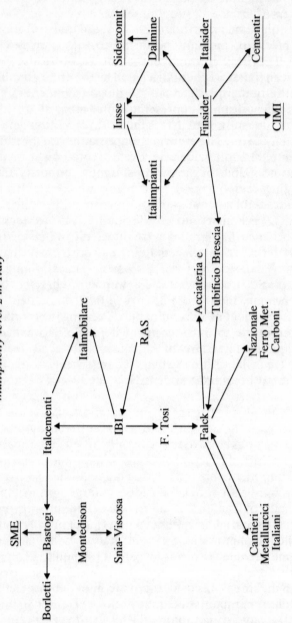

Figure 11.2 Main components in the directed graph of primary interlocks at multiplicity level 2 in Italy

Note: State-owned companies are underscored.

both belonged to the 'other' group, were found to have a very interesting position in the component. The first one held a very peripheral position in the private side and the latter was just a bridge between the two subsets.

If the division between primary and induced lines is retained, it is possible to give a further interpretation to the connections of the centre. Looking at the 21 companies that form the overall centre of the network, it can be seen that, unlike most of the other countries discussed in this book, the system of interlocking directorships did not involve centrally positioned banks. The centre of the network contains only two banks, Efibanca and IMI, which both supply long-term credit important for industry. The other largest banks in Italy are not devoted to long-term credit and do not have a central position in the network. The bank law of 1936 brought the most important banks under state control and they ceased to play a central role in the overall network. This was the result of previous structural crises in the Italian banking system in 1893, 1921 and especially 1930, which resulted from the fact that banks behaved like financial holdings and were investing customers' short-term deposits in long-term loans to the industrial sectors (Luzzatto, 1968; Grifone, 1971). These loans were often granted in the form of shares in debtor companies, so that interlocks between banks and industries were frequent.

For the 1976 network it would be misleading to conclude that financial functions are *not* concentrated in the network centre. If primary and induced lines are distinguished and the primary lines are divided into financial and production lines, there was evidence of a higher concentration of financial lines in the centre, while the primary production lines were concentrated in the outer margin.

THE IDENTIFICATION OF LOCAL INTEREST GROUPS

Since the study of the National Resources Committee in the USA in 1935, attention has been drawn to the relevance of interlocking directorships for the identification of local interest groups. In Italy the process of industrialization was concentrated in the northern regions of the country. In particular the area between Turin, Milan and Genoa has been called the 'industrial triangle'. Only since the Second World War has Rome become the headquarters of the public financial sector that became closely allied to political power. These two factors, together with the small size of the country compared with the USA, can explain the main characteristics of the findings reported in this section.

The country was divided into eight different regions, as shown in table 11.2. Although Milan represents the main economic centre in Italy, it is possible to distinguish at least three other economic centres:

Table 11.2 Density by region in Italy

Region	Rome (city only)	Milan and region	Turin and region	Genoa and region	Islands	North-eastern region	Southern regions	Central regions	Distribution of corporations %	N
Rome (city only)	0.068								21	51
Milan and region	0.028	0.031							44	108
Turin and region	0.041	0.024	0.052						11	26
Genoa and region	0.064	0.027	0.036	0.105					6	15
Islands	0.011	0.016	0.016	0.009	0.048				3	7
North-eastern region	0.030	0.020	0.009	0.062	0.022	0.026			5	13
Southern regions	0.043	0.030	0.042	0.067	0.014	0.023	0.022		4	10
Central regions	0.014	0.009	0.000	0.010	0.022	0.012	0.000	0.013	5	13

Rome, which is not an industrial centre but the administrative capital in which financial power can be found alongside political power; Turin, the centre of the automobile industry; and Genoa, a centre of heavy industry. The other regions are of less importance. The north-eastern regions, central regions, southern regions and the islands (Sicily and Sardinia) have been distinguished according to their socio-economic characteristics (Bagnasco, 1978). The results of the analysis are shown in table 11.2, in which densities for each regional group are given in the diagonal.

Rome, Milan, Turin and Genoa formed regional groups because each density was higher than the corresponding bipartite density with each other group. By contrast, the north-eastern, central and southern regions did not form a group because their bipartite densities were somewhat higher than the densities inside the corresponding region. The islands cannot be considered a group because there was only one interlock between two companies belonging to the chemical sector. The industrial triangle included three different groups. In fact, if it is considered as a single group, there is a lower density than that computed for the three groups taken separately. In particular, the Genoa group showed the highest density and also had the highest bipartite densities within the industrial triangle and with Rome. If we look at the most central companies inside each group, according to the neighbourhood at distance 1 and 2, the most central companies in Rome were Finsider, IMI, Finmeccanica and Banco di Roma. All of these were state-owned financial companies. The central position in the Milan group was held by strictly private companies: RAS, Italcementi, F.Tosi and IBI were controlled by the Pesenti family and Falck was the biggest heavy industrial still controlled by a family. Snia Viscosa was the only 'management-controlled' company as defined by Berle and Means (1932). Although the Milan group had the lowest density, it was the largest and also had the densest centre (12 companies had at least a neighbourhood of ten at distance 1, while the Rome group had only three cases and Turin and Genoa had one). Fiat and Olivetti were in the very centre of the Turin group and in this region there was also a state-owned company (Stet, a holding in the communication sector). The central companies in the Genoa group were also state-owned but all of them in the heavy-industry sector. This explains the high bipartite density with the Rome group. An analysis of the other regions shows that their bipartite densities with the Rome group and the industrial triangle were usually higher. This is especially true with Genoa and Rome. This can be considered as a result of the industrial policy carried out by the public sector after the Second World War, a policy aimed at industrializing the under-developed southern regions of the country.

Table 11.3   Regional structuring of board networks in Italy

Mean density	First board	Second board
Intraregions	0.045	0.033
Interregions	0.025	0.015
Intraregions/interregions	1.8	2.2

Some final remarks can be made about the regional structuring of the second-board network. A comparison for the two boards of the mean density within each regional group with the mean bipartite density between them (table 11.3) shows that the bipartite density for the second board was lower than for the first board. This indicates that the second board had a greater tendency to interlock regionally, since the sindaci are mainly professionals and they would be expected to exercise their activities mainly within one region.

CONCLUSION

It has been shown that the two boards formed completely different networks in the Italian system. No centre existed in the second-board network, the most central companies according to adjacencies were completely different for the two networks, the two boards interlocked only in a limited number of cases and the second board had a somewhat higher tendency to interlock at the regional level. These structural differences have been attributed to the different functions that are carried out by the two boards. The first board is the most relevant for co-ordination, information and control functions, while the second one is related to the professional functions exercised by the sindaci.

The analysis of centrality has shown decreasing densities from a relatively small centre to the periphery, a centripetal character of a large outer margin and a centrifugal tendency in the periphery. Although it was possible to identify a centre, this was mainly the result of the relations between two separate centres that did not interlock so frequently and were denser than the overall one. The kind of ownership was the factor used to identify these centres. While multinational corporations were isolated from the rest of the intercorporate national structure, the main private corporations shared their central positions with the state-owned ones. The integration of state and economy and the central position of the state-owned corporations can be explained by two phenomena: the importance of the state in economic activities and the shareholding formula which is typical of the Italian system.

Finally we have shown that the partition between private and public economic sectors has also an impact at the regional level, although the Italian economy is very concentrated in the north-western part of the country. Public-corporations headquarters are mainly located in Rome, while the private industrial corporations mostly form the so called industrial triangle.

Our starting hypothesis has been supported by the network analysis but seems related to the history and the institutional characteristics of Italy. Therefore we can conclude that the mode of state intervention in the Italian economy affected the network structure in a specific way. The state shareholding formula seems to be designed in order to integrate public economic policy with private initiative in a free market. The network of interlocking directorships had two separate centres, the first one dominated by state property and the second one by private property. Between these two, joint ventures and mixed companies have been established as a means of integration and co-ordination.

NOTES

1   The Italian part of the research work has been supported by ADPSS (Archivio Dati e Programmi per le Scienze Sociali, Milano). Valuable suggestions in data collection and sources have been given by CIRIEC (Centro Italiano di Ricerche e Informazione sull'Economia delle Imprese Pubbliche e di Pubblico Interesse, Milano) and by the staff members of Banca Commerciale Italiana. The help of these institutions is gratefully acknowledged.

2   For a reconstruction of the political debate about the nationalization and an account of the positions taken by the different parties, see the journalistic but accurate book by Scalfari (1964).

3   Chiesi (1979) shows that the density between electricity-supply companies in 1962 was 0.41.

4   The interlocks of the first board formed seven components with 1,380 lines. The biggest one had 180 points. Fifty-two points were isolated. The diameter of the component was eight and the mean distance was 3.04. The interlocks of the second board, which had 518 lines, formed only four components, of which the biggest one had 179 points. Sixty-two points were isolated. The diameter of the large component was 11 and the mean distance was 4.18. The whole network, taking into account all possible lines, formed a large component of 218 points, four components of two points each and 21 isolates. The diameter was nine and the mean distance 2.87.

5 　The number of interlocks inside the first-board network was 1,408, while the interlocks inside the second-board network were 545.

6 　We are speaking about components because, if we take into account only multiplicity $\geqslant 2$ the original strong component can loose its properties by definition.

7 　SME is an example of the balance between private and public directors in those cases where private interests are only an important minority in the share capital. Bastogi, a private holding company, owned 15 per cent of the shares, while the state has formal control through the public holding company IRI. Therefore the presidente e amministratore delegato of SME is a member of the board of a state-owned corporation operating in the heavy-industry sector. The vice-presidente was also presidente of Bastogi, whose board had another three members in common. On the other side, the interlocks with the state-owned corporations were dispersed in some 20 different boards. As a result, the influence of private property is overrepresented compared with its percentage of shares.

12

Bank Spheres of Influence in the British Corporate Network

JOHN SCOTT and CATHERINE GRIFF[1]

The notion of a split between 'the City' and industry has become a widely cited explanation for British economic inefficiency. The financial interests of the City of London, it is held, have failed to invest in British industry and have concentrated their attention on overseas investments and such 'unproductive' sectors as property development (Wilson Committee, 1980). Alternatively, it has been argued that manufacturing industry has gradually become subordinated to the rule of City interests (Aaronovitch, 1955, 1961). Unfortunately, very few studies have attempted even to describe the relations between the financial and non-financial sectors of the economy and a number of those studies which have been carried out remain impressionistic and unsystematic.[2] The present study of the major British companies in 1904, 1938 and 1976, is one of the first to approach this question on the basis of a rigorous investigation of the *structure* of interlocking directorships.[3] The aim of this chapter is to describe the structure of the British network of interlocking directorships over the period 1904 to 1976 in order to approach the question of the relationship between the financial and non-financial sectors. A discussion of general features of the network will be followed by a report on the state sector and regional divisions in order to assess the extent to which the network can be said to have a 'centre' of tightly linked financial companies. It will be argued that the British intercorporate network does not have a distinct centre and an alternative view of the links between financial and non-financial companies will be presented.

GENERAL FEATURES OF THE NETWORK

Companies in Britain have a single-board system of administration, within which supervisory and executive functions are combined. Although executive committees, management committees and various *ad hoc* boards have existed as adjuncts to the main board of directors, these bodies have no legal status and are subordinate to the main board. This board has legal responsibility for the company's affairs and is the locus of control within the enterprise (Scott, 1982b). The British data relate to interlocks generated by those who sit on the boards of major companies. The 200 largest non-financial companies and 50 largest financial companies were selected for each year investigated, giving comparable selections of 250 enterprises for each year.[4] The total number of directors fell slightly from 2,204 in 1904 to 2,173 in 1938 but had increased substantially to 2,682 by 1976. By contrast, the number of multiple directors increased from 303 in 1904 to 329 in 1938, i.e. multiple directors came to form a more significant proportion of the total directorate. Between 1938 and 1976 the number of multiple directors fell by 47 to 282, representing a reduction in their proportionate size from 15 per cent to 11 per cent. This was matched by a change in the proportion of directorships held: from 27 per cent in 1904, to 31 per cent in 1938 and 22 per cent in 1976. These figures show that the multiple directors had become a smaller group, accounting for a smaller proportion of directorships, within a vastly increased directorate. Nevertheless, the multiple directors in 1976 still held almost a quarter of all the directorships in the top 250 companies. The network of interlocks generated by the multiple directors became more extensive over the period, though the peak level was reached in 1938: the number of lines were 401 in 1904, 578 in 1938 and 542 in 1976. It would appear that the smaller number of multiple directors were directing their efforts more efficiently: the 303 directors of 1904 generated only three quarters of the number of lines generated by the 282 directors of 1976. It is noteworthy that the average multiplicity of the lines altered from 1.27 in 1904 to 1.41 in 1938, but then fell to 1.10 in 1976. The network of interlocking directorships contained less 'noise' in 1976 than it did before.

The pattern of movement in the network parameters discussed above suggests that the overall level of interlocking increased markedly between 1904 and 1938 but fell back in the post-war period. The period between the First and Second World War saw very little change in the number of uninterlocked companies but this number rose significantly to a level of 61 in 1976. Of particular significance in this respect is the growth in the number of companies owned from the USA or Europe. While the domestic part of the network tightened up in the post-war

Table 12.1   Control types and interlocking in 1976 in Britain

Mode of Control	Non-financial companies		Financial companies		Total
	Interlocked	Uninterlocked	Interlocked	Uninterlocked	
State corporation	11	2	0	0	13
Exclusive majority	24	35	5	0	64
Shared majority	5	0	7	0	12
Exclusive minority	19	7	10	0	36
Shared minority	6	2	4	0	12
Constellation of interests[a]	77	12	15	1	105
Mutual	0	0	6	2	8
Total	142	58	47	3	250

Note:
a So far as could be discovered, no companies had a widely dispersed share capital. In each case at least ten per cent of the shares, often more, was held by the 20 largest shareholders.

period, the growing number of uninterlocked, foreign-controlled enterprises resulted in a fall in the connectivity of the network from 60 per cent in 1938 to 55 per cent in 1976.

It can be seen from Table 12.1 that there was a definite association between mode of control[5] and interlocking in 1976. Those companies which were least likely to have any interlocks were those where one particular interest held a majority of the shares. Many of these were family-owned concerns such as Associated British Foods[6], Sainsbury, Littlewoods, Union International and Heron but the majority were subsidiaries of foreign enterprises. Of the 21 American subsidiaries only five (Ford, Chrysler, IBM, Standard Telephones and Gallaher) were interlocked. It is difficult to draw any firm conclusions about subsidiaries of other nationalities. Hoechst (German), Petrofina (Belgian) and Ciba-Geigy (Swiss) were all interlocked, but Philips (Dutch) and Nafta (Russian) were not. From France, Total was interlocked but Michelin, Cavenham[7] and Louis Dreyfus were not; and from Canada the Massey-Ferguson and Alcan subsidiaries were interlocked while those of Thomson and Inco were not.

The trend away from majority family ownership has led to the inclusion of more of the domestic companies in the network of interlocks. A high proportion of companies subject to minority control or to shared minority control were interlocked: as ownership came to be spread more widely, so the enterprises were more likely to be interlocked.[8] The largest category of companies, almost all which were interlocked, was those which were classified as controlled through a constellation of interests. This refers to the situation where the 20 largest shareholders hold ten per cent or more of the shares and so collectively have minority control. The dominant shareholders in these companies were the large insurance companies, the pension funds and funds managed by the merchant banks, though a number had substantial residual family holdings. These companies constituted the heart of the network in 1976. The massive growth of 'institutional' shareholdings occured in the post-war period and so there were few examples of companies controlled through a constellation of interests in either 1938 or 1904.[9] In both of these years many of the uninterlocked companies were controlled by families òr were amalgamations of family firms. The interlocking of foreign subsidiaries was similar to the pattern found in 1976: indeed, Ford was interlocked in 1938 and in 1976, whilst Woolworth and Anglo-American Oil (now Esso) were uninterlocked in both years.

Table 12.2 shows the ten companies with the highest adjacency in 1904 and 1976. It can be seen that the most central companies in 1904 covered a variety of types: four railways, two insurance companies, two banks and two non-financial companies. A similar pattern held in

Table 12.2   Companies ranked by adjacency in 1904 and 1976 in Britain

1904		1976	
Company	Adjacency	Company	Adjacency
North British and Mercantile Insurance	18	Lloyds Bank	28
London and North Western Railway	17	Bank of England	26
Royal Exchange Assurance	14	Midland Bank	21
Bank of England	13	British Petroleum	19
North Eastern Railway	13	Barclays Bank	18
Dunderland Iron Ore	12	Commercial Union Assurance	18
Guest Keen & Nettlefolds	11	National Westminster Bank	18
Forth Bridge Railway	11	Finance For Industry	17
Union of London and Smiths Bank	11	Delta Metal	16
Great Northern, Piccadilly and Brompton Railway	11	Hill Samuel	16

1938, when the ten most central companies comprised four banks, three railways, two non-financial and one insurance company. By 1976 the pattern was very different: seven of the ten most central companies were banks. Three main factors can be adduced to explain this trend. First, the banking sector underwent a massive process of concentration after 1904. By 1938, clearing-bank business in Britain was dominated by five banks and so the company connections of the 1904 banks became aggregated into a smaller number of large units. Second, the railway companies were nationalized in 1948 and underwent considerable reorganization.[10] The nationalized British Railways in 1976 had an adjacency of just 4. Third, the adjacency of companies ceased being simply a function of board size and came to reflect the growing interdependence of the financial and industrial sectors. The emergence of 'spheres of influence' – discussed later in this chapter – transformed the network functions performed by the major banks. It is perhaps important to point out that in 1976 the same companies appear as central regardless of whether centrality is measured in terms of adjacency, sum distance or rush.[11]

Within the largest component in 1976 there were a total of 17,020 pairs of companies. The longest distance between any two companies in this component was distance 8. Almost one-quarter of all the pairs were connected at distance 3. The mean distance between points was 3.26. An important question, which is frequently overlooked, concerns which companies were most peripheral in the large component. While many studies examine the central enterprises in a network, relatively few examine those which are peripheral. In 1976, the ten most peripheral companies (as measured by their sum distance) were all non-financial and they comprised four companies subject to exclusive majority control, one subject to exclusive minority control and five controlled through a constellation of interests. In all of the latter[12], founding families remained as important participants in the controlling constellations. The ten peripheral companies included two foreign subsidiaries (Petrofina and Ciba-Geigy). The peripheral companies, therefore, show similar characteristics to those which were completely uninterlocked. Over the whole period, relatively few financial companies have been peripheral. The large component of 1976 included 30 companies (16 per cent) which had just one interlock and only two of these were financials. Six of the ten most peripheral companies were amongst these 30. In 1904, 37 of the 177 companies in the large component (21 per cent) had just one interlock and just three of these were financials.[13]

THE PROBLEM OF THE MISSING CENTRE

A significant group of state-controlled enterprises has existed only since the Second World War and the 1976 data show little evidence of the formation of a distinct state centre. In 1976 there were 13 state enterprises[14], one company in which the state had majority control, two in which the state had indirect majority participation and four in which the state had indirect minority participation. Out of this total of 20 companies, ten were interlocked into a single component. This component included 11 lines, of which just three were based on primary interlocks. Only two of the state enterprises had no interlocks amongst the top 250 (Electricity Council and National Coal Board) and the National Enterprise Board had no interlocks with its two main subsidiaries.[15] Most of the state enterprises had links to non-state concerns and two findings are worthy of note: Marks and Spencer seems to have been a popular source of board-level expertise for state enterprises; and British Steel had important functional interlocks, some of which were associated with financial participations.[16] Perhaps the most important feature of the state enterprises is the large number of interlocks with Hill Samuel and its associates. British Leyland, Rolls Royce, British Rail and British Airways all had interlocks with this group of companies.

The 1904 and 1938 networks showed some signs of regional clustering and other forms of sectionalism but this had largely disappeared by 1976. The only regional grouping to survive into 1976 was that in Scotland and this was increasingly fragmented by the links of the three Scottish banks to their English parents and associates.[17] In 1904 the network of multiple lines was disaggregated into 24 components, these often having a regional basis or being associated with a particular entrepreneur or financier. By 1976 both the number of companies and the number of components in the network of multiple lines had fallen. This confirms the trend towards a less intensive and more diffuse corporate system in Britain. The figures for 1938, however, show that this was not a simple smooth trend. In 1938 there were a large number of components of size 4 and, more importantly, the largest component included 63 companies. This figure of 63 compares with a maximum component size of 17 in 1904 and 13 in 1976. It appears that the network became *more* clustered and intensive between 1904 and 1938 and only subsequently moved towards its 1976 pattern. This interpretation is confirmed by some provisional results for 1957 which suggest the existence of 15 components, the two largest of which included 12 and 34 companies. Prior to the First World War, the network was both localized and personalized. During the inter-war years many industrial companies were brought together with financial companies on a national basis and the financial difficulties of many companies led to bank-sponsored attempts at reconstruction and rationalization. Combined with the continuing importance of family and personal control, this resulted in a highly clustered network. The 1930s were a period in which many interlocks reflected vertical and horizontal integration between companies, often by region, or were associated with financial participations by holding companies. Indeed, British Electric Traction, Thomas Tilling, Power Securities, Edmundsons Electricity and the Gas Light and Coke Company operated in the transport, electricity and gas sectors almost like modern Belgian holding companies: they tended to involve an amalgam of family and investment company participations in a holding company which took control or participations in a number of operating companies.[18] These regional and financial groupings can be understood in the context of what Mintz and Schwartz have termed 'hegemonic domination' (Mintz and Schwartz, 1984), i.e. one enterprise significantly, regularly and directly influences other enterprises which do not have the power to counter this influence.

appearance of this functional and regional pattern. Both interlocks and participations have been consolidated into a structure of wholly owned subsidiaries. The fact that many of the clusters were to be found in heavy industry, energy and transport, has meant that nationalization in these industries has reinforced this trend. In particular, the regional, heavy-industry combines were incorporated into state enterprises operating at a national level. In the post-war period, intensive linkages became fewer in number and, as a result, the national features of an extensive network predominated by 1976.

Although the network had become more national in scope, the disappearance of regional groupings had not resulted in the emergence of a national 'centre' in the network. If the centre of a network is defined as the maximal subset of central enterprises which meet at distance 2, then the British network of 1976 had a nominal centre but it does not seem to have been an important structural feature of the network. The British centre has been consistently small and insignificant: in 1904 the centre included only two companies, in 1938 it included seven companies and in 1976 there were nine companies. The centre in a network can best be considered as a consequence of the level of interlocking. A high level of interlocking will produce a large centre (Snijders, 1981). The British network has had a consistently low level of interlocking compared with the levels for other European countries. The real problem, therefore, is not to explain why the British network has no real centre but to explain why other networks have such high levels of interlocking.

A number of reasons can be given for why Britain has not found it necessary to adopt the high level of interlocking found in many other European countries. Most important is the fact that British boards meet more frequently: at least once or twice every month. For this reason, multiple directors will meet one another more frequently and so will be in constant and close contact. In this respect Britain is similar to the USA. Almost as important in the explanation is the fact that the boards of British banks do not operate primarily as general forums of business discussion but are concerned mainly with the affairs of the specific bank. The reason for this is to be found in the existence of alternative forums outside of company boardrooms. In Britain there has been an 'establishment' – a dominant status group within the business class – which provided a myriad of informal forums and settings for business discussion.[19] The gentlemen's clubs of London, the social events of the London season, the Houses of Parliament and numerous dinners and luncheons were venues in which the members of this small and compact establishment came together and were able to discuss their common affairs. To the extent that multiple directors were part of this establishment, it was unnecessary for them to use company boardrooms as general business forums. The consequence of this for the centralization of the network was that fewer interlocks were required for the smooth operation of the business system. Interlocks constitute 'functional alternatives' to kinship, residence, clubs, and so on. Societies with such cohesive establishments will not, other things being equal, have centralized corporate networks.[20] Only with the decline of the institutions of the establishment have more formal mechanisms of interest formulation and representation been required and formal 'corporatist' bodies have increasingly taken on this role (Schmitter, 1979). Although the decline of the establishment since the 1930s has resulted in a slight increase in the centralization of the network, it remains to be seen whether its continued decline will be associated with even higher levels of interlocking or whether corporatist institutions will be able to provide satisfactory forums of business discussion. The only bank which takes the role of a general business forum, the nationalized Bank of England, has always maintained a policy of not recruiting directors of clearing banks to its board. This policy has further limited the degree of centralization which can exist in the network. Indeed, the Bank of England can best be understood as part of the emerging corporatist forms of interest representation.

BANK-CENTRED SPHERES OF INFLUENCE

The discussion of centrality in the network shows the increasing prominence of banks, especially of the London clearing banks. In 1904 the 18 companies with the highest numbers of contacts included only four of the numerous banks. The big five banks of 1938 were all to be found among the 20 most-central companies of that year. Table 12.3 shows that the number of companies to which the London banks were connected increased between 1904 and 1938 and then fell back slightly, though the average number of contacts per company increased steadily from 4.4 to 16.6. Many of the non-financial interlocks of the London banks in 1904 were with railway, canal, shipping and dock companies and much of this pattern persisted into the inter-war years. The data for 1938, however, show a great increase in the number of interlocks between the banks and manufacturing industry, a trend which led to this sector being the most important source of bank interlocks by 1976. This suggests that some features of the split between 'the City' and industry persisted into the 1930s but that in the post-war period the two sectors grew much closer together. Equally important as an expression of this move towards finance capital is the growth in the number of bank interlocks with other financial companies. In 1904 most of these

Table 12.3   Bank interlocks with the top 250 enterprises between 1904 and 1976 in Britain

| | Number of companies connected with | | | | |
	Transport and utilities	Manufac- turing	Other non-financial sectors	Financial sector	Total
13 London banks of 1904[a]	28	11	7	11	57
6 London banks of 1938	19	27	21	23	90
5 London banks of 1976	3	41	12	27	83

Note:
a London banks are here defined as the Bank of England and the London joint stock clearing banks.

Since the 1930s, mergers and diversification have led to the dis-
interlocks were with the major assurance companies. By 1976 the
clearing banks had built up links with merchant banks, property
companies and specialist credit banks. The financial interlocks of the
clearing banks had become more diversified.

The coming together of the financial and industrial sectors is
apparent from 1976 data on the pattern of interlocks generated
through financial companies. The number of distance 2 connections
carried by a non-financial company as a result of its interlocks with a
financial was dependent upon the centrality of the financial companies
to which it was connected. The importance of the financials is brought
out even more clearly in the network of primary interlocks. The
network generated by primary financial interlocks, ignoring all
induced and secondary interlocks, contained a large component of 100
companies. Large industrials acquired many of their indirect industrial
connections from their direct interlocks with financial companies.
Shell, for example, received two inside directors from financial
companies and, as a result, acquired distance 2 relations to 21 other
industrials. The eight most central financial companies in terms of
primary financial interlocks comprised three clearing banks, four
merchant banks and one insurance company. In contrast, those
financial companies which received the most inside directors from
non-financial companies were the Bank of England and insurance
companies. The only exception to this was Lloyds Bank, which was low
in terms of primary financial interlocks but high in terms of primary
industrial interlocks.

It is in the light of the above findings that we can approach the
question of the so-called bank-centred nature of intercorporate networks, a question which has particularly been raised in American
discussions. Considerable evidence has been brought forward to show
that the commercial banks in the USA play a central role in
the articulation of the financial and industrial sectors (Bearden et al.,
1975). In the British project this has been examined on the basis of the
formation of cliques in the network of primary interlocks. The large
component in this network included 156 companies and this component contained eight 2-cliques varying in size from 10 to 15. Each clique
took the form of a star though there was much overlapping of the
centres of the various stars. The central points in each of the eight stars
were the Hill Samuel merchant bank, the Bank of England, the four
clearing banks, the Commercial Union insurance company and
Imperial Chemical Industries. The eight cliques overlapped in such a
way as to produce distinct patterns of associations among the stars. In
particular, the Barclays Bank, ICI and Commercial Union cliques
overlapped to such an extent that they might reasonably be treated as a

distinct 'super cluster'.[21] Similarly, the Midland Bank clique[22] and the Hill Samuel clique[23] were closely linked through Eagle Star and Shell. The remaining cliques were distinct from one another and from the other cliques in the component.[24] It would seem that the five super clusters (Lloyds, National Westminster, Bank of England, Midland/ Hill Samuel and Barclays/ICI/Commercial Union) were distinct spheres of influence in the network and that they were linked together through the 'bridging' role played by a number of major industrial companies and two consortium banks.

The bridging role of large companies is particularly important. In 1904, one railway, two shipping and one dock company were inter-locked with two or more of the London banks but the main bridges between banks were assurance companies. In 1938, 15 non-financial companies were interlocked with two or more London banks and although many of these were railway and shipping companies, four came from manufacturing and heavy industry. In 1976, there were 16 non-financial companies with interlocks to two or more London banks and all but three were from the manufacturing and heavy-industrial sectors. Insurance companies were also important bridges: in 1976 five insurance companies had interlocks with two or more London banks.

The banks tend to interlock with a large number of companies to form what might be called 'spheres of influence', the central members of which tend to be stable over time. The evidence does not support the contention that banks exercise control or co-ordination over the members of these spheres. The spheres are loose communities of interest which have their foci on the bank boards. Some examples might clarify what is involved in a bank sphere of influence. In the case of the Midland Bank, the Birmingham connections of Dudley Docker in the 1930s constituted the heart of a sphere of influence which included the various Docker family interests, Birmingham Small Arms and the Roger group of telephone and cable companies. During the 1940s and 1950s these companies were supplemented by the closely allied Eagle Star, Philip Hill and Drayton companies. The Midland Bank's 1976 interlocks with Eagle Star, BICC and the Rank Organi-zation represent a continuation of this pattern of interlocks. Similarly, the National Provincial Bank had enduring links which were carried through to the National Westminster board. These links were centred around the interests of the first Lord Aberconway in John Brown, various colliery companies, Sheepbridge Engineering and English China Clays. In 1976 these interests were represented on the National Westminster board by the third Lord Aberconway and his cousin, W.R.Norman.

If bank spheres of influence are important structural features of the intercorporate network it is to be expected that removal of the banks would result in a loss of network structure. Deleting all those interlocks generated by those who sat on bank boards in 1976, whether as insiders or outsiders, in fact resulted in very little alteration to the overall structure of the network: there were four components, the largest of which included 165 companies. Although the bank directors linked 82 companies through 164 lines, there were enough alternative lines to prevent the total fragmentation of the network. The important question, however, is whether the structure of spheres of influence persists after deletion of the banks. An analysis of 2-cliques with minimum size 10 in the network of primary interlocks showed that deletion of the banks resulted in the number of cliques falling from eight to three. The spheres of influence did not survive the removal of the banks: clique structure was dependent on the banks as foci. Nevertheless, sufficient structure persisted to support a hypothesis that companies within a sphere were linked not only through the bank but also engaged in mutual interlocks.

The nature of these spheres of influence can best be understood in terms of the recent argument of Ratcliff (1980a and 1980b), who sees banks as capital-accumulation units for the groups and interests to which they are most closely connected. Banks tend to direct their loans in ways that best meet the capital needs of these groups. Bank spheres of influence, as units of *finance capital*, express the unity of banking and industry:

> Much of the money in the commercial banks comes from a diverse range of deposits, including individual checking and savings accounts, government accounts, certificates of deposit held by pension funds and other similar non-business institutions, accounts of churches and other private organisations and small business accounts, and would not be as available for corporate loans if banks tied to corporate interests did not serve to accumulate these funds. (Ratcliff, 1980a, p. 567)

Of particular importance are the bank trust departments and the nominee companies which they operate for clients, both of which give the banks a role in the co-ordination of capital owned and controlled by pension funds, unit-trust groups and other investment groups.[25]

This should not be seen as a variant of the 'bank power' theory. Power is an attribute of groups located within 'larger structures of propertied interests that tie banks and corporations together' (Ratcliff, 1980a, p. 567). Banks can be seen as the means through which dominant capitalist interests are able to exercise influence over a specific sphere of the economy. The bank interlocks are not associated with financial participations, although they do seem to involve a certain amount of preferential lending. The spheres do not result from the presence of bankers on industrial boards but from loose alliances of industrial, commercial and financial companies seeking representation on the bank boards. Banks recruit their directors over time from their main customers and associates and the resulting spheres of influence are the bases for some limited degree of co-operation among their members.

FINANCE CAPITALISTS AND NETWORK SPECIALISTS

Turning from the network of enterprises to its 'dual' – the network of persons – it is possible to identify the cliques and clusters of individuals who form the 'decision-making' centres within the spheres of influence. At the narrowest, such cliques may correspond to a particular foundation or family office. More typically, clusters of individuals associated with particular spheres of influence will overlap with those associated with other spheres. The potentially disaggregating effects of banking-centredness are countered by the overlapping pattern of clusters of persons who bridge the spheres.

Table 12.4   Distribution of lines in network of persons
between 1904 and 1976 in Britain

Value of line[a]	1904	1938	1976
2	166	242	73
3	10	25	—
4	—	11	—
5	—	5	—
Total	176	283	73

Note:
a A line of value 1 exists between any two people who are directors of the same company. These lines are not counted in the present analysis.

What is the structure of the network of multiple directors? It can be seen from table 12.4 that the trend for the number of lines has followed the same trajectory as that for the number of lines in the network of companies. A line exists between two people simply as a result of them sitting on the same board and therefore the analysis has been limited to multiple lines: those lines involving directors who meet one another on two or more boards. The 303 multiple directors of 1904 generated 401 lines between companies and 176 multiple lines among themselves. The 329 multiple directors of 1938 generated 578 lines between companies and 283 multiple lines among themselves. The 1976 directorate generated 542 lines between companies and 73 multiple lines amongst themselves. A line represents a 'meeting' between two multiple directors on a company board and multiple lines in particular might be expected to enhance the cohesion and solidarity of those who participate in the corporate system. The network of multiple lines of 1904 included 135 of the directors and contained 43 components, the largest of which were of sizes 11 and 10. The network of 1938 contained 42 components: the larger number of multiple lines were contained in a less-fragmented network. In 1976, the plural network contained 25 components, 14 of these being pairs of directors. There was an increase in the average number of meetings of directors over the period 1904 to 1938: in 1904 only two directors had adjacencies of 30 or more, the highest being 34; in 1938 there were 15 such directors and the highest adjacency was 55; by 1976 there were only four directors with 30 or more contacts, the highest number being 31.

Table 12.5   *Primary interests of directors in 1976 in Britain*

Primary interest	Initial allocation	Final allocation
Top 50 financial (current)	84	97
Top 50 financial (former)	—	7
Other financial	—	14
Top 200 industrial (current)	95	112
Top 200 industrial (former)	—	17
Other industrial	—	13
Other	103	22
Total	282	282

Perhaps the clearest way of understanding the network of persons is through the analysis of primary interests given in table 12.5. The primary interest of a director was initially given by whether he or she had a full-time executive position within one of the 250 companies. These primary interests were used to generate the network of primary interlocks between companies (there is no equivalent of primary interlocks in the network of persons). The 84 directors with primary interests in financial companies generated 133 primary interlocks and a further 74 induced interlocks. The 95 directors with primary interests in industrial companies generated 146 primary interlocks and a further 74 induced interlocks. A total of 103 directors had no inside position and their 168 interlocks (28 per cent of the total) were regarded as 'unclassified'. Many of the 103 people could, in fact, be allocated to a particular base company and therefore played a similar network role to those who carried the primary interlocks. By examining the background of the people involved, it was possible to produce the reallocations shown in table 12.5. Those who had their primary business interests in the top 250 companies (whether or not they were executives) were added to those who carried the primary interlocks. A similar strategy was followed for those who had retired from executive positions but remained board members of their base companies. This reduced the number of 'other' directors to 73, of whom 27 had primary interests in companies outside the top 250, 24 had retired from a top-250 company (and left its board) and 22 were 'outsiders' to the corporate system. The only real candidates for the role of 'network specialist' in the narrow sense were the 24 retired businessmen (seven financial and 17 non-financial) and certain of the 22 'other' people. The latter 22 included six past or present politicians and eight retired civil servants.

We may define *finance capitalists* as those who have business interests in two or more large business enterprises and thus the multiple directors can be regarded as the core of a slightly larger group of finance capitalists. Such finance capitalists are to be distinguished from those *internal capitalists* who have simply one corporate position as an executive of a large company and those *entrepreneurial capitalists* who have a single interest in a large company, owned and controlled by them or their families (Scott, 1982a, ch. 6). It is the group of finance capitalists as a whole who play an integrating and co-ordinating role in the network of intercorporate linkages. Those finance capitalists who carry primary interlocks play a dual role: in relation to the system as a whole and in relation to particular dyadic relations. It might be suggested that the group of finance capitalists who operate simply as 'network specialists' will be those who have retired from executive positions or from positions within the state and who now concentrate their attentions exclusively on the affairs of the corporate system as a whole. There may, in fact, be a *career* phenomenon at work. Those who begin their careers as internal capitalists or entrepreneurial capitalists may later acquire outside directorships and so become finance capitalists; at a later stage in their careers they may give up their executive responsibilities to become the 'elder statesmen' of the business world. If this is true, we would expect the network specialists to be successful and prominent businessmen at the ends of their careers and to have received some recognition of their achievements in terms of the award of a knighthood or peerage. That this is in fact the case is clear from an analysis of the network of companies generated solely by the group of 103 'other' directors. These people generated a network of 129 companies, formed into 13 components: one of 94 companies, one of six, one of five, four of three and six pairs. The ten companies with the highest adjacency in this network were interlocked through 26 directors, of whom 20 had titles. Three of the six central directors without titles were from a consortium bank (FFI) and would not have played a network role but for this company. Seven of the 20 were lords and the remainder were baronets or knights. This proportion compares with an overall figure of 47 per cent of the 282 multiple directors having titles.

CONCLUSIONS

The British network has a low level of centralization and the recent period shows no evidence of separate state and private sectors and little evidence of regional groupings. The high degree of integration between the financial and industrial sectors in 1976 suggests that the finance-capital model may be important in explaining some of the main features of the network in that period. The role of clearing banks in the formation of bank-centred spheres of influence also points in that direction. The spheres were not formed by the executives of banks sitting on industrial boards – as would be predicted by the bank-control model – but are best seen as expressing the coalescence of dominant business interests from both the financial and the non-financial sectors. The sources of disunity represented by the bank-centredness of the network were countered by the important bridging role, played by major industrial and insurance companies and by the clustering of the network of persons. The overall pattern of interlocks created a high level of cohesion among the inner circle of multiple directors. Particular importance in explaining the structure of interlocks must be ascribed to the career progression of those finance capitalists who achieve the position of network specialist. These people – the elder statesmen of the business world – seem to form the most obvious link between the corporate directorate as a whole and the wider establishment. As such, they play a key role in the operations of the corporate system and in perpetuating the privileges of a dominant, propertied class.

NOTES

1   This research has been financed by the Social Science Research Council under grant HR6992. We are grateful to Charlotte Kitson, Jill Scott and Martyn Taylor for their research assistance on the project.
2   Reports produced by journalists include Sampson (1962), Ferris (1960), Spiegelberg (1973) and McRae and Cairncross (1973). More systematic studies include Whitley (1973, 1974), Stanworth and Giddens (1975), Thompson (1977) and Useem and McCormack (1981).

3   A full discussion of the selection criteria for companies, a summary of the data and listings of all the companies included in the study are contained in Scott and Griff (1983). The research is an extension of work on Scottish capital presented in Scott and Hughes (1976, 1980a, 1980b). For earlier studies on Britain see Johnson and Apps (1979) and Overbeek (1980).

4   Selection of companies for 1976 was based on the general criteria adopted by the research group. For 1904 and 1938 company size was based on issued share capital rather than turnover. See Scott and Griff (1983).

5   These modes of control are defined in Scott and Hughes (1980b, p. 269). The categories are derived from the debate over ownership and control, some aspects of which are discussed in Scott (1979). The data are drawn from annual reports and from share registers.

6   ABF was owned by the Canadian Weston family but was not a subsidiary of their Canadian company.

7   Cavenham was a subsidiary of James Goldsmith's French master company.

8   Companies subject to family minority control were Blackwood Hodge, Costain, Inchcape, Kleinworth Benson, Ladbroke, Marchwiel, Morgan Grenfell, Pilkington, S.Pearson, Rowntree Mackintosh, Schroders, W.H.Smith, Thorn and United Biscuits. In some of these cases control was vested in family foundations.

9   The present study involves a full examination of shareholdings and these data will be presented elsewhere.

10   Initially all rail and road transport was controlled by the British Transport Commission. Later the railways were organized separately as British Railways.

11   It has not yet been possible to see whether this is also true for 1904 and 1938. The existence of any regional groups in these earlier periods might be expected to cause the measures to diverge.

12   C.T.Bowring, Brooke Bond, Croda, Guinness Peat and Fitch Lovell.

13   In 1904 there were 50 companies with adjacency 1: 12 were in isolated pairs, one was joined to a small component and 37 were members of the large component. In 1976 there were 34 companies with adjacency 1: 4 were in isolated pairs and 30 were members of the large component.

14   The state enterprises took the legal form of public corporations and not joint stock companies. A public corporation is established by Act of Parliament and has no share capital.

15   These subsidiaries were British Leyland and Rolls Royce. John Gardiner joined the BL board during the year 1976–77 as a representative of the NEB. Because of a mistake in the relevant volume of the *Directory of Directors* he was counted as two separate people. At some stage in 1976, therefore, BL and the NEB were interlocked.

16   British Steel had interlocks with, *inter alia*, Bridon, Clarke Chapman and Tube Investments.

17   See Scott and Hughes (1980b, chs 3 and 4). See also Scott (1983).

18   Edmundsons Electricity Corporation was controlled by the great American holding company Utilities Power and Light.

19   On the notion of the 'establishment' see Scott (1982a, ch. 7). See also Sampson (1962), Lupton and Wilson (1959) and Haxey (1939).

20   On the situation in the USA see Domhoff (1971).

21   The exclusive members of the stars were as follows: Barclays Bank (Tozer Kemsley and Milbourn, GKN, Robert Fleming, Union Discount, Booker McConnel and Agricultural Mortage); ICI (Reed, Carrington Viyella, Royal Insurance, Ford and the NEB); and Commercial Union (Debenhams, Barings, Kleinwort Benson, Trafalgar House, P & O, Plessey and British Steel).

22 The exclusive members of this clique were Standard Chartered Bank, UDT, Rowntree Mackintosh, Rank, Rothmans, Allied Breweries and Clydesdale Bank.

23 The exclusive members of this clique were BPB, Beecham, Rolls-Royce, British Leyland, Stone-Paltt, Marchwiel and Alcan.

24 The exclusive members of these cliques were as follows: Lloyds Bank (Grindlays Bank, Lucas, Lead Industries, National and Commercial Banking, Ocean Transport and Fisons); National Westminster Bank (Touche Remnant, Powell Duffryn, Redland, IBM, General Accident, Guardian Royal Exchange and Associated Portland); and the Bank of England (Laing, Rio Tinto Zinc, United Biscuits, Pilkington, Cadbury Schweppes, Hambros, Mercury Securities and Rothschild). The role of the Bank of England can best be understood as part of the corporatist tendencies discussed above.

25 The role of trust departments in the American banks is discussed in Herman (1980). It is important to recognize the role of merchant banks in mobilizing investment and pension funds and in smoothing corporate access to other sources of money (see Minns, 1980).

13

Regionality and Integration in the American Interlock Network

JAMES BEARDEN and BETH MINTZ

The first giant industrial firms in the USA appeared in the 1880s and, within a few decades, had come to dominate business enterprises. During this 'age of giant corporations' (Sobel, 1972), the American economy was transformed from a collection of relatively small regional firms to a system characterized by large national and international organizations (Chandler, 1977).

The growth of these corporations required large sums of capital and an institutional structure to provide it. Capital formation became dominated by large financial institutions: investment banks, insurance companies and commercial banks. Around the turn of the century a handful of investment banks with close connections to European capital dominated the promotion of corporate securities. They channelled the capital needed to build the railroads into the country and the increasing importance of these sources produced the age of finance capital. Financial institutions centred in New York and maintaining European connections created the industrial structure and dominated the economy for a number of years (Vatter, 1975).

The ties between financial institutions and industrial corporations were extensive. In order to protect their interests and to assure their own sources of capital, the leading investment and commercial banks participated actively in the direction of the newly formed corporations. Network analysis has revealed the unique place bankers held in the corporate structure. In 1904, 12 of the 20 most-central corporations in a directed graph of primary interlocks among a sample of 166 large corporations were financial institutions (Mizruchi, 1982a, p. 67). Prior to the development of large corporations, the American economy was composed of a series of relatively isolated regional centres. The creation of a mass national market changed the nature of these regions and increased competition for a time. Price wars and cutthroat competition were common. Through concentration, the giant corporation brought order and domination to the national economy. By the turn of the century the concentration ratio, as measured by the percentage of total value added produced by the four largest firms in an industry, was in the order of 30 per cent (Historical Statistics of the United States, 1970, p. 687). By 1917, there were 278 non-financial companies with assets of $20 million or more. Of that number, 236 (85 per cent) were manufacturers concentrated in the following areas: primary metals, food, transportation equipment, machinery, petroleum and chemicals (Chandler, 1977, p. 346).

The basic pattern of the American corporate structure has remained essentially the same for decades. A group of a few hundred large national and international corporations dominate a periphery of thousands of middle and small businesses. In this dual economy the large corporations have taken leadership in technology, capital intensity, price and wage setting and growth (Averitt, 1968). As a result of merger waves in the 1920s and 1960s there has been an increase in the share of corporate assets held by the major corporations. The 100 largest manufacturing companies held 39.7 per cent of all manufacturing assets in 1950 and 45.5 per cent in 1976. In the latter year, 2,050 corporations held assets of at least $250 million; together they controlled 65.8 per cent of total corporate assets (Historical Statistics of the United States, 1970, p. 576).

THE NETWORK OF INTERLOCKING DIRECTORSHIPS

Despite the vast concentration of industrial capacity and the dominant role played by large, financial institutions in this development, the American network did not contain an integrated centre. Instead, identification of the maximal subset of central firms with distance 2 or less produced a 12-corporation grouping which was not highly cohesive. Although each company was well connected to the larger system, these firms collectively maintained only ten lines based on primary interlocks among themselves.

Table 13.1 presents a description of the corporations included in the centre. Note that this group was dominated by financial institutions – nine of the 12 were commercial banks or insurance companies. Many were among the largest financials in the country, including Citibank and Chase Manhattan, the second- and third-largest commercial banks in the system. Prominent production companies were quite central as well: American Telephone and Telegraph (AT&T) ranked third in total sales and in terms of assets it was the largest company in the world; General Motors, the third-ranking non-financial, was present. Only Kraft did not fit this pattern, as, in 1976, it ranked 46th in sales.

Table 13.1   The network centre in the USA

Corporation	Sector	Corporate rank[a]	Adjacency	Rush
AT & T	Telephone	3	37	0.068
Metropolitan Life	Insurance	5	34	0.063
Citicorp	Commercial bank	2	35	0.061
Chemical New York	Commercial bank	8	35	0.056
First Chicago Corporation	Commercial bank	12	28	0.048
Mutual of New York	Insurance	42	28	0.044
Chase Manhattan	Commercial bank	3	27	0.042
Bankers' Trust	Commercial bank	10	27	0.038
Manufacturers Hanover	Commercial bank	6	28	0.037
General Motors	Vehicles	2	24	0.032
J. P. Morgan	Commercial bank	7	26	0.031
Kraft	Food	46	23	0.028

Note:
a Non-financials were ranked by sales and range from 1 to 202. Financial institutions were ranked by assets and range from 1 to 50.

The lack of integration among these units is illustrated by an investigation of 2-cliques. Based on primary interlocks only, the American interlock system contained 17 2-cliques of ten or more corporations. Eleven of these 17 were stars, indicating that the group was held together by ties to one corporation. Nine stars were organized by companies included in the network centre.[1] A tenth star was formed by links to Bankers Trust, although it contained only nine firms. Analysis of connections among the corporations forming these ten stars demonstrates the sparseness of ties. AT&T linked to more of these firms than any other corporation included in the group: it maintained five interlocks. Kraft ranked second, maintaining interlocks with Bankers Trust, First Chicago and Manufacturers Hanover. The remainder linked to two or fewer of the companies at issue.

Although interlocking directorships among competing commercial banks have been illegal since the passage of the Clayton Act in 1914, this proscription does not explain the low number of interlocks maintained among these centre stars. Director exchanges among banks operating in different regions are legal and interlocks between commercial banks and insurance companies are allowed as well. Nevertheless, First Chicago, for example, while legally allowed to link to all corporations selected, maintained only one relevant line.

Similarly Morgan, potentially able to send to or receive directors from four centre stars, maintained none. Thus, it can be concluded that the low level of interlocking among these corporations was the result of something more than legal proscriptions.

Moreover, this lack of cohesion is underscored by the minimal number of firms to which star nuclei mutually tie. Using primary interlocks only, the number of meeting-points for firms constituting the nuclei of stars can be considered. Of 45 such paired corporations, 25 did not share an interlock partner, 15 pairs met on the board of one firm and only five pairs met on two boards. These data indicate then, that not only did the companies occupying the network centre which were nuclei fail to link directly with each other, they did not tie to the same companies to any great extent. Each maintained interlocks with a fairly discrete collection of less-central firms.

These findings are consistent with the results of earlier interlock investigations. Most studies have found commercial banks and insurance companies to be among the most important corporations in the American economy, although little evidence has been generated to suggest co-ordination among these units (Dooley, 1969; Levine, 1972; Allen, 1974; Bearden et al., 1975; Mariolis, 1975; Sonquist and Koenig, 1975; Mintz and Schwartz, 1978 and 1981; Mizruchi, 1982a). The prominence of financial institutions, coupled with their lack of integration, has invited analyses of financial-interest-group formation in the American economy. And while some studies have uncovered autonomous subgroups of corporations organized into interest groups (Rochester, 1936; Sweezy, 1939; Temporary National Economic Committee, 1940; Perlo, 1957; Kotz, 1978), others have not (Sweezy, 1953; Dooley, 1969; Allen, 1978).

Analysis of the 1976 interlock network generates some support for the interest-group notion. Of the 17 2-cliques (minimum size 10) formed by primary interlocks in the overall network, eight were stars with financial institutions at their centre, three were production-company stars, two were Chicago cliques and four had no obvious unity. The eight 2-cliques organized by financial institutions were relevant in this analysis. The slightly smaller group formed by Bankers Trust was included since this firm was included in the network centre and was thus among the most important banks in the network. The question at issue is whether each nucleus interlocks with a unique set of non-financial corporations.

Table 13.2 lists the financial nuclei, the number of member companies in their 2-cliques and the number of group members which do not maintain interlocks with other financial nuclei. Note that Citicorp's 2-clique was the largest: it contained 17 member firms, of which 13 did not tie to the other nuclei. While in most of the groupings a majority of

J

Table 13.2   Financial nuclei of 2-cliques in the USA

Nucleus of star	Rank in assets	Size of star	Number of companies which do not tie to other financial nuclei
Citicorp	2	18	13
Manufacturers Hanover	6	14	8
J. P. Morgan	7	14	8
Continental Illinois	11	13	4
First Chicago Corporation	12	12	7
Chase Manhattan	3	12	8
Chemical New York	8	10	7
Metropolitan Life	5	10	4
Bankers' Trust	10	9	7

Note: Continental Illinois is not included in the network centre. The 2-cliques are based on the network of primary interlocks.

member firms did not tie to the other financials, there were two exceptions: Continental Illinois and Metropolitan Life. They both organized 2-cliques in which over half of their members maintained interlocks with the other nuclei. Continental Illinois, a Chicago commercial bank, was most extreme in this regard: eight of its 12 member companies tied to the other financials. In the case of Metropolitan Life, five of its nine members maintained interlocks with other nuclei.

Metropolitan Life and Continental Illinois, therefore, organized groupings which were less discrete than the other financials under consideration. They can be distinguished from these other nuclei in additional ways as well. Metropolitan Life was an insurance company, while the other nuclei were commercial banks. Continental Illinois was the only financial in the network to organize a 2-clique of minimum size 10 which was not a member of the network centre. It was also the only selected commercial bank which was not among the major money banks of the USA.

These findings suggest that the major foci of interest-group formation in the USA were the largest commercial banks and that the seven banks included in the network centre organized discrete groupings. The last column of table 13.2 shows that many of the largest corporations in the 1976 network maintained primary interlocks to one and only one of these major financials. These findings can be interpreted as support for the existence of financial interest groups but some differences between our results and those of earlier studies should be noted. In the USA the question of interest-group formation has been framed in terms of the domination of industrial corporations by financial institutions. Guided by the theory of bank control (Fitch and Oppenheimer, 1970), this tradition has attempted to uncover a series of co-ordinated groups organized around and subordinated to the interests of financial firms. While recent work has failed to uncover groups of this type (Mariolis, 1977; Mintz and Schwartz, 1983, 1984; Mizruchi, 1982b), our method does not directly address domination and hence our results are not comparable with those studies. Nevertheless, our findings demonstrate the existence of bank-centred groups within the interlock network and, although we cannot evaluate the extent to which the groups approach the types suggested by bank-control theory, we find an identifiable interest-group structure within the system.

REGIONAL CHARACTER OF THE NETWORK

Previous research on the American interlock network has identified regional groupings within the larger system (Allen, 1978; Dooley, 1969; Sweezy, 1953). Typically characterized by dense pockets of director exchanges, analyses of these subsets should offer important information about the shape of the larger network. In recent years especially, geographical variation has attracted much attention as the northern industrial corridor has been threatened by the economic growth of the sunbelt.

To evaluate the role of regionalism in the overall structure, the extent to which geographical proximity effects interlock patterns was investigated. For this, the network was divided into four sections: the north-east, north-central, west and south. Due to the importance of New York City as a major commercial centre, additional analyses of New York City as a subset were carried out when relevant. The north-east contained the most corporations (108) while the south (27) contained the fewest. The north-eastern network contained a large component of 94 members, with an average distance between companies of 2.5 steps. Moreover, this area included many highly central firms: nine of the 12 companies included in the network centre were headquartered in the north-east. The north-central was second in importance to the north-east as measured by number of selected corporations contained (83), size (71) and density of its large component (0.08). The smallest components were found in the south, where 12 corporations formed four components ranging in size from 2 to 4. Regional differences are apparent then in the number of corporations in an area, the level of connectedness within the area and the number and density of components forming the locale.

Table 13.3 Regional densities in the USA

	North-east	North-central	South	West	New York City	Number of corporations
North-east	0.06 (376)	0.03 (268)	0.02 (49)	0.02 (65)	—	108
North-central		0.06 (207)	0.01 (22)	0.01 (39)	0.04 (181)	83
South			0.03 (11)	0.01 (10)	0.02 (37)	27
West				0.07 (41)	0.02 (41)	34
New York City					0.10 (176)	61

Note: Numbers in parentheses indicate number of lines.

Regional effects are underscored when density is considered. As table 13.3 illustrates, corporations consistently maintained a greater proportion of lines with firms in the same region than with companies in other areas. The western section is most autonomous in this regard: it maintained 7 per cent of potential lines within its locale, compared to 1 per cent with its southern and north-central neighbours and 2 per cent with the north-east. The north-east and the north-central regions each maintained 6 per cent of all possible internal lines and each showed a low level of external connections. When New York City was investigated as a separate region, it became the most densely connected area, maintaining 10 per cent of potential lines. These results are striking when it is recalled that the overall system had a density of only 3 per cent.

These findings suggest that the American interlock network was divided into regional groupings within which corporations maintained denser connections to local concerns than to distant companies. These results are consistent with earlier studies which have found regional organization within the larger system (Allen, 1978; Dooley, 1969; Mintz and Schwartz, 1981). At the same time, however, this is best understood as local pockets of densely interlocked corporations tied into a larger network, rather than as autonomous centres. This is illustrated by an investigation of the composition of regional centres.

When the network is partitioned into geographical areas and the maximal subset of central firms with distance 2 or less are identified, it is found that each locale produces a small collection of highly central companies. The north-east contained the largest number: six corporations (AT&T, Bankers' Trust, Chemical New York, Citicrop, Metropolitan Life and Morgan), all of which were also included in the centre of the overall system. Each firm was a nucleus of a 2-clique (minimum size 8) formed by primary interlocks maintained within the north-east.[2] Each firm was also a nucleus of a 2-clique (minimum size 9) formed by primary interlocks in the larger network. The analysis of the network centre presented above showed that these nuclei did not form an integrated centre. Since the same corporations are at issue, they cannot form an integrated regional centre either.

Nevertheless, geographical proximity remains an important feature of the interlock system. When primary interlocks are considered, for example, we see that corporations occupying the network centre accumulated more centrality from ties to other firms in their area than through interlocks to companies in all regions of the country. For north-east-based nuclei, 68 per cent (65) of their primary interlocks were with companies within the region, 27 per cent (26) were with the north-central companies, while only four interlocks (4 per cent) were with the south or west.

Similar patterns were present for the north-central area. Of the four nuclei of 2-cliques (minimum size 10) of the overall system, formed by primary interlocks, which were located in the north-central region, 80 per cent (33) of their lines were within the region, while 19 per cent (8) were to firms in other areas, seven of which were to the north-east. However, the centre generated by lines maintained within the area contained only four corporations (International Harvester, Continental Illinois, First Chicago and Mellon National), two of which were nuclei of 2-cliques (minimum size 8) formed by primary interlocks within the area. Although this was too small to define a regional centre, the locale forms a densely interlocked subset within the larger system, a subset which was not autonomous but linked to other areas of the country.

Although the western section of the USA was the densest of all regions, the most-central companies were less integrated than in other areas. The three most-central firms (Pacific Gas & Electric, Western Bancorp and BankAmerica) did not link. Only one, BankAmerica, was a nucleus of a 2-clique formed by primary interlocks (minimum size 5), thus indicating that in the west, companies typically did not maintain a high number of interlocks. In fact, 57 per cent of all intraregional lines were created by companies with four ties or less, as compared to 30 per cent for the north-central region. Thus, we conclude that the western centre was neither integrated nor connected to a large number of corporations within the group. Similarly, a cohesive centre was not generated in the southern section. The largest component contained only four corporations, a number too small to be of interest in this respect.

Finally, there remains one regional partitioning which might be expected to produce autonomous centres within the system. Since the late 1960s the USA has experienced a vast migration of population and capital from the traditional centres of industrial activity – the north-east and mid-west – to the southern and south-western corridor of the country. At times described as a split between the established financial interests of the north-east and the new electronic and defense industries of the south-west, this shift has been referred to as the Yankee-Cowboy Theory. This theory suggests a growing division between the regions (see Johnson, 1976; Rifkin and Barber, 1978) and to test it the interlock network was divided into three sections: the greybelt, consisting of 16 states; the sunbelt, consisting of 15 states; and those remaining. The number of corporations in each grouping was 183, 53 and 16 respectively.

As in other partitionings, corporations in each locale maintained denser ties internally than across regions. Within the greybelt, 5 per cent of potential lines were maintained; in the sunbelt, the figure was 3 per cent; while between areas, the density was 2 per cent. While it was not expected that the greybelt would contain an autonomous centre, since the most-central firms in the region were almost identical to the most-central companies of the overall system, the organizing principle of the sunbelt was of interest. Results suggest, however, that this area did not contain an integrated centre and that little additional information about the structure of regional groupings can be obtained from this analysis. We find that the most central companies in the sunbelt (Pacific Gas & Electric, BankAmerica and Transamerica) are all western firms. Of these three, only BankAmerica was the star of a 2-clique (minimum size 5) formed by primary interlocks and all member firms were from the west. These findings indicate that the sunbelt was not an integrated area, that corporations maintained a higher proportion of lines when geographical areas are defined more narrowly and that the shifts of capital and economic power have not generated solid alliances. From this we conclude that the rise of the sunbelt has not created a new organizational structure and that geographical proximity remains the most important variable in predicting the density of intercorporate interlocks.

TYPES OF INTERLOCKS WITHIN THE NETWORK

Given the regional structure of the American system, there is a particular interest in similarities and differences in the type of interlocks which form local areas, as well as in a comparison of intraregional and cross-regional types. For these analyses, interlocks were divided into primary, induced and unclassified types. Primary and induced interlocks were subdivided into financial and production types, while unclassified interlocks were divided into those carried by directors holding four or more board positions and those carried by directors with less than four.

Over half (55 per cent) of all interlocks in the 1976 system of director exchanges were unclassified interlocks – held by individuals who were not primarily affiliated with corporations in our sample. Such directors occupying at least four board positions accounted for almost half of that number or 24 per cent (295) of all interlocks in the network. While 16 per cent of interlocks were induced by primary interlocks, 29 percent were primary (primary production, in particular, accounted for 24 per cent). These findings demonstrate that directors generating unclassified interlocks, responsible for 55 per cent of all interlocks, were the most important actors in the formation of the overall interlock system that network specialists were crucial to that for-

Table 13.4 Types of interlocks within the regional networks in the USA (%)

	Primary		Induced		Unclassified		Total
	Financial	Production	Financial	Production	By network specialists (≥ 4 positions)	By others	
North-east	9	20	3	12	28	27	100 (467)
New York City	9	19	3	10	37	21	100 (223)
North-central	2	34	2	14	22	26	100 (277)
West	10	31	2	2	2	53	100 (51)
South	0	18	9	0	0	73	100 (11)

Note: Absolute numbers are in parentheses.

mation and that directors who were executives of very large corporations typically maintained a limited number of outside board positions. These findings underscore the importance of distinguishing between primary and secondary interlocks in an analysis of intercorporate interaction.

Turning to an investigation of the types of interlocks forming specific regions, several differences among locales are immediately apparent. First, as table 13.4 illustrates, the north-central region of the USA was less dependent on primary financial interlocks than other parts of the country. Only 2 per cent of interlocks within the region were formed by primary interlocks maintained with financial institutions, versus 9 percent for the north east and New York City, 10 per cent for the west and none for the south.[3] Second, when we consider the proportion of primary production interlocks, we see that they predominated in the north-central and western regions. This reflects the economic composition of the various regions and hence is not startling.

The western region is more interesting in this regard. Although 29 per cent of the firms in the category were financials, 31 per cent of all interlocks were primary production interlocks. Thus, although the north-east in general, and New York City in particular (29 per cent financials), had about the same financial–non-financial composition as the west and their proportions of financial primary interlocks were roughly the same, their primary production interlocks were quite different. This indicates that in the west, executives of production companies sat on fewer boards than in the east and, thus, induced production interlocks accounted for a very small proportion of all interlocks in the region.

Moreover, network specialists – directors with four or more directorships and no inside position – were less involved in the west. Only two per cent of western interlocks were formed by these individuals. In the north-central region 22 per cent of all interlocks were created by these big linkers, while the north-east was stronger still with a 28 per cent total. When we consider New York City as a separate area, we find that its network depends on big linkers: 45 per cent of its interlocks were produced by directors with at least three board memberships. Looking only at network specialists, New York City still stood out: 37 per cent of its interlocks were produced by these individuals.

Given previous research on the USA, network specialists would be expected to tie regions together into an integrated whole. This is partially true. First we note that unclassified directors, in general, are crucial to the maintenance of a unified interlock network. Depending on region, these individuals accounted for between 50 per cent (linking the north-central section with the west) and 73 per cent (uniting the south and the west) of interregional interlocks. Network specialists were most important in tying the north-east to other areas of the country. In the case of interlocks connecting the north-east and the north-central section, for example, 23 per cent were formed by network specialists. North-east to west and north-east to south figures were roughly comparable: 26 per cent and 25 per cent respectively. North-central ties to other areas were less dependent on network specialists: 13 per cent of interlocks connecting it to the south and 17 per cent of interlocks connecting it to the west were formed by these directors. South to west interlocks were less dependent still on network specialists: nine per cent of all their interconnections were formed by these individuals.

Network specialists then, are not evenly distributed within the 1976 interlock network. Both in terms of intraregional composition as well as cross-regional ties, unaffiliated big linkers were most important in the north-east.

TYPE OF INTERLOCKS MAINTAINED
BY FINANCIAL INSTITUTIONS

Financial institutions have been identified as among the most-central corporations in the interlock network. In this section, the sources of financial centrality are examined on the basis of the division into primary, induced and unclassified interlocks.

Unclassified interlocks help form the network created by financial institutions and unaffiliated board members were dominant in all partitioning of the interlock system. They account for over half (55 per cent) of the interlocks in the full network, over half (55 per cent) of the interlocks maintained by non-financial corporations, as well as about half (53 per cent) of all ties involving financial institutions. Network specialists were evenly distributed as well: they account for 23 per cent, 24 per cent and 22 per cent respectively.

Differences among financial institutions are apparent, however, when the total number of interlocks are considered. Dividing financials into two categories – those with the most interlocks versus those with the fewest – it was found that the companies maintaining the least number of interconnections had a larger proportion of unclassifed interlocks: 60 per cent compared to 54 per cent. As might be expected, the less-integrated financials maintained few interlocks created by network specialists: only 6 per cent versus 26 per cent for companies maintaining the greatest number of interlocks. When we add the proportion of induced interlocks, we find that at least 46 per-cent of the

Table 13.5 *Types of interlocks involving financial institutions in the USA (%)*

	Primary		Induced		Unclassified		Total
	Financial	Production	Financial	Production	By network specialists (≥ 4 positions)	By others	
Commercial banks (N=28)	12	22	0	19	19	28	100 (517)
Insurance companies (N=13)	12	9	3	7	29	39	100 (202)
Investment banks (N=6)	13	10	6	15	25	32	100 (72)
All financials (N=47)	12	17	2	15	22	31	100 (791)

Note: Absolute numbers are in parentheses.

interconnections of the most-integrated financials were created by individuals holding three or more board positions as opposed to 19 per cent for the less-connected firms. Thus, financial institutions which accumulated high adjacencies did so because of the big linkers who sat on their boards.

Comparing interlock distributions across types of financial institutions (table 13.5), we find that other factors are at work as well. Examining differences between commercial banks and insurance companies, it can be seen that a large proportion of insurance-company interlocks were created by unaffiliated directors (68 per cent versus 47 per cent). Note also that insurance companies had a much larger proportion of interlocks which were created by network specialists (29 per cent versus 19 per cent).[4] Finally, note that induced interlocks were more important to the composition of commercial-bank interconnections than to those of insurance companies (19 per cent versus 10 per cent).[5] These differences indicate that commerical banks and insurance companies played different roles within the system of interlocking directorships. The predominance of interlocks created by unaffiliated directors, including network specialists, suggests that insurance companies help tie the overall network together. Commercial-bank linkages, on the other hand, were dominated by interlocks created by directors who were affiliated to corporations in the system. Primary interlocks accounted for 33 per cent of their ties and primary and induced together for 53 per cent. Hence, commercial-banking networks were created by and as a result of the direct placement of executives of major corporations. They were, therefore, more likely to represent one-to-one relationships than were insurance-company interlocks. We thus conclude that commercial banks have more specific orientations than insurance companies.

CONCLUSION

The portrait which emerges from our analysis is of a loosely integrated system characterized by financial centrality, interest-group formation and regional density. There were two unifying mechanisms within the network: insurance companies and unaffiliated directors. Both tie corporations and regional and financial groupings into the larger system.

Financial institutions played a special role. They were consistently the most-central corporation in the whole network, in the regions and in the interest groups. Insurance companies can be distinguished from commercial banks in this regard. Their centrality was disproportionately due to unaffiliated directors, network specialists in particular. Banks, on the other hand, owed their centrality to the larger number of directors attracted from production companies. Thus, while major banks were the foci of interest groups, insurance companies were not. In fact, 29 per cent of the corporations in the selection were tied to a bank-centred interest group. While it is unclear whether these groups were dominated by banks, their existence is one of the most striking features of the network and suggests the continued importance of major commercial banks in the American economy.

Interaction patterns then, were associated with the corporations most directly involved with capital-flow decisions: financial institutions. Commercial banks played a particular role in this regard. They organized discrete groupings, while insurance companies functioned as organizational links between these groups.

Additionally, geographical proximity is related to interaction patterns. The ties to neighbouring corporations were denser than those to distant firms. Tendencies towards regional autonomy were counteracted, however, by significant numbers of interregional ties, especially those formed by unaffiliated directors. Popular notions that the sunbelt states had become the new centre of American economic activity are not supported by the network analysis. Within the regions, the pattern of financial centrality was maintained. Thus, the regional organization of the American network interacts with the financial organization rather than conflicts with it.

NOTES

1   These companies are Citicorp, AT&T, Morgan, Manufacturers Hanover, First Chicago, Chase Manhattan, Metropolitan Life, Kraft and Chemical New York.
2   We analysed 2-cliques with different minimum sizes when comparably sized groups were not available. We report results on the largest 2-cliques generated in each analysis.
3   Due to the small number of lines in the southern region, little emphasis will be placed on the area in the present analysis.
4   Fourteen of the 28 banks and six of the 13 insurance companies were included among the most-interconnected financials in the system. Thus, this difference cannot be explained by differences in the total number of lines maintained.
5   That commercial banks maintain a higher proportion of primary production lines than other financial institutions can be explained by board compositions. Commercial banks typically have very large boards with few inside directors, while insurance companies and diversified financials have a more even inside–outside mix. They therefore have a larger number of directors to send out and fewer seats earmarked for outsiders. Hence, the difference in primary-production lines between types of financials was but the result of differences in board make-up.

14

The Transnational Network

MEINDERT FENNEMA and HUIBERT SCHIJF[1]

In the preceding chapters of this book national interlock networks have been analysed from a historical and comparative perspective. In this chapter, two *international* networks of corporate interlocks will be analysed: a network of international interlocking directorships and a network of international financial participations. Such networks constitute business structures above the national level which cement the different national systems into an international structure.

The network of foreign ownership relations is clearly a network of control. The network of interlocking directorships, on the other hand, is predominantly a network of communication. An international network of control, stemming from international direct investment, creates economic interdependence among nation-states, a situation which has been characterized as the problem of territorial non-coincidence, i.e. the economic and political decision-making structures do not coincide (Murray, 1971). The structure of such territorial non-coincidence will be analysed for nine countries: Finland has been excluded because the data on financial participations were not available, while for the interlocking directorships it was clear from the start that there were no international interlocks. Subsequently, the analysis will concentrate on a very specific kind of international control, namely that involved in the transnational firms in which *ownership* has been internationalized. These companies differ from the simple multinational corporation and stem from international mergers which took place in Western Europe, mainly during the 1960s. A number of parent–subsidiary relations were expected to be paralleled by interlocking directorships between the parent company and its subsidiaries and such interlocks would clearly indicate control relations. Likewise the transnational corporations were expected to have interlocking directorships between the two (or more) national headquarters, due to the fact that they often had overlapping or nearly identical boards.

Such interlocks also indicate control, though here the 'direction' of the control relation is not straightforward. All other interlocks, however, will be considered as communication channels providing for international business consultation and co-ordination and they will be analysed in the last part of this chapter.

This chapter is based on an analysis of the transnational network of interlocking directorships among the most central firms from the nine countries. This network is compared with the one found by Fennema (1982), also for 1976, but based on a selection of the largest rather than the most central firms from several countries.

FINANCIAL PARTICIPATIONS

To investigate international participations all of the 250 largest firms in each country were taken into account. For nine countries this amounted to 2,250 corporations, among which 252 international financial participations were found. Only participations of 50 per cent or more were taken into consideration. Minority participations were not included, even though such participations might be regarded as the most interesting in terms of network analysis. The reason for this was that data on minority participations are incomplete and unreliable, especially if so many firms from different countries are taken into account. By excluding minority participations the type of interlock associated with international financial participations is limited to joint ventures, in which both participations hold 50 per cent of the stock. Such joint ventures are very rare indeed: none of the participations in this sample is such a joint venture. In fact, nearly a half of the 252 international participations were parent–subsidiary relations in which the parent held 100 per cent. For this reason the analysis in this section is, in effect, restricted to a mapping of the foreign subsidiaries of the multinational corporations in the data set. The distribution of these foreign subsidiaries over the nine countries is presented in table 14.1.

The asymmetry of the financial links is striking. The American corporations had, in 1976, 116 majority financial participations in the eight European countries, while there were only two financial participations by European corporations in the USA (Shell and Cavenham). Among the European countries there were also remarkable differences: Austrian corporations had no international participations, Belgian only 5 but French corporations had 33. Conversely, there existed 72 participations in Belgian corporations (among them 32 American), 25 participations in Austrian corporations and 17 in Swiss corporations. The network of interlocking financial participations

Table 14.1 Distribution of financial participations

Country of parent	Country of subsidiary									Total
	Austria	Belgium	Switzerland	Germany	France	Britain	Italy	Netherlands	USA	
Austria	—	0	0	0	0	0	0	0	0	0
Belgium	0	—	0	1	0	1	1	2	0	5
Switzerland	6	1	—	2	1	1	3	0	0	14
Germany	3	7	2	—	1	1	5	1	0	20
France	1	14	3	2	—	3	6	4	0	33
Britain	5	6	1	2	2	—	0	8	1	25
Italy	3	2	1	1	0	0	—	2	0	9
Netherlands	4	10	4	4	3	1	3	—	1	30
USA	3	32	6	15	6	18	22	14	—	116
Total	25	72	17	27	13	25	40	31	2	252

looks completely different from the other networks analysed in this book. Only in one case was there a link between two independent corporations via a joint venture. The network effectively took the shape of a number of 'stars', each comprising a parent company surrounded by its subsidiaries. Only in five cases did the star contain two levels and thus included a 'tree'[2]. This, for instance, applied to British Petroleum, which had seven 100 per cent participations and two 50 per cent participations in the sample. One of the 50 per cent participations was in Société Française des Petroles BP, which in turn had a 50 per cent participation in Total Belgium.

The 252 participations were held by 143 corporations. Among the corporations with five or more subsidiaries in the sample, the Dutch and American multinationals predominated: Philips (10), British Petroleum (8), Exxon (7), Chrysler (6), Mobil Oil (6), Shell (6), Peugot-Citroen (5), Unilever (5), Ford (5), General Motors (5) and Xerox (5). Do financial participations coincide with international interlocking directorships? For the American multinationals this was the case for only 25 of the 116 subsidiaries they had in Europe (22 per cent). These 25 companies generated 12 lines with a multiplicity greater than 1. Four banks (Bank of America, First Chicago Corporation, Chemical Bank and Morgan) had nine or more interlocks with their Belgian subsidiaries. At the same time, they had none or very few interlocks with their subsidiaries in other countries so that the Belgian subsidiaries seemed to be the European headquarters of these banks.

Another interesting phenomenon worth mentioning is that in a dozen cases there were no interlocks between an American parent and its European subsidiaries, although there were interlocks among these subsidiaries. There were, in such instances, regional executives who did not sit on the board of directors of the parent company but served as big linkers between the European subsidiaries. A good example of such a regional big linker was J.G.Maisonrouge, who was director of all four European subsidiaries of IBM without being an executive of the American parent. These observations underline the relative autonomy of American subsidiaries in Europe, which were controlled by sophisticated financial auditing techniques rather than through the direct and personal surveillance of the managers. Another factor contributing to the existence of regional big linkers was the fact that many American firms started their multinationalization in the 1960s in an effort to stay in the race for the European markets:

> In nearly every case, expatriate managers with headquarters' experience supervised start-ups, or the integration of acquisitions into the multinational system. Sometimes, as in the case of Du Pont, the *same* U.S. expatriate started U.K., then Dutch, then Swiss, French and German operations. (Franko, 1972, p. 18).

Such persons became the regional linkers of the network of American subsidiaries in Europe.

Although the most central American corporations were hardly inter-locked with European corporations, they might be expected to have been interlocked with the European networks through their sub-sidiaries. However, this was not the case. Almost all of these subsidiaries were in the periphery of the national networks or were completely isolated, especially in Belgium. The only American subsi-diaries which had rather central positions were the Belgian ACE (a 68 per cent participation of Westinghouse Electric), the Dutch Van Nelle[3] (a 100 per cent participation of Standard Brands) and IBM United Kingdom Holding.

For the European corporations the story is different. Here 136 foreign subsidiaries were found and 70 of these were interlocked with their parent through one or more multiple directors. In 43 cases there were two or more interlocking directorships and in eight cases there were five or more interlocks.[4] Seven of these closely interlocked subsidiaries were Belgian. Like their American counterparts the European banks tended to remain closely interlocked with some of their Belgian subsidiaries, although the 44 interlocks between the Dutch ABN and its Belgian subsidiary was somewhat extreme. These banks had an almost complete overlap of Raad van Kommissarissen and Raad van Bestuur.

In Europe, the parent–subsidary relations indeed corroborate the findings of Franko:

> Continental European enterprises maintained highly personalized relations with their foreign manufacturing subsidiaries. The nineteenth century practice of appointing relatives of company owners as heads of foreign subsidiaries gradually gave way to less familial ties. Nevertheless, at the beginning of the 1970's, the most important bonds between the centre and periphery in European multinational systems were still the personal relationships between president and presidents of foreign ventures. (Franko, 1976, p. 187)

As Franko has convincingly shown, the typical European parent-subsidiary relation permits a lesser degree of financial control than the American firms are able to exercise: 'When European managers described their mother–daughter organizations, they invoked analo-gies of control systems used in roman or feudal times.' (Franko, 1976, p. 170) Such personal surveillance through interlocking directorships is less efficient for such highly complex multiproduct organizations as the modern multinational corporations.

BI-NATIONAL FIRMS

Some firms can be regarded as bi-national firms, Royal Dutch/Shell and Unilever being the best known and most established examples. Both are Anglo-Dutch and were formed at the beginning of the century. The Royal Dutch/Shell group resulted from the 1907 merger of the Koninklijke Nederlandsche Petroleum Maatschappij and 'Shell' Transport and Trading. The group as it operated in 1976 had two group holding companies, each owned on a 60/40 per cent basis by the Dutch and the British parent companies. Shell Petroleum NV had its headquarters in The Hague, while Shell Petroleum Limited was based in London. The group was administered by a Committee of Shell Petroleum Limited and the presidium of Shell Petroleum NV. While the Royal Dutch/Shell group was based on a joint subsidiary principle, Unilever had a more complex structure. Unilever originated in a merger between the Van Den Berg & Jurgens Margarine Unie and Lever Brothers in 1929. Rather than bringing together complementary business formations, as was the case with Royal Dutch/Shell, the two merging companies brought together related products. The organizational chart also differed considerably. Unilever was a straightforward 50/50 union between Unilever Limited in London and Unilever NV in Rotterdam. The two parents were separate companies but were so closely linked that they worked as one. Each director was on the board of both and at the top there was a special committee of three to which the boards delegated most of their functions and which took virtually all the major decisions. Both Shell and Unilever seemed to have profited from their bi-nationality, especially during the Second World War when operations could be shifted smoothly from one headquarter to another. The lack of identification with one specific country also had advantages during the process of decolonization. In Indonesia, for example, both Shell and Unilever withdrew their Dutch employees and acted as British companies, thus escaping for some time the anti-Dutch campaigns of 1957 to 1960. Although the preferential treatment of both companies by the Indonesian government cannot be ascribed solely to their bi-nationality, it certainly played a role.

For a long time the two Anglo-Dutch firms were without followers but from the 1960s a number of firms in Europe negotiated international mergers. The first occured when AGFA and Gevaert formed a German–Belgian bi-national, AGFA-Gevaert, in 1964. In 1968 FIAT negotiated an association with Citroen, though this was dissolved in 1973 under pressure from the Michelin family who owned the majority of the shares of Citroen. Citroen was subsequently taken over by Peugeot. In 1969 the Dutch Fokker merged with the German Vereinigte Flugtechnische Werke to form Fokker-VFW and in the following year an attempt by Crédit Lyonnais, Commerzbank and Banco di Roma to amalgamate was prevented by the veto of the French government. As an alternative, these banks formed the international bank consortium, Europartners. Dunlop and Pirelli adopted a similar organization to Royal Dutch/Shell in 1971, Pirelli being jointly owned by Italian and Swiss family holding companies. And in 1972 the Dutch state-owned Hoogovens and the German privately owned Hoesch formed ESTEL.

None of the recently formed bi-national companies survived the 1980s. Dunlop-Pirelli split up in 1980, as did Fokker-VFW. 'VFW is an organization embedded in German politics', said Fokker's president Swarttouw in 1981.[5] In that same year Fokker engaged in a new transnational co-operation, this time with the American McDonnal Douglas. This co-operation also failed and by 1983 Fokker seemed to be in trouble. ESTEL broke up in 1982. Again it was suggested from the Dutch side that political pressure from the German government played a decisive role.[6] In both cases the German part of the bi-national merged shortly afterwards with another German firm (VFW with Messerschmidt-Bölkow-Blohm; Hoesch with Krupp). The only bi-national firm still in existence, AGFA-Gevaert, became a German firm in 1981, because Bayer – which already owned 91.5 per cent of the AGFA-parent – took over the Gevaert interests in AGFA.[7] In nearly all these cases the main reason for the failure seems to be that the government support which was needed in the economic crisis was not given unconditionally and a national approach proved incompatible with a bi-national company structure. Thus the economic crisis had a strong negative effect on the international concentration which took place in the 1960s and the beginning of the 1970s. Only Royal Dutch/Shell and Unilever seemed to continue unshaken by the crisis.

It may be useful at this point to recall the results of the previous study on interlocking directorships at the international level. Fennema (1982) found that the international network, though very loose when compared with the national networks, had grown denser and more connected between 1970 and 1976. This was caused by a spectacular increase in the number of big linkers, who carried 37 per cent of the international interlocks in 1976 as against 25 per cent in 1970. A rapidly growing, international corporate elite was shown to carry an integrated Atlantic network in which banks were very central. At the time of writing (1983), it remains to be seen whether, in the face of the economic crisis and the impending nationalist reactions of the governments, the international business elite still strives for institutionalized forums for general business discussion and co-ordination at the international level. Data for the 1980s has yet to be gathered and so few hypotheses can be formulated. It is intriguing to ask, however, whether decreasing economic interdependence is associated with a decline in the communication structure or whether the reverse is true.

THE TRANSNATIONAL NETWORK

So far, the international financial participations among 2,250 firms from nine countries have been investigated. To do the same for interlocking directorships would have exceeded the capacity of the research team. For this reason it was decided to limit the number of corporations to the 40 most central from each of the nine countries. As has been seen in the chapters on national networks, central corporations tended to be densely connected with each other. In our transnational analysis we therefore want to investigate whether this is also the case across frontiers. The criterium used for centrality is simply the number of connected corporations within the national networks. The transnational network studied in this chapter consists of the 360 firms and the international interlocks between them. There were no international interlocks among 202 of these 360 enterprises and among the remaining 158 firms there were 232 international lines carried by 111 persons.

Table 14.2   International linkers and their international interlocks

Number of Positions	Number of persons	Number of International Interlocks
2	63	63
3	16	33
4	11	39
5	7	42
6	6	37
7	5	38
≥ 9	3	43
Total	111	295

Table 14.2 gives the distribution of positions among the multiple directors and it can be seen that the majority held only two directorships. Among these were many directors of the bi-national firms Royal Dutch/Shell and ESTEL. Thirty-two persons, however, sat on the boards of at least four corporations, thus creating at least six interlocks (national *and* international). Accordingly, less than a third of the multiple directors carried 496 out of 580 interlocks in the network as a whole. A tiny business elite seemed to carry a large part of the network.

These persons also tended to be of importance in their national networks: 272 national lines were carried by the 111 international interlockers and they had still more positions in the 210 remaining firms in their national networks. About a third of the multiple directors with only two positions had more positions, while three-quarters of the multiple directors with three or more positions had more directorships. The global network connecting the 360 enterprises and carried by the international interlockers contained 504 lines based on 580 interlocks. The transnational network (disregarding interlocks *within* national economies) contained 295 interlocks formed into 232 lines. Some bi-national firms, such as Shell, Unilever, ESTEL and Brown Bovery (see table 14.4), were interlocked internationally through almost identical boards and accounted for most of the international lines of high multiplicity. Very few of the remaining lines had a multiplicity of more than 1 and so an analysis which disregards the multiplicity results in the loss of little information.

The density of the transnational network was very low (0.004) compared with the densities of the national networks and the network studied by Fennema (1982). This latter difference can be explained in several ways. First, in the transnational network the interlocks carried by purely 'national' interlockers were not taken into account. Second, the number of firms included here was twice as large as Fennema's sample and the density measure is very sensitive to the number of points in a graph. Third, the advisory-board interlocks were not taken into account and a third of the international interlocks in the Fennema study were advisory interlocks. This may also explain part of the most surprising difference from the previous analysis. Whereas Fennema found that the 33 *largest* American firms carried 76 international lines, the investigation of this transnational network found that the 40 *most central* American firms carried, in the same year, just six international lines. The exclusion of the advisory interlocks, however, explains only part of the difference. Deleting advisory interlocks, the 33 largest American firms in Fennema's data set still carried 26 international interlocks. Four of these were with Canadian firms and one was with the Luxembourg company, ARBED; none of these firms was included in the transnational network. This leaves some 15 interlocks to be explained by the difference in interlocking behaviour between the largest firms and the most central firms.

This finding underlines the fact that the most central firms in the American network were not the most internationally oriented. A clear example is the American subsidiary of Royal Dutch/Shell, Shell Oil, which was among the ten largest companies in the USA and, according to Fennema's study, was heavily interlocked with European firms. It

Table 14.3 International lines

	Austria	Belgium	Switzerland	Germany	France	Britain	Italy	Netherlands	USA
Austria		2	10	7	5	2	9	1	0
Belgium			1	1	46	3	0	6	1
Switzerland				20	9	4	16	1	1
Germany					4	1	3	48	0
France						14	5	0	0
Britain							2	6	4
Italy								0	0
Netherlands									0
USA									

was not, however, among the 40 most central firms in the USA. This particular example illustrates a general feature of the American network: the most central firms were not the ones which had an international orientation with respect to interlocking.

The network studied here was typically a European network, which had another striking characteristic: bi-national lines were predominantly between neighbouring countries. Table 14.3 shows that bi-national density was very high between Belgium and France, and between Germany and the Netherlands and was high between Germany and Switzerland, between Italy and Switzerland and between France and Great Britain (see figure 14.1). A high number of lines might have been expected between Belgium and the Netherlands, given the high number of lines between Belgium and France and the equally high number of lines between the Netherlands and Germany. But the Flemish part of Belgian business was not at all integrated with the Dutch business community. The Walloon business elite, on the other hand, had many ties with the French business community. Drawing on financial-participations data (see the first section) it can be shown that both the Flemish sectors of Belgian business and the Dutch economy were heavily penetrated by German and American multinationals. These business systems thus looked like dependent economies and exhibited few 'horizontal' relations. The Walloon bourgoisie, on the other hand, was still relatively self-contained and had historically been linked with the French steel industry. This can be seen in tables 14.3 and 14.4. A further historical factor which kept Belgian and Dutch business separated was the geographical distance of their respective colonial empires. Belgian colonial business was oriented towards Africa (the Congo), whereas Dutch colonial enterprises were pre-

Figure 14.1   Bi-national integration

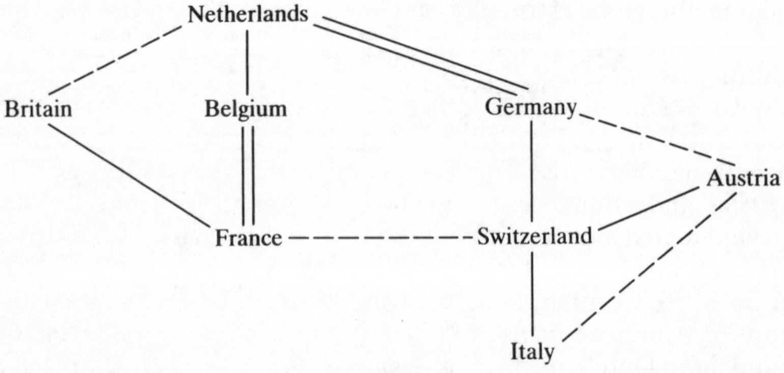

Note: Double lines = > 20 lines; single = 11 lines ≤ lines ≤ 20; broken lines = 6 ≤ lines ≤ 10.

dominantly oriented towards South-East Asia (Mommen, 1982, Baudet and Fennema, 1983).

Table 14.4 shows the international lines with multiplicity 3 or more. All lines with multiplicity 4 or more were between companies of the same concern. Those lines with multiplicity 3, however, indicate strong financial links. These links include those between AKZO and Deutsche Bank and those in the French and Belgian steel industry, where Paribas had a dominant position through Chiers-Chatillon and COBEPA.

Table 14.4   International lines with multiplicity 3 or more

	Multiplicity
Estel (Dutch) – Hoesch (German)	15
KNPM (Dutch) – Shell T & T (British)	8
AKZO (Dutch) – ENKA (German)	6
AKZO (Dutch) – Deutsche Bank (German)	3
Semperit (Austrian) – Kléber-Colombes (French)	4
Brown Boveri (Swiss) – Brown Boveri (German)	4
Chiers-Chatillon (French) – Cockerill (Belgian)	3
Chiers-Chatillon (French) – Forges de Thy-marcinelle et Moncau (Belgian)	3
Chiers-Chatillon (French) – Electrobel (Belgian)	3
Chiers-Chatillon (French) – Intercom (Belgian)	3
Chiers-Chatillon (French) – COBEPA (Belgian)	3
Chiers-Chatillon (French) – Forges de Clabecq (Belgian)	3

The closely linked economies, those of Belgium and France and those of the Netherlands and Germany, were even more closely linked by multiple interlocks than by single interlocks. The only substantial change in the global structure was that the Netherlands and Great Britain became highly interlocked when multiplicity was taken into account. This was largely due to the interlocks between the companies of the Royal Dutch/Shell group (Unilever was not among the 40 most central Dutch firms). The Dutch firms occupied central positions in the transnational network. There were historical links with German industrial and commercial interests and Royal Dutch/ Shell and Unilever created a community of interest between parts of the British and Dutch business system. Hence the Netherlands had strong ties with both the German and British networks. The financial participations of American firms in Dutch firms was also high (see the first section) and Dutch investment in the USA was considerable (see Overbeek, 1981).

AN INTERNATIONAL BUSINESS COMMUNITY?

Notwithstanding the dominance of direct cross-border relations, the network of internationally interlocked firms had a high connectivity. Of the 158 internationally interlocked firms, 142 formed one large component with a density of 0.02. The remaining 16 firms were connected pair-wise.[8] Five British and two American firms belonged to such pairs which were thus isolated from the large financial and industrial firms. This means that the large component was even more 'continental' than it appears in table 14.3.

Table 14.5   The most central firms in the large component

Nationality		Number of firms with which directly connected
1. Swiss	Schweizerischen Bankverein	24
2. Dutch	ESTEL	14
3. German	Deutsche Bank	12
4. German	ENKA	11
5. Italian	Riunione Adriatica di Sicuritá	10
6. Swiss	Société Internationale Pirelli	9
7. Belgian	Electrobel	9
8. Belgian	COPEBA	9
9. French	Kleber Colombes	8
10. Dutch	AKZO	8
11. Swiss	Schweizerische Kreditanstalt	8
12. French	CFDE (Companie Financière de Dévelopment)	7
13. Belgian	Intercom	7
14. Belgian	Entreprises	7
15. Italian	Medio Banca	7
16. French	Chiers-Chatillon	6

From table 14.5 it can be seen that financial institutions were central in the network. Of the 16 most central firms, six were financials; and if the Belgian holdings are regarded as financial institutions, then nine of the 16 most central firms can be regarded as financial. The most central firm in the component, Schweizerische Bankverein, had 24 foreign neighbours, Deutsche Bank, ranking number three, had 12 and Riunione Adriatica di Sicuritá had interlocks with 10 foreign companies. It is less surprising to find many foreign neighbours of the bi-national ESTEL and the same goes for ENKA (part of the AKZO group). The Belgian holding company COBEPA was part of the Paribas group.

A large number of international interlocks were created by a relatively small number of big linkers, especially C. Pesenti (12 directorships), J.R.M. v.d. Brink (nine), G. Rambaud (nine), H. Abs (seven), A. Frère (seven), H.L. Merkle (seven) and J.M. Levèque (seven). Since all of these had a directorship in at least one financial institution, they can properly be called finance capitalists.[9] Such big linkers, with seven or more directorships in the most central firms of the national networks, created many interlocks. For example a director with seven directorships would generate six bi-national lines if just one of these directorships was in a foreign firm. And if that multiple director had two positions in one country and five in another the number of transnational interlocks would become ten. In fact, it could be said, with only a little exaggeration, that the international network among continental European firms was a network of neighbouring countries carried predominantly by big linkers whose directorships induced many international interlocks. Since adjacency was taken as a measure of centrality and the big linkers contributed greatly to the centrality of the firms of which they were directors, the big linkers played an even more important role in this transnational network than in the network based on the largest firms (Fennema, 1982). Nevertheless, the fact that these big linkers carried many international interlocks is a sign of the existence of a continental European business elite which differed from the American or British elites by the number of their directorships. None of the American or British directors had seven directorships, not even among the largest 250 firms of their own countries. This suggests the existence of structural differences among business elites, which tended to be more hierarchical and family-oriented in the continental European countries. These differences also had economic roots. The business environment in Europe was more negotiable than that in the USA, as markets were often cartelized and fragmented. In such circumstances, 'knowing the right people' is very important for entrepreneurial strategies. Tight relations with national governments may have been another factor in contributing to the existence of a more integrated network in Europe, especially in countries like Italy and France. Big linkers can play a very important role here and this not only on a national level. Franko (1976, p. 220) recalls that when Belgium's public purchasing authorities decided in 1970 to discriminate against the dominant American computer firms they discriminated in favour of Philips of the Netherlands and Siemens of Germany. Finally, the family ownership relations probably are in Europe more transnationalized than anywhere else.

CONCLUSIONS

Some of the most obvious but nevertheless crucial conclusions from this chapter concern the selection of the boards and firms. Fennema's study has made it clear that the international advisory boards played a crucial role in cementing the transatlantic network of interlocking directorships. Moreover, these boards were set up for international consultation and co-ordination and were thus likely to produce networks which were more purposive than the networks resulting from the historical patterns of elite co-optation which seemed to flourish among European firms. Without such advisory interlocks American business was far less interlocked with European firms.

The selection criteria for the firms also matter greatly. Taking the most central firms for each country produced a network which differed considerably from the network based on the largest firms per country. Especially for the American firms it became clear that the most central firms were not those which maintained most international interlocks. The inverse relation between international orientation and national centrality can also be illustrated by looking at financial participations. Only 17 of the 64 American corporations which had financial participations in Europe were among the 40 most central corporations, while 27 belonged to the 40 largest industrials and eight to the 40 largest American commercial banks. Of the European firms, the Swiss, German, British and Dutch internationals were well integrated into their respective national networks, but the Belgian, French and Italian were less so. Thus it can be concluded that changing the selection criteria for the firms not only had a general impact on the network but also affected corporations from different countries differently.

What can in general be said about the network of the most central firms instead of the largest ones? First, the network emphasizes the elite cohesion aspect of the network, because the big linkers in the national networks had a direct impact upon the centrality of the firms in which they were directors. Accordingly, the number of big linkers in the transnational network was much higher than was the case in the Fennema data set. Second, the network largely excluded the transatlantic lines because the most central firms in the USA were not the largest and most international. In the Fennema data set there were 15 more transatlantic interlocks, even though fewer than half as many companies were studied. Furthermore, between American corporations and their European subsidiaries there were 21 interlocks. Third, exclusion of the non-director executives meant that a number of personal interlocks between American parents and their European subsidiaries were neglected.

The lack of an Atlantic structure to interlocking directorships is due not only to the selection procedures discussed above but also to the exclusion of Canadian firms from the present selection. In Fennema's study the Canadian firms served as a bridge between American and British business, just as the Dutch firms connected the British and continental European firms.

It was shown in the first section that the interlocking directorships between parent companies and their subsidiaries were far less frequent in the case of American firms than in the case of European firms. It was suggested that the difference is explained by the retarded development of the European multinationals towards multidivisional organization. Till the end of the 1960s the loose holding companies organization predominated in Europe, while American firms had already gone over to the more efficient global organization (see Franko, 1976). The interlocking directorship is typically a means of control in such a loose relation which is half-way between market and hierarchy. In a multidivisional structure, the relationship between parent and subsidiary had moved definitely in the direction of hierarchy. This also explains why the co-ordination among the European subsidiaries of American multinationals was often carried out by executives who were not on the board of directors of the American parent. The organizational hierarchy was so firmly established that regional contacts could be delegated to 'regional specialists' without fear of 'regional insurrections'. The exceptions to this pattern were the American commercial banks which maintained very close interlocks with their European subsidiaries, especially those in Belgium. Here it looks as if the Belgian subsidiaries functioned as regional headquarters for European banking. Why they should have so many interlocks with their parent bank is not clear. The European subsidiaries of American firms were peripheral in the national networks and many of them were even isolated. The strategy of appointing 'regional specialists' who are sometimes Europeans does not lead to an integration of these American subsidiaries into the network of interlocking directorships.

Another type of intracorporate relations where board overlap is overwhelming is that of the bi-national firms. In the second section it has been argued that transnational business marriages are rare and, with the exception of Shell and Unilever, not stable. All bi-nationals which were formed at the end of the 1960s had now been dissolved again. The main reason for this appears to be that the economic crisis required state intervention, which in turn tends to favour the national enterprises. The idea that multinational corporations and, *a fortiori*, transnational ones would globalize the national economies has not materialized. On the other hand, the results of Fennema's study show an increased international density of the network in 1976 compared to that of 1970. It would be highly intriguing to analyse the international network of 1982.

As in the national networks, the financial institutions tended to be the central companies in the international network. The commercial banks Schweizerische Bankverein and Deutsche Bank were most central but insurance companies and investment banks also ranked high in centrality. The European network can *summa summarum* be characterized as a network carried by finance capitalists, knitting firms from neighbouring countries together into a transnational network. In particular the lines between the Netherlands and Germany and between Belgium and France were frequent and often strong. Most striking perhaps was the lack of interlocks between Belgium and the Netherlands. This was explained in the third section by historical facts. The strong penetration of American capital in both the Dutch and the Flemish economy may be a structural factor providing an additional explanation.

NOTES

1   We thank all national teams for providing their data for this chapter, especially Donald Bender who converted the German and Austrian data, and Frans Wasseur who provided us with all data sets in comparable format.
2   For the definition of a tree see Harary (1972).
3   Van Nelle had no interlocking directorships with the American corporation. Its board is constituted of members of established families in Holland. Its central position is, therefore, not surprising.
4   Agfa-Gevaert with Belgian subsidiary Agfa-Gevaert (12 interlocks); BASF with Belgian BASF Antwerpen (6); BSN-Gervais-Danone with Belgian Glaverbel-Mecaniver (7); Banque National de Paris with Belgian Banque de Paris et des Pays-Bas (11); Crédit Lyonnais with Belgian Crédit Lyonnais (10); Algemene Bank Nederland with Belgian Algemene Bank Nederland (44); Clydesdale Bank with Belgian Barclays Bank International (11); Cavenham with American Grand Union (5).
5   *International Management*, October 1981.
6   *De Volkskrant*, 21 January 1982
7   See for the organizational charts of this bi-national firm Tugendhat (1973) and its Annual Report 1981.
8   The eight pairs were: ROBECO (the Netherlands)–Allianz Lebensversicherung (Germany); Delta Lloyd (the Netherlands)–Commercial Union (Great Britain); Rhône Poulenc (France)–Donau Chemie (Austria); Bendix Corp (USA)–British Leyland (Great Britain); Schindler (Switzerland)–Wertheim Werke (Austria); VMF (the Netherlands)–Davy International (Great Britain); Lazard Brothers (Great Britain)–Credit Chimique (France); Lloyds Bank (Great Britain)–Citycorp (USA).
9   All of them had more positions than were included in the data set. C. Pesenti had a total of 13 directorships, J.R.M. v.d. Brink 11, G. Rambaud 14, H. Abs 12, A. Frère 15, H.L. Merkle 10 and J.M. Levèque 10.

15

Conclusion

ROLF ZIEGLER[1]

It has sometimes been said about studies of interlocking directorships that they have resulted again and again in the same finding: the vast majority of corporations are tied into a large component, with the biggest companies and especially the financial institutions most densely connected. Despite this expectation, the great variations found among the ten countries studied are striking. Though formal proof is lacking, it seems unlikely that so much variation might be the outcome of a simple random process[2] or of one basic generating mechanism with similar boundary conditions. As the selection procedure kept the number of corporations actually studied within rather narrow limits – a factor to which the measures should be highly sensitive[3] – size of the data set cannot account for the observed differences. In the case of the position of banks, the results are also far from uniform confirmation of previous studies. The proportion of banks among the most densely connected companies varies greatly and in some countries they do not even seem to be very centrally placed. It is important to stress these 'deviant' results because they show the merit of a comparative cross-national study in preventing premature generalizations.

Appointment to executive positions and to the boards of directors takes place on very diverse grounds. Consequently, and because of the variations of power patterns in boards, the importance to be attached to interlocking directorships between two companies may vary considerably in individual cases. However, a broad classification of interlocks indicating the strength of the relation between two corporations was developed in chapter 2. This was based on both theoretical reasoning and on empirical covariation with financial participations. Primary interlocks involve an executive position on one side and are more likely to indicate a stronger institutional link between the two corporations. Indeed, the analysis of primary interlocks most clearly revealed the basic structure of the networks. A further distinction among the remaining, secondary interlocks also proved fruitful. Some of them were considered to be induced relations between two companies created when an executive of a third corporation sat as an outsider on their boards. The remainder, the so-called 'unclassified' interlocks, were further subdivided on the basis of the number of directorships accumulated by the person carrying them. Special attention was paid to the interlocks created by 'network specialists', i.e. those multiple directors who did not occupy an inside position in any of the corporations at the time of this study but who created many interlocks because of their large number of positions.

First the main features of the national networks will be briefly summarized without repeating all the historical and institutional details discussed in the national chapters; then special attention will be given to factors underlying the diversity and unity in intercorporate structures.

SUMMARY DESCRIPTION OF NATIONAL NETWORKS

The *British* network stood out for its low level of interlocking. Though average board size and total number of directors were intermediate compared with other countries, the cumulation of directorships and the strength of intercorporate links, as measured by their multiplicity, were both extremely low. This resulted in a less-dense and weakly tied network. This may be due to the existence of alternative forums outside company boardrooms. In Britain there has been an 'establishment' which provided a myriad of informal forums and settings for business discussion. The traditional way of recruiting and organizing the board seems also partially responsible. Frequent meetings, a less articulated or formal committee structure and a majority of inside directors are concomitant with a more active and less consultative or monitoring role of the board (Bacon and Brown, 1977, pp. 51ff.). The fact has to be stressed, however, that there is no necessary correspondence between the distinctions inside/outside and single/multiple director. Work taking the organizational perspective has sometimes mixed up these categories. Both inside and outside directors of a particular corporation may or may not sit on the board of another company. However, the fact that directors very seldom combined several inside positions, the general low tendency of British corporations to recruit their board members from outside and the low cumulation of directorships – which may also be due to the more demanding role of a director – reduce the likelihood of interlocking. There was no evidence of separation between state- and privately owned enterprises and little evidence of regional grouping. Among the most central corporations banks were strongly represented and formed the nuclei of distinct clusters which were linked together through the bridging role played by a number of major industrial corporations, insurance companies and two consortium banks. Disunity of the bank-centred spheres of influence was also countered by a high level of cohesion among a small inner circle of multiple directors. However, these forces did not create a large, cohesive centre. This may come as a surprise to those who expected 'the City' to act as an integrating centre.

Though rather more densely connected, the *American* network displayed a similar structure. It showed a low level of centralization too, with a very large number of banks being concentrated among the most central corporations. The commercial banks organized discrete groupings with only a modest amount of overlap. Insurance companies functioned as organizational links between these bank-centred groups, with a large proportion of their interlocks being created by unaffiliated directors. Geographical proximity raised the likelihood of interlocking but within regions the pattern of bank centrality was maintained. There was, however, no indication of an autonomous, integrated centre existing in the sunbelt. The shifts of capital and economic power to this area do not seem to have generated solid intercorporate alliances.

Finland presented a very different picture from that of the two Anglo-American countries. Its network was dense and there existed a few very cohesive groups of enterprises. Sectoral interests (agricultural industries versus other manufacturing sectors) and ideological factors (the old language cleavage between Finnish- and Swedish-speaking Finns or the strong co-operative movements) were reflected in the composition of the groups. Their integration into a large and densely connected centre was especially due to a few corporations functioning as important meeting-points. These 'integrators' were under the joint control of government and private business and were established or reorganized to facilitate national trade and provide long-term credit for industries.

The structure of the *Belgian* network resembles the Finnish in important aspects, though for quite different reasons. It was dense, centralized and contained several groups of enterprises each strongly tied to a big holding company. The dominant position of the holding companies has been a peculiar institutional feature of Belgium, rooted in the tradition of the mixed banks which were compelled to give up all permanent industrial participations in the mid 1930s. Nowadays, banks do not occupy a very central position in the network. This at least suggests that in the presence of large, ownership-based, financial

K

interest groups the role of banks as suppliers of credit in itself does not increase their likelihood of being interlocked. Though some of the holding companies could still be considered as family-controlled, there were quite a number of holding companies in which different interest groups, family and non-family alike, met. This resulted in much overlapping and the lack of any pronounced separation among the financial interest groups together with the dominant position of the largest, the Société Générale, created a large, densely connected centre.

The importance of the nationalized sector in the *Austrian* economy was clearly recognizable from its intercorporate structure. The largest state-owned holding company and the two nationalized banks (which also functioned as holding companies), together with their subsidiaries, formed distinguishable though overlapping clusters. They and a few privately and foreign-owned corporations made up the centre. A densely connected cluster of co-operative banks and manufacturing companies operating in agricultural products was located outside the overall centre, being linked through one company only. No split between public and private sectors existed. However, a great part of these interlocks was due to a few big linkers who held or had occupied leading positions in the main institutions of the corporatist system of interest intermediation, i.e. the federations and chambers of labour, business and agriculture.

Though perhaps not quite as pervasive as in Austria, state intervention in *Italy* has a long-standing record and has gradually enlarged the share of the public sector. It provides a good case for studying the consequences of different organizational strategies for the network of interlocking directorships. While nationalized companies run as departmental agencies tended to be isolated, the application of the shareholding formula to public enterprises led to their integration into the corporate network. However, the most conspicuous feature was the existence of two dense centres, one consisting predominantly of privately owned corporations and the other of publicly controlled enterprises. Though a few companies acted as bridges, they did not integrate the parts into an overall centre. Traditional socio-economic differences among regions were reflected in the network. Regional groups in the 'industrial triangle' of Turin, Milan and Genoa showed signs of internal cohesion and were predominantly composed of private companies, many of them still being family-controlled. Rome was headquarters mainly for public corporations and ranked second in terms of internal density. All other regions exhibited the typical characteristics of a periphery: they are more densely connected to at least one of the central regions than internally.

Because of the post-war nationalizations and the interventionist policy of the *French* government in promoting the concentration and restructuring of the corporate sector, one might have expected to find public corporations to be well connected with private companies. However, the public sector turned out to be neither well integrated nor closely connected to private enterprise. Ownership-based interest groups, many of them organized around a holding company, characterized the structure of interlocking directorships. Two financial interest groups, Paribas and Suez, were outstanding. The tendency to keep their spheres separate, which also characterized some smaller groups, prevented the formation of a sizeable centre and created a segmented, less centralized structure in the French interlocking system.

In the *Netherlands*, primary financial interlocks revealed a hierarchical structure with the largest banks on top, insurance companies intermediate and two joint ventures of financial institutions (providing for long-term credit and equity capital) ranking lowest. The neighbourhood of the two big banks overlapped considerably, contributing to the integration of an overall centre. Interlocks created by network specialists – most of them being former executives of large production corporations – strengthened the centralized structure. As in Austria a separate local centre of financial and manufacturing companies oriented towards the agricultural segment of the Dutch economy was found.

The three big banks together with the largest domestic multinationals formed the core of the *Swiss* network. Its high density was mostly due to unaffiliated big linkers who often, however, held intermediate positions as chairmen on supervisory boards of one of the large corporations. The other corporations in the centre were large but more nationally oriented, measured by the proportion of domestic turnover but especially by the low number or absence of subsidiaries abroad. The direction of primary interlocks revealed an interesting pattern. While the three big banks acted as meeting-points of executives of production companies in the centre, they were more likely to send their own executives on the supervisory boards of usually smaller production corporations outside the centre rather than receiving executives from outside.

The central position of the big *German* banks, noted in earlier studies since the turn of the century, was confirmed. Together with the biggest insurance company they ranked top in terms of the number of outgoing primary interlocks. Their 'domains', however, overlapped to a high degree, as large production corporations especially were able to attract executives from two financial institutions. No separation of bank-centred groups was therefore observed but instead banks acted more like integrators cross-connecting industrials from various economic sectors. Network specialists contributed to the cohesion of the network. Most of them had a firm institutional basis and usually an extended career in top business.

Finally, the main results of the analysis of the *transnational* network will be summarized. It should be kept in mind that only those holdings of at least 50 per cent of the shares among all the 250 largest corporations selected and common directorships among the 40 most central companies of nine countries (excluding Finland) were studied. The asymmetry of financial participations was striking. The dwarfing posture of the USA was, of course, to be expected, though the proportion might have come as a surprise: there were 116 American subsidiaries or joint ventures among the 2,000 largest corporations in the eight European countries which themselves had majority-ownership in only two American companies. Belgium seemed to be a favourite place for American subsidiaries, especially those of American banks. However, the asymmetry, though less pronounced, extended further. A clear ranking could be detected among the eight European countries which was not violated in a single case, i.e. a country 'further down the ranks' never held more subsidiaries or joint ventures in a country 'above it'. This 'pecking order' reads: the USA, France, Great Britain, the Netherlands, Germany, Switzerland, Italy, Belgium and Austria. Interlocking between parents and subsidiaries was far from common: only half of the European and a fifth of the American subsidiaries (here mainly banks) were tied to their parent companies by common directorships. As foreign subsidiaries tended to be isolated in the national networks, the activities of multinational corporations seem to follow a strategy of penetration of foreign markets without integration and co-optation into national inter-corporate structures. The transnational network of interlocking directorships had a very low density, though it was somewhat denser among the founding countries of the EEC. Only six lines existed between European and American corporations, much less than was found in a previous study (Fennema, 1982) which selected on the basis of size instead of centrality. Obviously the most central firms in the American network were not the most internationally oriented. Two factors seem to account for most parts of this loose transnational network: strong connections between bi-national firms; and the interlocking activity of a few continental European financial institutions, the latter being carried out by a small number of big linkers. Regarding the development of transnational interlocks, two general conclusions may be drawn from this analysis. First, the international-ization of production and trade by multinational corporations has created very little integration among national intercorporate structures, especially across the Atlantic. Second, the somewhat higher integration among the European countries on the continent was mainly due to a few big linkers, most of whom had a directorship in at least one financial institution. Refering to Fennema's study mentioned above, which found about a third of all transnational interlocks to involve specially designed, international advisory boards of corporations, it is possible to suggest that much transnational interlocking was used for getting general advice and gaining respectability.

This brief overview has deliberately neglected many interesting national details which are documented in the individual chapters. Characteristic features and differences have been emphasized within a comparative perspective and these will be more systematically elaborated in the next section.

UNITY AND DIVERSITY IN
INTERCORPORATE STRUCTURES

So far, variations and differences in intercorporate structures have been stressed. There were, however, some general tendencies discernible across all countries. The first to be mentioned relates to the size of companies. In all countries the most interlocked corporations tended to be the largest and economically most important. If smaller companies – as measured by size criteria like assets, sales, value added or number of employees – were highly connected, this was almost always due to close ties with other large and central corporations on which they were dependent. Similarly, smaller financial companies sometimes had a central position because of their specialized function in acting as meeting-places for larger corporations. It has sometimes been argued that this size/interlock correlation is an 'artefact' of sheer board size. This seems to be a misleading argument as it overlooks the fact that the size of the board may itself be a strategic variable. Partialling out its effect would amount to erroneously controlling for an intervening or dependent variable.

Few other factors which generally raised the likelihood of interlocking could be found but there were a few characteristics which were persistently found to be associated with the more peripheral or isolated positions. Corporations with a strong regional base and outlook were less central, though part of this correlation was undoubtedly due to their usually smaller size. A second group consisted of trading companies, especially those operating in the retail sector. Third, foreign-owned companies, especially wholly owned subsidiaries, were poorly integrated into the national network. Finally, privately owned family companies, though sometimes quite large, also showed little tendency for interlocking. It could be argued that this is simply the consequence of legal regulations which required that board members should have a particular ownership status in this kind of company. However, this is an insufficient explanation. First, by no means all privately owned companies had this kind of legal status: the requirement applied to the partnership but many were set up as limited liability or joint stock companies. Second, as legal status is a matter of strategic choice, the possibility of recruiting outsiders to one's own board did not seem to carry much weight in that decision. Third, there is nothing in the legal status itself which prevents the (owner-) managers from being asked by other corporations to join their boards.

In trying to relate these results to the models outlined in chapter 1, certain problems become immediately apparent. Some simply do not speak to the point and others are hard to relate without further untested assumptions. The size/interlock correlation and the tendency of multiple directorships to occur more frequently among large corporations seem most easily to be explained by a prestige seeking and generating mechanism. Prestige can be accumulated by publicly observed association with others of even higher prestige and through visible formal positions in organizations of high importance. Assuming a corporation's status to be dependent on its size (which is very unequally distributed) the observed correlation would follow. It would also predict a general incremental process of 'career development', at least with regard to outside positions, with perhaps sudden gains or losses depending on changes in executive directorships held. This kind of explanation is, of course, explicitly stated in the managerial model, though the other approaches do not seem to contradict it.

The low level of interlocking of retail companies may perhaps best be accounted for by the resource-dependence model. There is no way to co-opt the main sources of uncertainty on the consumer side because they are generally too diverse; and there is little need for large retailers to co-opt their suppliers, which are often more dependent on them than vice versa. Keeping co-ordination and control in the hands of an ownership group has often been noted as a reason for avoiding extensive interlocking. However, the tendency of even large, family-owned companies not to share directorships with other big corporations poses some problems for a strict class-cohesion approach. If interlocks simply map the cohesion of the capitalist class, then why should the classical capitalist firms be so weakly integrated?

A similar argument can be put forward to explain the peripheral position of foreign subsidiaries. Through various organizational measures, parent companies abroad hold tight control over their subsidiaries and obviously have little incentive to allow domestic corporations a closer look at their internal operations. On the other hand, co-opting a subsidiary may not be considered an efficient way for domestic corporations to exercise influence when final decisions are made at higher echelons abroad. National and cultural barriers did certainly play a role but the lack of an incentive to establish co-optive relationships, given the locus of ultimate control, seems to be more important. While foreign subsidiaries tended to be located on the periphery, even when their parent was headquartered in a country of very similar cultural background, they became more integrated when a sizeable minority-holding by a domestic corporation or a number of domestic shareholders existed.

Having discussed some rather invariant relationships found across all countries, it is now possible to turn to an analysis of the differences between the national networks. The impact of variations in board systems has already been stressed in chapter 2. First, the German two-tier system with its strict separation between an executive board of full-time employed directors and a supervisory board of outsiders (common membership of the two boards not being allowed) does not raise the problem – often posed in a single-board system – of how the proportion of insiders to outsiders should be fixed. The differences between the USA and Great Britain have already been noted. The latter is said to prefer a majority of insiders, while the American boards seem to have increased the proportion of outsiders in the last two decades (Bacon and Brown, 1977, pp. 22ff.). All four countries with a Latin two-tier system kept the number of directors, to whom executive power was delegated, on the first administrative board very low. These variations in board composition do partially account for overall similarities and differences of intercorporate structures. Second, the Italian case provides an interesting example of the effects differences in board functioning have on the structure of interlocking. The network of the second board, which in practice acted as an auditing committee, looked very different from that of the administrative board. It was very loose, showed a higher regional density, had no centre at all and overlapped very little with the first board network. Furthermore, the most central companies in both networks were not the same. This indicates that the two boards were recruited from very different sets of persons. A narrow managerialist view which takes boards simply as places to be filled with prestigious and well-known, trustworthy people should have some difficulties in accounting for this different set up. Any explanation has to rest on the distinction between boards responsible for post hoc approval and auditing according to professional standards and boards involved in decision-making, even if the latter are restricted to providing advice and counsel or to serving as some sort of discipline for management (Mace, 1971).

The summary presentation of the national networks was not based on distinctions of board systems but on two characteristics of inter-

Figure 15.1 Typology of national networks

	CLUSTERING				CENTRALIZATION		
	Cumulation ratio	Multiplicity	Co-occurrence of interlocks with financial participation	Few large clusters present	H-index of primary interlocks	Percentage of highly inter-locked corporations	Size of centre
Britain	–	–	–	–	–	–	–
USA	+	–	?	–	–	–	–
Switzerland	–	+	–	–	+	+	+
Germany	–	–	+	–	+	+	+
Netherlands	–	–	–	–	+	+	+
France	+	–	?	+	–	–	–
Italy	+	+	–	+	–	–	–
Austria	–	+	+	+	+	+	+
Belgium	+	+	+	+	+	+	+
Finland	+	+	+	+	+	+	+

Note: Indicators are dichotomized in low (–) and high (+) levels. In the fourth column (–) refers to no and (+) to yes. ? indicates missing data. For exact figures see tables in chapter 2.

corporate structure: the degree of *clustering* and *centralization* in the networks. Relying on both the qualitative descriptions and the quantitative measures given in chapter 2 and the national chapters, the ten countries can be placed into the four cells of a cross-classification. The two dimensions of this cross-classification are clustering and centralization, each of which is dichotomized into 'high' and 'low'. Recognizing the simplification introduced when a continuous variable is dichotomized, figure 15.1 presents the results.

Clustering is here defined in terms of whether a few large, distinct groups of enterprises were distinguishable. Countries with low clustering in this sense either exhibited many groupings or showed a low level of separation between them. Clustering thus defined tended to be associated with a high cumulation of directorships, a greater prevalence of stronger (i.e. multiple) ties among companies and more financial participations being reinforced by common directorships. Higher centralization is here defined in terms of the existence of a sizeable centre and is strongly associated with a larger proportion of densely connected corporations and a high value on Snijder's index H. If dichotomized, these three measures classify the ten countries the same way but their rank orders do not perfectly correlate. Figure 15.1 shows Finland, Belgium and Austria to be both clustered and centralized, while France and Italy were less centralized though containing a few large and distinct groups of enterprises. The other five countries showed less clustering but while Switzerland, the Netherlands and Germany were centralized, the USA and especially Great Britain exhibited extremely low degrees of centralization.

Given the number of cases available, any variables used to 'explain' these differences would be strongly overdetermined. The analysis is therefore confined to looking for suggestive associations, concentrating on three major factors: ownership structure and mode of organizational control, extent and mode of state intervention, and differences in banking systems and capital markets. It will be argued that these factors do not work independently but may jointly account for the different national structures. It should be stressed again that these ideas are merely suggestive.

Extended ownership links between corporations seemed to give rise to distinct clusters of interlocking directorships, especially if organized around a holding company. The kind of ultimate ownership did not turn out to be an important factor in itself. Sometimes a few families but more often government or no specific group of owners were found to prevail. When the latter occured, cross-participations and cyclical chains of financial links among the corporations were often found. Frequently, a proportion of the shares were dispersed among many shareholders, indicating that these financial interest groups were relying on the public for finance and were acting as financial intermediaries. Though often comprising companies from diverse industries, they should not be confused with the conglomerate, multidivisional enterprise as they lack the organizational devices for coordination and monitoring of the day-to-day production and marketing operations (Chandler and Daems, 1980). It has been argued that they are institutions for organizing and structuring the corporate control market where there are conflicting interests among large investors because of uncertainty, differences in beliefs about the likely occurence of some events and incomplete markets (Daems, 1978, p. 122). The formation of these financial interest groups seems to come closest to the finance-capital model. It should be noted, however, that while banks were often closely affiliated with one group, they were not always the organizing pivots of these interest groups.[4]

Two conditions seemed to reduce the segmentation of this clustered structure. If one ownership group predominated (as in Belgium with the Société Générale and in Austria with the state-controlled enterprises) or if joint ventures existed which functioned as integrating meeting-points (as in Finland with active participation by government) then the intercorporate network was characterized by a large and densely connected centre. Low centralization resulted if neither condition was met, as in France or Italy. In neither country had state intervention been accompanied by extensive interlocking between private and public enterprise. The state had relied on budgetary and fiscal policy and on direct negotiation with private business (Vernon, 1974).

The remaining five countries did not exhibit a few large, distinct clusters but they differed greatly in their degree of centralization. This was probably due to differences in their banking systems. Switzerland, the Netherlands and Germany were all characterized by a high degree of *absolute* concentration in banking. Three or four big banks dominated on a national scale and ranked, of course, high in number of interlocks. Three points need to be stressed as they have contributed to the formation of large, densely connected centres. First, these big banks were linked through primary interlocks to corporations, especially large ones, from various industries. Second, the fact that their spheres of influence overlapped to a high degree did not indicate a one-sided bank-control situation, as large industrial corporations were obviously able to attract directors from several banks or to send their executives to the boards of more than one of the very big banks.[5] Third, these banks tended to have more outgoing than incoming primary interlocks. As bankers accumulated several directorships, they created many induced interlocks and so reduced the distance between the corporations and contributed to the enlargement of the centres in these countries.

With Great Britain and the USA the situation was quite different. Here the absolute concentration of banking has been lower as a result of the strict separation between commercial and investment banking. Consequently there were more commercial and investment banks among the most frequently interlocked corporations. Among the top 20 companies there were eight banks[6] (including the Bank of England) in Britain and eight in the USA, while in the Netherlands and Germany there were only four and in Switzerland there were three. This high degree of 'bank-centrality' in the Anglo-American countries, far from creating centralized networks, was actually preventing the formation of large centres. In all countries, commercial banks, if not linked through financial participations, tended to have no directors in common.[7] Two banks would therefore not be neighbours and could have distance 2 relations – a necessary condition for both of them being included in the centre – only if their directors met on the board of a third corporation. To be part of a centre, all central banks must therefore have had pair-wise overlapping 'spheres of influence'. The more banks there were, the less likely that seems to have happened. There was another process at work which raised the likelihood of longer distances among industrial corporations. As compared with Switzerland, the Netherlands and Germany, bankers in the Anglo-American countries less often sat on the boards of industrials than the other way round, creating therefore fewer induced lines among them. Other things being equal, this tended to enlarge their distances.

The following conclusions may be drawn from this analysis. The tendency towards clustering in interlocking directorships seemed very much dependent on the existence of ownership-based groups and was especially pronounced when holding companies acted as financial intermediaries allocating and monitoring capital among corporations from various industries. Whether ownership ultimately belonged to families, government or was dispersed, made for little difference. While interlocking directorships might be a clumsy technique for co-ordinating the activities of independent firms (Stigler, 1968, p. 261) and might be inferior to managerial techniques for organizing production and marketing of well-integrated, diversified enterprises (Chandler, 1977), they seemed to be satisfactory devices for monitoring capital allocation among financial interest groups. It is, of course, this function which has been stressed by writers on finance capitalism.

Turning now to the second characteristic, centralization of clustered structures resulted either from one financial interest group predominating or from joint ventures acting as meeting-places which have usually been set up together with government in order to promote common interests such as foreign trade or investment policy. All the less-clustered networks were invariantly characterized by banks occupying the most central positions. They were, however, less centralized when a number of very large banks existed, because these banks did not interlock, had only partially overlapping 'spheres of influence' and lacked overall meeting-places. It should be added that insurance companies fulfilled this integrating function to a certain degree in these countries. If on the other hand only a few banks dominated, they acted as integrators giving rise to the development of a large centre. It is hypothesized that these differences were related to variations in banking systems – especially the degree of separation between commercial and investment banks.[8] In countries where banks combine different functions – taking deposits and giving loans, underwriting and trading securities, holding financial participations and voting by proxy – their position *vis-à-vis* industrial corporations is strengthened. But this should not be interpreted as confirming a simple model of bank control. Even in Germany where banks are said to have held a traditionally strong position they did not form separate competing groups of co-ordinated companies around banks but had largely overlapping neighbourhoods. Though basically competing and not directly interlocked among themselves they have often acted in concert to rescue corporations or to take part in restructuring whole industries.

There is some indication that these variations in intercorporate structure are associated with broader societal differences which have been discussed in the literature on corporatism. This has been defined as a system of interest intermediation in which large interest organizations – being hierarchically ordered, functionally differentiated and having compulsory membership – are strongly co-opted into governmental decision-making (Schmitter and Lehmbruch, 1979, p. 13; Lehmbruch and Schmitter, 1982, pp. 5ff.). It is an interesting fact calling for further clarification that precisely those four countries having the least centralized networks of interlocking directorships (France, Great Britain, Italy and the USA) also show weak forms of corporatism (Schmidt, 1982, p. 245). An explanatory hypothesis may be suggested by the Austrian example: under a corporatist system of interest intermediation, holding a prominent position in the associations of interest representation is more strongly correlated with being a big linker among central companies than in other societies.

Finally, we will take up the problem of *density*. Though it is an interesting and important characteristic of interlocking directorships, which are considered as potential channels of communication, it is better explained as an unintended by-product of other generating mechanisms. In trying to account for its variation one should not, however, focus on the overall density of the total network as this was largely determined by the proportion of isolated firms, which was in turn highly dependent on the degree of penetration by foreign capital. There was almost complete agreement between the ranking of countries noted in the first section, which was based on the financial participations reported in chapter 14, and a ranking based on the proportion of companies outside the largest component. To avoid this confounding factor explanations should concentrate on variations in density of the largest components and in particular on that of the partial network of primary interlocks. This should be the case for two reasons. First, primary interlocks constitute the backbone of the network, their establishment being most likely a matter of deliberate choice by the corporate and individual actors involved. Second, leaving out induced and unclassified interlocks makes interlocks statistically independent. The strong but imperfect correlation between density and centralization discussed in chapter 2 could therefore not be dismissed as an artefact but should be seen as an important empirical finding. We may now again try to account for the imperfect correlation. Both centralization and clustering tend to raise the density of the network, though the latter in a less straightforward manner. As table 2.10 shows, all three centralized and clustered countries (Belgium, Austria and Finland) had the densest component. The two uncentralized and weakly clustered networks (the USA and Great Britain) were the least dense and the three centralized but weakly clustered countries (Switzerland, the Netherlands and Germany) ranked intermediate. Centralization being low, density very much depended on the kind of clustering. When the few clusters actually had developed into a bi-polar structure with two separate centres, as in Italy, overall density was high but when the dominant groups were not at the apex of two separate yet centralized subclusters but still surrounded by smaller groupings, as in France, density was rather low. Though centralization by a few banks raised density to only intermediate levels, in a way it was more efficient than clustering. Taking the ratio of pairs of companies connected at distance 2 to those directly interlocked, this ratio is largest for the Swiss, Dutch and German networks, while it was low for the clustered networks, especially the Italian. This is, of course, to be expected. The tendency towards 'transitive closure', i.e. the 're-dundant' linking of two corporations already tied to a third company, has long been pointed out as one of the basic mechanisms accounting for the emergence of separate clusters in a network (Leinhardt, 1977; Holland and Leinhardt, 1979).

CONCLUDING REMARKS

This is the first study of interlocking directorships between large business enterprises in ten countries which employs network analysis as a technique of investigation and adopts a strictly comparative method. Its descriptive empirical findings may contribute to the growing theoretical debates on intercorporate structure, as they demonstrate some of the regularities and variations in structure which the theoretical approaches should try to account for.[9] The data was analysed from an interorganizational perspective, focusing on the structural properties of the networks. An effort was made to outline generating mechanisms which helped to explain broad qualitative distinctions among the countries. The models presented in chapter 1 highlighted different aspects of the intercorporate structure but none was successful in satisfactorily explaining all the findings. Institutional peculiarities of individual countries which were due to their historical development had to be taken into account.

Many interpretations of interlocking directorships, especially those based on the organizational perspective, have related them to economic performance and the capital structure of corporations. Chapter 3 reports the results of an inductive statistical analysis along these lines with data from Belgium, the Netherlands and the USA. Though most of the findings could be provided with a consistent and plausible interpretation, only a few relations seemed to hold across all countries.[10] While in the Netherlands and Belgium a positive relation between profitability and interlocking with banks was found, this was not observed in the USA. For that country profitability was even negatively correlated with the 'rush', considered as a measure of the linking or meeting-point role of enterprises. The negative association of economic performance with various types of holding interlocks in Belgium fits the often-cited image of the 'industrial conservatism' of the main financial-industrial groups in that country. Highly indebted companies both in Belgium and in the Netherlands seemed less able to attract bankers or 'network specialists' to their boards. If they were especially dependent on short-term loans, interlocking with other production companies tended to be higher. This indicated perhaps some resource dependence with respect to credit from customers and suppliers. In the USA large, central production companies tended to be characterized by a high turnover velocity of capital, as measured by their sales on net assets ratios, which might indicate a relative independence of these corporations from external finance. As with similar studies, the causal interpretation of these statistical relationships is by no means always clear as a plausible argument for reversing directionality can often be set up, e.g. by referring to the effects of anticipatory action.

This points, of course, to one of the limitations of our study. While its comparative scope helped to avoid some of the pitfalls leading to premature generalizations, it still shares the weaknesses of a cross-sectional study. These were probably less severe and consequential as far as explaining the structure of the national networks was concerned. Interlocking directorships were basically treated as indicators of significant social relations among the corporations, the existence of which was substantiated by additional independent evidence. Yet time-series or panel data would permit more stringent tests of the generating mechanisms. Interlocks result from a person sitting on the board of two or more corporations. The accumulation and discontinuance of directorships is a process in time and the career progression of certain types of persons, especially the network specialists, has been stressed by several authors in this book. Many of these elder statesmen have been former top businessmen and an important question to answer is how they accumulated their directorships and when, particularly whether this was before or after their retirement from executive officership. But even the basic distinction between different types of interlocks, which proved to be very fruitful, poses the problem of temporal sequence. The basic generating mechanisms were conceptualized to work mainly on the level of primary and unclassified interlocks. The induced interlocks may sometimes have constrained the choice, e.g. if an executive of an industrial company would connect two competing banks by holding outside directorships on their boards, but usually they were thought of only as unintended consequences of primary interlocks. However, the fate of these induced interlocks when an executive director changes his primary affiliation is by no means clear and would require panel data to be fully investigated. This is just one example of the problem of retention mechanisms which cross-sectional analysis does not usually deal with. Another example would be the continued presence of a bank which played an important role in founding or restructuring the corporations. To study the impact of past periods and events on present interlocking and to dissect the causes of inertia would again call for longitudinal data. Perhaps this 'inertia' may partly – though certainly not completely – explain the low rates of replacement of broken ties reported in recent studies (Ornstein, 1982; Palmer, 1983).

Several times it was stressed that this study concentrated on interlocking directorships as *potential* channels for communication, influence and power. We did not pretend to analyse the actual flow of communication and the exercise of power with regard to specific issues. This is not to deny the importance of these questions but they would have required a far more extended research design. Even then it would be impossible to gather and process data on all ties so as to be able to describe the extent to which interlocks are actually used in a controlling or co-optive manner. Case studies aimed at such detailed description of decisional processes and outcomes would have to concentrate on strategically selected corporations, persons and issues. The results of this study might help in the selection of the types of companies and directors to be studied.

A lesson to be learned from the literature is that there is no easy and plain answer to the deceptively simple question, Who controls the large corporation?. Even if one restricts the analysis to the making of the key decisions in a company and leaves out all the problems of implementation, the question cannot be answered without taking into account relations to outside actors and the constraining effects of various institutionalized incentive systems. This is, of course, one of the main topics in the long-lasting debate about the extent and consequences of the 'separation of ownership and control'. As Herman has recently argued in the USA, 'the managerial revolution has been one of the increasing, but sharply constrained, management control, with the controlling managers operating within behavior boundaries that have not widened over time.' (1981, p. 20) Some recent theoretical approaches try to describe this development as a more efficient institutional arrangement due to the specialization of two functions, i.e. managing and holding the residual claim, which were fused in the classical concept of the entrepreneur. Their separation entails, however, the costs of controlling the agents, and the functioning of some controlling mechanisms are analysed: for example, the structure of the managerial labour market, compensation policies or the implication of the capital market as a market for corporate control. [11]

Regarding the other question often posed, How powerful are corporations in realising their interests?, it is again necessary to look beyond the individual corporation to the network of structural constraints created by the other actors which control resources relevant to the realization of their interests. It is important to conceptually distinguish and separately measure these different components and to develop precise models which relate them in a theoretically meaningful and empirically testable way. Interlocking directorships are here considered as a means for reducing transaction costs in a context mid way between 'markets' and 'hierarchies' (Williamson, 1975)[12] and have to be compared with other kinds of interorganizational relations such as cartels, joint ventures, license agreements, long-term contracting, parent–subsidiary realtionships and mergers (Poensgen, 1980).

There are, in general, three questions that can be asked about these networks of relations. The first is mainly descriptive: What do the networks look like? The task of describing complex structures is not an easy one but there are now methods available which have been used in this book and can be applied to other fields of research as well. The other two questions are theoretically and analytically more demanding if dealt with in a precise and not merely discursive manner. One is the question of consequences: How do these networks of relations affect behaviour and outcomes? The other relates to causes: What accounts for the existence of the networks?[13] This study has mainly contributed to the topics raised by the first question, especially by treating them in a comparative perspective. We would not pretend to have offered any definite answers to the other two questions but it is hoped that the hypotheses suggested and the evidence presented may stimulate research for a better understanding of co-ordination and control among large-scale businesses.

NOTES

1   The final chapter was written while the author was visiting as a Fellow of the Netherlands Institute for Advanced Study in the Humanities and Social Sciences at Wassenaar.

2   The hypothesis of interlock networks being structurally similar to random graphs should not be easily dismissed on the basis of intuitive reasoning about the purposeful behaviour of individual and corporate actors having created these structures. As one scholar has stated, they may appear as if 'the facts of corporate data, which some sociologists are at pain to endow with meaning and to adduce in the explanation of current events, are, in fact, the work of some whimsical spirit who shoots 'craps' into the universe.' (Levine, 1975, p. 36) However, it is just the work of the Hungarian mathematician Erdös, to which Levine refers, which allows for the refutation of a *simple* random-graph model as inconsistent with our empirical data. Erdös and Rényi (1973) proved that for a simple random graph, where each line has the same and independent probability of occuring, five phases may clearly be distinguished depending on the ratio of edges (lines) to vertices (points). In the first phase, with only a few lines, the random graph consists only of a few small trees. In the second phase, with an increasing number of lines (but still less than half of the number of points), more and more yet unconnected trees and a few cycles occur. When the number of lines passes the threshold of half the number of points, the structure of the random graph abruptly changes. There suddenly appears one 'large' component, the other components being small trees besides still many isolated points. In the fourth phase, characterized by a ratio of lines to points between 0.5 and 3 (given the number of points of our networks), the graph almost surely becomes connected into one component with a few isolated points. Finally in the fifth phase, as the ratio further increases, the whole graph is not only almost surely connected but all points tend to have the same number of lines incident. If we now consider the networks of primary interlocks (these are taken to avoid the 'obvious' statistical dependence due to induced interlocks) the ratio of lines to points varies between 1 and 3, i.e. all networks would belong to the fourth phase. However, they are far from being completely connected, as the proportion of isolated points ranges from 20 to 48 per cent and is far above the expected proportion under a simple model. Even where predicted and observed

proportions of isolated points come closest there is still a large difference: 6 per cent expected against 25 per cent observed in the American network of primary interlocks.

3   There are, of course, no standards of selection which might not be objected to on certain grounds. The final decision – to select according to a fixed uppermost number of corporations – was mainly made to control for varying size as an obvious explanation of any differences among the national networks. Selecting a fixed uppermost percentage of a nation's total set of appropriate firms or applying uniformly some absolute criterion of firm size would have caused this ambiguity. Besides, the number selected then would have depended both on the total number of firms in a national economy and on the distribution of firm sizes as well. Variations in this distribution more heavily reflect national differences in 'small (or medium) business' while this study was focused on 'big business'. Using turnover as a standard of selection for the industrials and assets for the financial institutions there remained a certain amount of incommensurability. However, a common yardstick, e.g. value added, was not available at the level of individual companies in all countries. But its biasing effect may be perhaps less severe as the financial sector of each national economy accounts for a roughly comparable proportion of total economic activity, in contrast to the prevailing differences in composition of gross industrial product across countries.

4   In Belgium, banks were prohibited by law from holding financial participations in production companies.

5   This statement does not postulate a simple relation between the number of bank interlocks and the status of an industrial corporation. There were quite a few cases where this association was the consequence of several banks having joined to rescue an industrial company threatened by bankruptcy.

6   Only commercial and/or investment banks were counted, while other financial institutions (e.g. insurance companies, national banks, banks rendering specialized services to the banking sector) were excluded. But even if all financial institutions were put together they were more numerous among the most central corporations in the Anglo-American countries (12 among the top 20) than in others where this number varied between seven and ten.

7   In the USA, interlocking directorships among competing banks have been illegal since the passage of the Clayton Act. But as pointed out in chapter 13, even if interlocks among specific banks were not prohibited they did not tend to occur. Though banks quite often co-operated rather extensively in specific fields, e.g. through joint ventures, they kept their boards separate, indicating a basic competitive relationship among them.

8   Mizruchi (1982b, pp. 123ff.) uses a similar argument to account for the decline in centrality of the investment banks since the separation of commercial and investment banking by the Glass-Steagall Act of 1933.

9   The data will also be made available for secondary analysis through Social Science Data Archives.

10   In comparing his results with those from previous studies, Pennings (1980, p. 191) also points to the lack of agreement.

11   See Alchian (1975), Fama (1980) and Ridder-Aab (1980) for a discussion of this 'property-rights' approach. Although still lacking empirical research, it seems to be more promising than quibbling about the exact percentage of shareholding where the boundary line between minority-control and managerial-control should be drawn.

12   Research has demonstrated that interlocks tend to increase with product-market constraints on corporate profit. While this agrees with the hypothesis of

purposeful co-optive behaviour, evidence for its success is far more inconclusive. Though established as if intended to control sources of market constraints, interlocking directorships seemed only marginally successful in raising profits (Schiffels, 1981; Ziegler, 1982; Burt, 1983).

13 These questions are not always completely distinct. A network may be created in order to bring about certain consequences, though even then intentions and consequences should be kept separate. But often this is not the case. One may argue that, whatever their causes, interlocking directorships have the function of building trust and fostering the development and enforcement of conventions about proper business behaviour in a recurrent social situation of the prisoners' dilemma type (Schotter, 1981).

References

Aaronovitch, S. (1955) *Monopoly*. London: Lawrence and Wishart.

Aaronovitch, S. (1961) *The Ruling Class*. London: Lawrence and Wishart.

ABVV (1956) *Holdings en Economische Demokratie*. Brussels: Algemeen Belgisch Vakverbond.

Alba, R.D. (1973) 'A Graph-Theoretic Definition of a Sociometric Clique', *Journal of Mathematical Sociology* 3:113–126.

Alchian, A.A. (1975) 'Corporate Management and Property Rights'. In H.G. Manne (ed.) *The Economics of Legal Relationships*. St. Paul: West Publishing Company.

Aldrich, H. (1979) *Organizations and Environments*. Englewood Cliffs, N.J.: Prentice-Hall.

Allard, P., M. Beaud, B. Bellon, A.-M. Lévy and S. Lienart (1978) *Dictionnaire des Groupes Industriels et Financières en France*. Paris: Editions du Seuil.

Allen, M.P. (1974) 'The Structure of Interorganizational Elite Cooptation', *American Sociological Review* 39:393–406.

Allen, M.P. (1978) 'Economic Interest Groups and the Corporate Elite Structure', *Social Science Quarterly* 58:597–615.

Andrews, J.A.Y. (1982) *The Interlocking Corporate Director: A Case Study in Conceptual Confusion*. Dissertation for the degree of Master of Arts. Illinois: University of Chicago.

Annuaires Desfossés – SEF (1978) Paris: DAFSA.

Anscombe, F.J. (1967) 'Topics in the Investigation of Linear Relations Fitted by the Method of Least Squares', *Journal of the Royal Statistical Society*, Series B.

Anthonisse, J.M. (1971) *The Rush in a Directed Graph*. Amsterdam: Mathematisch Centrum.

Aron, R. (1959) *Une Grande Banque d'Affaires: la Banque de Paris & des Pays-Bas*. Paris: Editions de l'Epargne.

Augustin, W. (1982) *Aufsichtsräte ohne Executivmandate*. Munich: Unpublished thesis.

Averitt, R.T. (1968) *The Dual Economy*. New York: Norton.

Bacon, J. and J.K. Brown (1977) *The Board of Directors: Perspectives and Practices in Nine Countries*. New York: The Conference Board Inc.

Bagnasco, A. (1978) *Le Tre Italie*. Bologna: Il Mulino.

Baltzell, E.D. (1958) *Philadelphia Gentlemen*. New York: Free Press.

Barratt Brown, M.(1973) 'The Controllers of British Industry'. In J. Urry and J. Wakeford (eds) *Power in Britain*. London: Heinemann.

Baudet, H. and M. Fennema (1983) *Het Nederlands Belang bij Indië*. Utrecht: Het Spectrum.

Baumier, J. (1967) *Les Grandes Affaires Françaises. Des 200 Familles aux 200 Managers.* Paris: Julliard.

Bearden, J., W. Atwood, P. Freitag, C. Hendricks, B. Mintz and M. Schwartz (1975) *The Nature and Extent of Bank Centrality in Corporate Networks.* Paper presented at the Annual Meeting of the American Sociological Association, San Francisco.

Beekenkamp, G.G. (1982) *An Elite Within the Dutch Economic Elite.* Paper presented at the Workshop on Empirical Elite Research, Florence.

Beekenkamp, G. G. and J. Dronkers (1984) 'Rotterdam, Delft, Leiden. De Plaats van het Onderwÿs in de Rekrutering van President-Directeuren'. In F. N. Stokman and J. Dronkers (eds) *Nederlandse Elites in Beeld: Recrutering, Samenhang en Verandering.* Deventer: Van Loghum Slaterus.

Bellon, B. (1977) 'Méthodologie de Délimitation et de Repérage des Ensembles Financiers', *Recherches Economiques et Sociales* 7/8 (July–October): 99–116.

Bellon, B. (1980) *Le Pouvoir Financier et l'Industrie en France.* Paris: Editions du Seuil.

Benson, J.K. (1975) 'The Interorganizational Network as a Political Economy', *Administrative Science Quarterly* 20:229–249.

Benson, J.K. (1977) 'Organizations: A Dialectical View', *Administrative Science Quarterly* 20:1–21.

Berkowitz, S.D. (1982) *An Introduction to Structural Analysis.* Toronto: Butterworth.

Berle, A. and G. Means (1932) *The Modern Corporation and Private Property.* New York: Macmillan.

Bertrand, H., C. Mansuy and M. Norotte (1981) 'Vingt Groupes Industriels Français et le Redéploiement', *Economie et Prévision* 51(6): 3–42.

Bhaskar, R. (1979) *The Possibility of Naturalism.* Hussocks, Sussex: Harvester Press.

Boon, M. (1975) *Netwerkanalyse in de Beeldende Kunst.* Amsterdam: Dr. E.Boekmanstichting.

Bosman, H.W.J. (1973) *Het Nederlandse Bankwezen.* Deventer: Kluwer.

Bundesministerium der Finanzen (1979) *Bericht der Studienkommission 'Grundsatzfragen der Kreditwirtschaft'.* Bonn: Wilhelm Stollfuss Verlag.

Burt, R.S. (1980a) 'On the Functional Form of Corporate Cooptation', *Social Science Research* 9:146–177.

Burt, R.S. (1980b) 'Cooptive Corporate Actor Networks: a Reconsideration of Interlocking Directorates Involving American Manufacturing', *Administrative Science Quarterly* 25:557–582.

Burt, R.S. (1982) *Toward a Structural Theory of Action.* New York: Academic Press.

Burt, R.S. (1983) *Corporate Profits and Cooptation: Networks of Market Constraints and Directorate Ties in the American Economy.* New York: Academic Press.

Chandler, A.D. (1962) *Strategy and Structure.* Cambridge, Mass.: MIT Press.

Chandler, A.D. (1977) *The Visible Hand: The Managerial Revolution in American Business.* Cambridge, Mass.: Harvard University Press.

Chandler, A.D. and H. Daems (eds) (1980) *Managerial Hierarchies.* Cambridge, Mass.: Harvard University Press.

Channon, D. (1973) *The Strategy and Structure of Business Enterprise.* London: Macmillan.

Chiesi, A.M. (1978) 'I Legami Personali tra Consigli di Amministrazione in Italia', *Studi Organizzativi* 10(4): 25–72.

Chiesi, A.M. (1979) *Interlocking Directorates in Italy: a Study in their Functions and Trends.* Paper presented at ECPR Joint Sessions of Workshops, Brussels.

Cianci, E. (1977) *Nascita dello Stato Imprenditore in Italia.* Milan: Mursia.

Clark, G. (1979) 'Modernization Without Urbanization or Switzerland as a Model of Job Development Outside Large Urban Areas', *Schweizerische Zeitschrift für Soziologie* 6: 1–42.

Claude, H. (1969) *Histoire, Réalité et Destin d'un Monopole: la Banque de Paris & des Pays-Bas.* Paris: Editions Sociales.

CRISP (1962) *Morphologie des Groupes Financiers.* Brussels: CRISP.

Cuyvers, L. and W. Meeusen (1976) 'The Structure of Personal Influence of the Belgian Holding Companies – A Quantitative Analysis', *European Economic Review* 8.

Cuyvers, L. and W. Meeusen (1981) *Note on the Belgian Data Set.* Discussion Paper, ECPR Research Group on Intercorporate Structure.

Cuyvers, L. and W. Meeusen (1982) *The Belgian Intercorporate Structure in 1976.* Discussion Paper, ECPR Research Group on Intercorporate Structure.

Daems, H. (1978) *The Holding Company and Corporate Control.* Leiden/Boston: Martinus Nijhoff.

Delion, A.G. and M. Durupty (1982) *Les Nationalisations 1982.* Paris: Economica.

De Vannoise, R. (1977) 'Etude Économique et Financière de 18 Groupes Industriels Français en 1972', *Economie et Statistique* 87 (March): 11–28.

De Vroey, M. (1973) *Propriété et Pouvoir dans les Grandes Enterprises.* Brussels: CRISP.

Domhoff, G.W. (1967) *Who Rules America.* Englewood Cliffs, N.J.: Prentice-Hall.

Domhoff, G.W. (1971) *The Higher Circles.* New York: Vintage Books.

Domhoff, G.W. (ed.) (1980) *Power Structure Research.* Beverly Hills, Cal.: Sage.

Dooley, P.C. (1969) 'The Interlocking Directorate', *American Economic Review* 59: 314–323.

Dyas, G.P. and H.T. Thanheiser (1976) *The Emerging European Enterprise.* London: Macmillan.

Eggen, A.Th.J. and P. Neijens (1979) *Intercorporate Networks in the Dutch Oil Industry: Interlocking Directorates at Different Levels.* Paper presented at the ECPR Joint Sessions of Workshops. Brussels.

Erdös, P. and A. Rényi (1973) 'On the Evolution of Random Graphs', pp. 569-617 in P. Erdös, *The Art of Counting.* Cambridge, Mass.: The MIT Press.

Eulenburg, F. (1906) 'Aufsichtsräte der deutschen Aktiengesellschaften', *Jahrbücher für Nationalökonomie und Statistik* 32: 92–109.

Fama, E.F. (1980) 'Agency Problems and the Theory of the Firm', *Journal of Political Economy* 88:288–307.

Fennema, M. (1982) *International Networks of Banks and Industry.* The Hague: Martinus Nijhoff.

Fennema, M. and H. Schijf (1979) 'Analyzing Interlocking Directorates: Theory and Method', *Social Networks* 1: 297–332.

Ferris, P. (1960) *The City.* London: Gollancz.

Fitch, R. and M. Oppenheimer (1970) 'Who Rules the Corporations', Parts I, II and III. *Socialist Revolution* 4, 5 and 6.

Francis, A., J. Turk and P. Willman (1982) *Power, Efficiency and Institutions.* London: Heinemann.

Franko, L.G. (1972) *Who Manages Multinational Enterprises?* Geneva: EEI.

Franko, L.G. (1976) *The European Multinationals. A Renewed Challenge to American and British Big Business.* London/New York: Harper and Row.

Freeman, L. (1979) 'Centrality in Social Networks. Conceptual Clarification', *Social Networks* 1:215–239.

Galbraith, J.K. (1967) *The New Industrial State.* Boston: Houghton Mifflin.

Gerretson, F.C. (1958) *History of the Royal Dutch.* Leiden: E.J. Brill.

Gerschenkron, A. (1962) *Economic Backwardness in Historical Perspective.* Cambridge, Mass.: Harvard University Press.

Giddens, A. (1979) *Central Problems in Social Theory.* London: Macmillan.

Giddens, A. (1981) *A Contemporary Critique of Historical Materialism.* London: Macmillan.

Gilly, J.-P. and F. Morin (1981) 'Les Groupes Industriels en France', *Notes et Etudes Documentaires* 4605–4606 (February 10). Paris: La Documentation Française.

Gogel, R. and T. Koenig (1981) 'Commercial Banks, Interlocking Directorates and Economic Power: An Analysis of the Primary Metals Industry', *Social Problems* 29: 117–128.

Grifone, P. (1971) *Il Capitale Finanziario in Italia*. Turin: Einaudi.

Hagemann, W. (1931) *Das Verhältnis der deutschen Großbanken zur Industrie*. Berlin: Wilhelm Christians Verlag.

Harary, F. (1972) *Graph Theory*. Reading, Mass.: Addison-Wesley.

Harary, F., R.Z. Norman and D. Cartwright (1965) *Structural Models*. New York: Wiley.

Haxey, S. (1939) *Tory MP*. London: Gollancz.

Heiskanen, I. (1977) *Julkinen, Kollektiivinen, Markkinaperusteinen*. Helsinki: Finnish Government Printing Office.

Heiskanen, I. (1982) *Top Interlocking Directorates as Quasi-Government in the Economic Sector*. Paper presented at the IPSA 12th World Congress, Rio de Janeiro.

Helmers, H.M., R.J. Mokken, R.C. Plijter, F.N. Stokman and J.M. Anthonisse (1975) *Graven naar Macht: Op Zoek naar de Kern van de Nederlandse Economie*. Amsterdam: Van Gennep.

Henning, F.W. (1979) *Das industrialisierte Deutschland 1914 – 1978*. Paderborn: Verlag Ferdinand Schönnigh. First published 1974.

Herman, E.S. (1980) 'Commercial Bank Trust Departments'. In *Abuse on Wall Street. A Twentieth Century Fund Report*. Connecticut: Quorum.

Herman, E.S: (1981) *Corporate Control, Corporate Power*. New York: Cambridge University Press.

Hilferding, R. (1981) *Finance Capital*. London: Routledge and Kegan Paul. Originally published in German in 1910.

Historical Statistics of the United States: Colonial Times to 1970. (1970) Washington: US Government Printing Office.

Höpflinger, F. (1974) *Gewerkschaften und Konfliktregelung in der Schweiz. Eine explorative Studie*. Zürich: Soziologisches Institut der Universität Zürich.

Höpflinger, F. (1980) *Das unheimliche Imperium*. Zürich: Eco-Verlags AG.

Hoffmann, W.G. (1959) 'Die unverteilten Gewinne der Aktiengesellschaften in Deutschland, 1871 – 1957', *Zeitschrift für die gesamte Staatswissenschaft* 115: 271–291.

Holland, P.W. and S. Leinhardt (eds) (1979) *Perspectives on Social Network Research*. New York: Academic Press.

Holland, S. (1972) *The State as Entrepreneur: The IRI State Share Holding Formula*. London: Weidenfeld and Nicholson.

Holliger, C.M. (1977) *Die Reichen und die Superreichen in der Schweiz*. Zürich: Exibris.

Immenga, U. (1978) *Beteiligungen von Banken in anderen Wirtschaftszweigen*. Baden-Baden: Nomos Verlagsgesellschaft.

Inoguchi, T. (1979) *Political Surfing over Economic Waves: a Simple Model of the Japanese Political–Economic System*. Paper presented at the IPSA 11th World Congress, Moscow.

Jeidels, O. (1905) *Das Verhältnis der deutschen Großbanken zur Industrie mit besonderer Berücksichtigung der Eisenindustrie*. Leipzig: Verlag von Duncker & Humblot.

Jenny, F. and A.P. Weber (1974) 'Concentration et Politique des Structures Industrielles'. In *Economie et Planification*. Paris: La Documentation Française.

Johnson, P.S. and R. Apps (1979) 'Interlocking Directorates Among the UK's Largest Companies', *Antitrust Bulletin* 24:357–369.

Johnson, S. (1976) 'How the West Was Won: Last Shootout for the Yankee-Cowboy Theory', *The Insurgent Sociologist* 4: 15–26.

Knowles, J.C. (1973) 'The Rockefeller Financial Group', *MSS Modular Publications*, Module 343.

Kocka, J. (1980) 'The Rise of the Modern Industrial Enterprise in Germany'. In A.D. Chandler and H. Daems (eds) *Managerial Hierarchies*. Cambridge, Mass.: Harvard University Press.

Kocka, J. and H. Siegrist (1979) 'Die hundert größten deutschen Industrieunternehmen im späten 19. und frühen 20. Jahrhundert'. In N. Horn and J. Kocka (eds) *Recht und Entwicklung im 19. und frühen 20. Jahrhundert*. Göttingen: Vandenhoeck & Ruprecht.

Kotz, D.M. (1978) *Bank Control of Large Corporations in the United States*. Berkeley, Cal.: University of California Press.

Langer, E. (1966) *Die Verstaatlichung in Österreich*. Vienna: Verlag der Wiener Volksbuchhandlung.

Lehmbruch, G. and Ph.C. Schmitter (eds) (1982) *Patterns of Corporatist Policy-Making*. London: Sage.

Leinhardt, S. (ed.) (1977) *Social Networks. A Developing Paradigm*. New York: Academic Press.

Le Nouvel Economiste (November 1978) Paris.

Les Liaisons Financiéres en France (1978) Paris. DAFSA.

Levine, J. (1972) 'The Sphere of Influence', *American Sociological Review* 37: 14–27.

Levine, J. (1975) *The Network of Corporate Interlocks in the United States: An Overview*. Paper presented at the Advanced Symposium on Social Networks, Dartmouth College.

Lévy-Leboyer, M. (1980) 'The Large Corporation in Modern France'. In A. D. Chandler and H. Daems (eds). *Managerial Hierarchies*. Cambridge, Mass.: Harvard University Press.

Lundberg, F. (1937) *America's Sixty Families*. New York: Vanquard Press.

Lupton, T. and C.S. Wilson (1959) 'The Social Background and Connections of Top Decision-Makers', *The Manchester School* 27.

Luzzatto, G. (1968) *L'economia Italiana dal 1861 al 1894*. Turin: Einaudi.

Mace, M.L. (1971) *Directors: Myth and Reality*. Cambridge, Mass.: Harvard University Press.

Maraffi, M. (1980) 'State/Economy Relationships: the Case of the Italian Public Enterprise', *British Journal of Sociology* 31.

Marin, B. (1981) *Die Paritätische Kommission als Zentralorgan autonomer Verbändekooperation*. Vienna/Linz.

Mariolis, P. (1975) 'Interlocking Directorates and Control of Corporations: The Theory of Bank Control', *Social Science Quarterly* 56: 425–439.

Mariolis, P. (1977) *Interlocking Directorates and Finance Control: A Peak Analysis*. Paper presented at the Annual Meeting of the American Sociological Association, Chicago.

Martinelli, A. (1981) 'Italian Experience: Historical Perspective'. In R. Vernon and J. Aharoni (eds) *State-owned Enterprises in the Western Economies*. London: Croom Helm.

McArthur, J.H., and B.R. Scott (1969) *Industrial Planning in France*. Boston: Harvard Graduate School of Business Administration.

McRae, H. and F. Cairncross (1973) *Capital City*. London: Eyre Methuen.

Miliband, R. (1969) *The State in Capitalist Society*. London: Weidenfeld and Nicholson.

Mills, C.W. (1956) *The Power Elite*. New York: Oxford University Press.

Minns, R. (1980) *Pension Funds and British Capitalism*. London: Heinemann.
Mintz, B. and M. Schwartz (1978) *The Role of Financial Institutions*. Paper presented at the ECPR Joint Sessions of Workshops, Grenoble.
Mintz, B. and M. Schwartz (1981) 'The Structure of Intercorporate Unity in American Business', *Social Problems* 29: 87–103.
Mintz, B. and M. Schwartz (1983) 'Financial Interest Groups and Interlocking Directorates', *Social Science History*..
Mintz, B. and M. Schwartz (1984) *The Structure of Power of the American Corporate System*. Chicago: University of Chicago Press.
Mintz, B., P. Freitag, C. Hendricks and M. Schwartz (1976) 'Problems of Proof in Elite Research', *Social Problems* 23:314–324.
Mizruchi, M.S. (1982a) *The American Corporate Network, 1904–1974*.Beverly Hills, Cal.: Sage.
Mizruchi, M.S. (1982b) *Interest Groups in the American Corporate Elite, 1900–1975*. Paper presented at the Annual Meeting of the American Sociological Association, San Francisco.
Mizruchi, M.S. and D. Bunting (1981) 'Influence in Corporate Networks: An Examination of Four Measures', *Administrative Science Quarterly* 26:475–489.
Mokken, R.J. (1977) 'Cliques, Clubs and Clans', *Quality and Quantity* 13:161–173.
Mokken, R.J. and F.N. Stokman (1974) *Interlocking Directorates Between Banks and Institutions in the Netherlands in 1969*. Paper presented at the Joint Sessions of the ECPR, Strasbourg.
Mokken, R.J. and F.N. Stokman (1978) *The 1972 Intercorporate Network in the Netherlands*. Paper presented at the Joint Sessions of the ECPR, Grenoble.
Mokken, R.J. and F.N. Stokman (1979) *Information and Cooptation: Comparative Analysis of Two Intercorporate Networks in the Netherlands*. Paper presented at the Joint Sessions of the ECPR, Brussels.
Mommen, A. (1982) *De Teloorgang van de Belgische Bourgeoisie*. Leuven: Kritak.
Monopolkommission (1978) *Fortschreitende Konzentration bei Großunternehmen, Hauptgutachten 1976/1977*. Baden-Baden: Nomos Verlagsgesellschaft.
Monopolkommission (1980) *Drittes Hauptgutachten 1978/1979*. Bundestagsdrucksache 8/4404. Bonn: Verlag Heger.
Morawetz, I. (1983) *Die Struktur personeller Verflechtungen zwischen Industrie und Bankwesen in Österreich*. Research Memorandum No.182. Vienna: Institute for Advanced Studies.
Morin, F. (1974) *La Structure Financière de capitalisme Français*. Paris: Calmann-Lévy.
Morin, F., A. Alcouffe, C. Alcouffe, X. Freixas and M. Moreaux (1977) *La Banque et les Groupes Industriels à l'Heure des Nationalisations*. Paris: Calmann-Lévy.
Murray, R. (1971) 'The Internationalisation of Capital and the Nation State', *New Left Review* 67.
Offe, C. and H. Wiesenthal (1978) 'Two Logics of Collective Action: Theoretical Notes on Social Class and Organizational Forms', *Political Power and Social Theory* 1.
Ornstein, M.D. (1982) 'Interlocking Directorates in Canada: Evidence from Replacement Patterns', *Social Networks* 4:3–25.
Österreichisches Statistisches Zentralamt (ed.) (1980) *Die österreichische Gemeinwirtschaft im Jahre 1976. Eine Sonderauswertung der nichtlandwirtschaftlichen Bereichszählungen*. Vienna: Verlag Carl Ueberreuter.
Overbeek, H. (1980) 'Finance Capital and the Crisis in Britain', *Capital and Class* 11.
Overbeek, H. (1981) 'Nederlandse Direkte Investeringen in het Buitenland'. In F. Crone and H. Overbeek (eds) *Nederlands Kapital over de Grenzen*. Amsterdam: SUA.
Pahl, R.E. and J.T. Winkler (1974) 'The Economic Elite: Theory and Practice'. In P.

Stanworth and A. Giddens (eds) *Elites and Power in British Society*. Cambridge: Cambridge University Press.

Palmer, D. (1983) 'Broken Ties: Interlocking Directorates and Intercorporate Coordination', *Administrative Science Quarterly* 28:40–55.

Pennings, J. (1980) *Interlocking Directorates*. San Francisco: Jossey-Bass.

Perlo, V. (1957) *The Empire of High Finance*. New York: International Publishers.

Pfeffer, J. and G.R. Salancik (1978) *The External Control of Organizations: A Resource Dependence Perspective*. New York: Harper and Row.

Poensgen, O.H. (1980) 'Between Market and Hierarchy – The Role of Interlocking Directorates', *Zeitschrift für die gesamte Staatswissenschaft* 136:209–225.

Poulantzas, N. (1975) *Classes in Contemporary Capitalism*. London: New Left Books. Originally published in French in 1974.

Ratcliff, R.E. (1980a) 'Banks and Corporate Lending: An Analysis of the Impact of the Internal Structure of the Capitalist Class on the Lending Behavior of Banks', *American Sociological Review* 45:553–570.

Ratcliff, R.E. (1980b) 'Banks and the Command of Capital Flows: An Analysis of Capitalist Class Structure and Mortgage Disinvestment in a Metropolitan Area'. In M. Zeitlin (ed.) *Classes, Class Conflict and the State*. Cambridge, Mass.: Winthrop Publishers.

Ridder-Aab, Ch.-M. (1980) *Die moderne Aktiengesellschaft im Lichte der Theorie der Eigentumsrechte*. Frankfurt: Campus.

Riesser, J. (1910) *Die deutschen Großbanken und ihre Konzentration im Zusammenhang mit der Entwicklung der Gesamtwirtschaft in Deutschland*. Jena: Gustav Fischer, 3rd edition.

Rifkin, J. and R. Barber (1978) *The North Will Rise*. Boston: Beacon Press.

Rittner, F. (1981) *Einführung in das Wettbewerbs- und Kartellrecht*. Heidelberg, Karlsruhe: C.F.Müller Verlag.

Rochester, A. (1936) *Rulers of America*. New York: International Publishers.

Roos, F. de (1982) *De Algemene Banken in Nederland*. Utrecht: Oosthoek.

Rutges, A. (1983) 'Theorievorming met Behulp van een simulatie-model: Twee Alternative Verklaringen van Dubbelfuncties'. In S. Lindenberg and F. N. Stokman (eds) *Modellen in de Sociologie*. Deventer: Van Loghum Slaterus.

Rutges, A. (1984) 'Deskundigheid versus Financiële Controle: Simulatiestudie van Benoemingen in het bedrÿfsleven'. In F. N. Stokman and J. Dronkers (eds) *Nederlandse Elites in Beeld. Recrutering, Samenhang en Verandering*. Deventer: Van Loghum Slaterus.

Sagou, M. (1981) *Paribas: Anatomie d'une Puissance*. Paris: Presses de la Fondation Nationale des Sciences Politiques.

Sampson, A. (1962) *Anatomy of Britain*. London: Hodder and Stoughton.

Saraceno, P. (1956) 'Rapporto su origini, ordinamenti e attività svolta'. In Ministero dell'Industria e del Commercio, *L'Istituto per la Ricostruzione Industriale, IRI*. Turin: UTET.

SBG (1977) *Die größten Unternehmen der Schweiz im Jahre 1976*. Zürich: Schweizerische Bankgesellschaft.

Scalfari, E. (1964) *L'autunno della Republica*. Milan: Etas Kompass.

Schaffner, H. (1970) *Dauer und Wandel in der Schweizerischen Wirtschaft*. Zürich: Vorort des Schweizerischen Handels- und Industrie-Vereins Zürich (ed.).

Schiffels, E.W. (1981) *Der Aufsichtsrat als Instrument der Unternehmenskooperation*. Frankfurt: R.G. Fischer.

Schijf, H. (1978) 'Een netwerk in het Bedrijfsleven in 1886: Een Eerste Beschrijving', *Cahiers voor Politieke en Sociale Wetenschappen* 1.

Schijf, H. (1984) 'Economische netwerkelites rond 1900'. In F. N. Stokman and J. Dronkers(eds) *Nederlandse Elites in Beeld. Recrutering, Samenhangen Verandering*. Deventer: Van Loghum Slaterus.

Schmidt, M.G. (1982) 'Does Corporatism Matter? Economic Crisis, Politics and Rates of Unemployment in Capitalist Democracies in the 1970s'. In G. Lehmbruch and Ph. C. Schmitter (eds) *Patterns of Corporatist Policy-Making.* London: Sage.

Schmitter, Ph.C. (1979) 'Still the Century of Corporatism', In Ph. C. Schmitter and G. Lehmbruch (eds) *Trends Toward Corporatist Intermediation.* London: Sage.

Schmitter, Ph.C. and G. Lehmbruch (eds) (1979) *Trends Toward Corporatist Intermediation.* London: Sage.

Schönwitz, D. and H.-J. Weber (1980) 'Personelle Verflechtungen zwischen Unternehmen: Eine wettbewerbspolitische Analyse', *Zeitschrift für die gesamte Staatswissenschaft* 136:98–112.

Schotter, A. (1981) *The Economic Theory of Social Institutions.* Cambridge: Cambridge University Press.

Schultze, C.L. (1975) 'Falling Profits, Rising Profit Margins, and the Full-Employment Profit Rate', *Brookings Papers on Economic Activity* 2.

Schweizerische Kartellkommission (1979) 'Die Konzentration im schweizerischen Bankgewerbe', *Veröffentlichungen der schweizerischen Kartellkommission* 1/2.

Schweizerische Nationalbank (n.d.) *Schweizerische Nationalbank 1907– 1957.*

Scott, J.P. (1979) *Corporations, Classes and Capitalism.* London: Hutchinson.

Scott, J.P. (1982a) *The Upper Classes.* London: Macmillan.

Scott, J.P. (1982b) 'Property and Control: Some Remarks on the British Propertied Class'. In A. Giddens and G. Mackenzie (eds) *Social Class and the Division of Labour.* Cambridge: Cambridge University Press.

Scott, J.P. (1983) 'Recent Trends in the Scottish Economy'. In D. McCrone (ed:) *Scottish Government Yearbook.* Edinburgh: Edinburgh University.

Scott, J.P. and C. Griff (1983) *Interlocking Directorships in Major British Companies, 1904 to 1976.* Final Report to Social Science Research Council.

Scott, J.P. and M.D. Hughes (1976) 'Ownership and Control in a Satellite Economy', *Sociology* 10.

Scott, J.P. and M.D. Hughes (1980a) 'Capital and Communication in Scottish Business', *Sociology* 14:29–47.

Scott, J.P. and M.D. Hughes (1980b) *The Anatomy of Scottish Capital.* London: Croom Helm.

SGB (1972) *Société Générale de Belgique 1822–1972.* Brussels: Société Générale.

Shonfield, A. (1965) *Modern Capitalism.* New York: Oxford University Press.

SHZ (1977) *Wer sind die größten Schweizer Unternehmen?* Zürich: Schweizerische Handelszeitung.

Simon, H.A. (1961) *Administrative Behavior.* New York: Macmillan.

Snijders, T.A.B. (1981) 'The Degree Variance: An Index of Graph Heterogeneity', *Social Networks* 3: 163–184.

Sobel, R. (1972) *The Age of Giant Corporations.* Westport, Conn.: Greenwood Press.

Sonquist, J. and T. Koenig (1975) 'Interlocking Directorates in the Top United States Corporations: a Graph Theory Approach', *The Insurgent Sociologist* 5: 196–230.

Spiegelberg, R. (1973) *The City: Power Without Accountability.* London: Quartel.

Stanworth, P. and A. Giddens (1975) 'The Modern Corporate Economy: Interlocking Directorships in Britain, 1906–1970', *Sociological Review* 23:5–28.

Stigler, G.J. (1966) 'The Economic Effects of Antitrust Laws', *Journal of Law and Economics* 9.

Stigler, G.J. (1968) *The Organization of Industry.* Homewood, Ill.: Richard D. Irwin Inc.

Stucki, L. (1968) *Das heimliche Imperium.* Zürich: Ex Libris.

Suleiman, E. (1978) *Elites in Modern France.* Princeton, N.J.: Princeton University Press.

Sweezy, P.M. (1939) 'Interest Groups in the American Economy'. In P.M. Sweezy *The Present As History.* New York: Monthly Review Press.

Sweezy, P.M. (1953) *The Present As History.* New York: Monthly Review Press.

Temporary National Economic Committee (TNEC) (1940) *The Distribution of Ownership in the 200 Largest Non-financial Corporations.* Monograph 29. Washington, D.C.: Government Printing Office.

Thompson, G. (1977) 'The Relationship Between the Financial and Industrial Sector of the United Kingdom Economy', *Economy and Society* 6.

Tilly, R. (1974) 'The Growth of the Large-scale Enterprise in Germany since the Middle of the Nineteenth Century'. In H. Daems and H. van der Wee (eds) *The Rise of Managerial Capitalism.* The Hague: Martinus Nijhoff.

Tugendhat, C. (1973) *The Multinationals.* Harmondsworth: Penguin Books.

Useem, M. (1982) 'Classwide Rationality in the Politics of Managers and Directors of Large Corporations in the United States and Great Britain', *Administrative Science Quarterly* 27:199-226.

Useem, M. and A. McCormack (1981) 'The Dominant Segment of the British Business Elite', *Sociology* 15:381-406.

Van der Knoop, J., F. N. Stokman and F. W. Wasseur (1984) 'Theoretische Herinterpretatie van Dubbelfuncties tussen Grote Bedrijven: Stabiliteit en Carrièreopbouw in de Periode 1960-1980'. In F. N. Stokman and J. Dronkers (eds) *Nederlandse Elites in Beeld. Recrutering, Samenhang en Verandering.* Deventer: Van Loghum Slaterus.

Vatter, H.G. (1975) *The Drive to Industrial Maturity: The US Economy 1860-1914.* Westport, Conn.: Greenwood Press.

Veckans affärer (1975) 'VA Kartlägger: De Okända Maktblocken i Finlands Näringsliv', *Veckans affärer* December 11.

Venturini, V.G. (1971) *Monopolies and Restrictive Trade Practices in France.* Leyden: A.W. Sijthoff.

Vernon, R. (ed.) (1974) *Big Business and the State. Changing Relations in Western Europe.* London: Macmillan.

Vinke, P. (1961) *De Maatschappelijke Plaats en Herkomst der Direkteuren en Commissarissen van de Open en Daarmee Vergelijkbare Besloten Naamloze Vennootschappen.* Leiden: Stenfert Kroese.

Vries, J. de (1978) *The Netherlands Economy in the Twentieth Century.* Assen: Van Gorcum.

Wagner, K.(1970) *Die deutsche Kreditwirtschaft. Aufbau und Aufgaben.* Frankfurt am Main: Fritz Knapp Verlag.

Warner, W.L. and D.B. Unwalla (1967) 'The System of Interlocking Directorates'. In W. L. Warner, D.B. Unwalla and J.H. Trimm (eds) *The Emergent American Society, Vol I: Large Scale Organizations.* New Haven, Conn.: Yale University Press.

Whitley, R. (1973) 'Commonalities and Connections Among Directors of Large Financial Institutions', *Sociological Review* 21:613-632.

Whitley, R. (1974) 'The City and Industry'. In P. Stanworth and A. Giddens (eds) *Elites and Power in British Society.* Cambridge: Cambridge University Press.

Wibaut, F.M. (1913) 'De Nieuwste Ontwikkeling van het Kapitalisme', *De Nieuwe Tijd* 18:284-339.

Williamson, O.E. (1975) *Markets and Hierarchies.* New York: Free Press.

Wilson, C. (1954) *The History of Unilever.* The Hague: Martinus Nijhoff.

Wilson Committee (1980) *Report of the Committee to Review the Functioning of Financial Institutions.* London: HMSO.

Wright, E.O. (1978) *Class, Crises and the State.* London: New Left Books.

Zeitlin, M. (1974) 'Corporate Ownership and Control: The Large Corporation and the Capitalist Class', *American Journal of Sociology* 79:1073-1119.

Zeitlin, M. *et al.* (1975) ''New Princes' for Old? The Large Corporation and the Capitalist Class in Chile', *American Journal of Sociology* 80:87-123.

Zeitlin, M. and R.E. Ratcliff (1975) 'Research Methods for the Analysis of the Internal Structure of Dominant Classes', *Latin American Research Review* 10.

Ziegler, R. (1982) *Market Structure and Cooptation*. Final Research Report. Munich: Institut für Soziologie.

Zijlstra, G.J. (1979) 'Networks in Public Policy: Nuclear Energy in the Netherlands', *Social Networks* 1:359–389.

Zijlstra, G.J. (1982) *The Policy Structure of the Dutch Nuclear Energy Sector*. Dissertation. Amsterdam: University of Amsterdam.

Zimmermann, B.R. (1980) *Verbands – und Wirtschaftspolitik am Übergang zum Staatsinderventionismus*. Bern, Frankfurt/M., Las Vegas: Peter Lang.

Index

INA 193
Inco 218
incoming interlocks; *see* directional
  interlocks
indebtedness 7, 46, 57, 65ff.
indegree 44
induced interlock 33, 38, 63, 128, 268
industrial conservatism in Belgium 63,
  153, 282
information 5, 9, 11, 24, 32, 62, 128
inner circle 11, 12-13, 39
inner margin 31
inside positions 34, 48
institutional groups in Finland 24-5,
  168-9, 173ff., 181
insurance 6-7, 81, 122-3, 135-8, 226,
  248, 280
Interbrabant 157, 165
Intercom 157, 165
interest groups 7, 8-9, 12, 63, 69, 149,
  185, 197, 237, 239, 271, 277-8
interlock 1-2, *passim*
intermediate positions 34, 48
internal capitalists 230
  see also executives
Internationa-Müller 114
International Harvester 242
international interlocks 7, chapter 14
  passim, 272
international participations 113-14,
  251ff., 272
international trade 92, 114, 131, 167
interorganizational perspective 4-5, 6,
  14, 21, 282
Italcementi 211
Italy 17-18, 21ff., 74, 84, chapter 11
  passim, 256, 260, 263, 264, 270, 272ff.
ITT 78

Jacobs 78
Jeidels, O. 92, 115
John Brown 226
joint stock companies 18
joint ventures 113, 118, 251, 253,
  279-80

Karstadt 100
kinecon group 8
Knorr 78
Knowles, J.C. 8
Kotz, D. 8
Kraft 236, 249

Kreditanstalt für Wideraufbau 98,
  100, 107
Krupp 96, 100, 256
Kuwait Investment Office 100

Lambert family 149, 150
latin board system 22-3, 34, 159, 202,
  275,
  see also administrative board;
  auditing board
Lazard 186, 187, 266
Levèque, J.M. 263, 266
Liebherr 78
Lille Bonnières Colombes 189, 194
Lindt & Spruengli 146
line 18, 24, 29
Littlewoods Organization 218
Lloyds Bank 225, 226, 233, 266
L'Oreal 185
Louis Dreyfus 218
Luxembourg 258
Lyonnaise des Eaux 189-91, 194

Maisonrouge, J.G. 253
majority control 71, 78, 81
management control 148, 211
managerial model 6, 10-11, 12, 64,
  274, 275
Mannesman 95, 100
Manufacturers Hanover 236, 249
Mariolis, P. 53
market relations 4, 9, 14, 15, 45, 284
Marks & Spencer 220
Marx, K. 3
marxist theory 3, 6
Massey-Ferguson 218
Mellon National Bank 242
Merkle, A. 263, 266
Merlin Gérin 187, 189, 190, 191, 192
Messerschmidt-Bölkow-Blohm 256
Metallgesellschaft 98
Metropolitan Life 238, 241, 249
Michelin 89, 191, 218
Midland Bank 226
Miliband, R. 5
Mills, C.W. 4, 39
minority control 72, 218
Mizruchi, M. 53
Mobil 79, 253
Mobiliar
  Versicherungsgesellschaft 135
Mokken, R 115